M000187521

RED
CALYPSO

RED CALYPSO

The Grenadian Revolution and its Aftermath

Geoffrey Wagner

**Regnery
Gateway**

© Geoffrey Wagner 1988

First published in 1988 in the U.S. by
Regnery Gateway Inc.
1130 17th Street NW Suite 620
Washington
D.C. 20036

ISBN: 0-89526-773-X

Printed in Great Britain

For Jack Farris

What is to is must is
Grenadian saying

ACKNOWLEDGEMENTS

Some of the material in this book has appeared in: *The American Spectator*; *Army Times*; *Chronicles of Culture*; *The Claremont Review*; *The Grenadian Voice*; *National Review*; *New York Tribune*; *The Paraglide*; *The Salisbury Review*; *The Spectator* (London); *The Wall Street Journal*. Editors are thanked for their permission to reprint.

PART ONE: BEFORE

1. BEFORE

We Chose the Windwards

"We reachin' by St. George's 'bout an hour, please God. You care for a smile of white, suh?"

The big man leant over me in his soaked shirt as I lay on the deck. The bottle he proffered was labeled Jeyes Fluid. Under the sentried motion of the stars his boat, the sail-assisted *Starlight*, had brought us overnight from Trinidad, where he had all-aboarded us, while saturnine ships smoked and skulked offshore. There had been bales to load, parts of car, cylinders of gas, doomed poultry, goats, and about twenty traffickers, one of whom, a lady without teeth but with a mustache – had been groaning by my side throughout the ride.

Dawn was breaking, the sun sneaking over the windward hills of the approaching island, lancing through leggy palms and staining scuddy clouds a faint gold above an oyster-silver sea. I sat up stiffly.

"Thank you, Mr. Williams. I'd love a smile."

The way he put it would have made it hard to refuse, had he offered gun oil.

As the wooden ship rolled under his feet the big man with the greying poll wiped an enamel cup on his work pants and poured me half a pint of white. It put firewater into my veins.

"Mistress Celia?"

Spray drenched the lady beside me, who now sat up to consider the prospect of a liquid breakfast. As the *Starlight* had sailed out of Port-of-Spain the kind soul had fixed a mattress of mace for me, with a cocoa sack for pillow.

"Tanks," she said, and slugged from the skipper's bottle.

Bodies lay all over the deck, some still sullenly vomiting, but as Captain Williams set off to revive more of them, and get his craft ship-shape for arrival, I could see figures making their way to the glassed-in cuddy, where a Father was preparing to say prayers. Skirts flapped in the breeze, revealing in Celia's case a shocking-pink sateen slip.

I stood up and shook myself. A deckhand coiled rope around a winch. The thick gray sail was slapping and I took another swallow of white; it was Carriacouan jack iron, the drink that doesn't leave you with a headache because it doesn't leave you with a head. Some West Indians can drink it like water.

Alone for a moment, I leant over the wet rail and watched the hull of land heave up ahead. A slice of manicured moon was gracefully subsiding and I saw the first gleams of beaches, like linen hung out to dry, each with a frou-frou of surf like lace on Celia's slip. We were sailing north up an endless crescent of vagabond islets and cays that straggle up the Windwards, impoverished relatives of the larger islands. All emerald isles and reef seas. You expect to see galleons, scattered like dreams. I was the only white man on board. I was sitting on a sack when a deckhand came up with a paper plate of paw-paw and cassava bread.

"Compliments of de skip." He opened a bottle of Sprite with his teeth and emptied it into my mug. "'Migration Officer be coming aboard soon, suh." He shook his head. "Dat man mos' obnoxious. I do not wanting you have any bad experience of Grenada now."

"It looks beautiful," I said.

In some surprise he stared to starboard where his country arose, a typical geologic convulsion of the area. "Dey calls it an island God make from de rainbow." He chuckled and padded off.

We were approaching the southernmost tip of the island, Pointe Salines, its lighthouse winking. This chubby tower, checkered black and white, was modeled on the old Eddystone

Light, and powered by the island's only solar voltaic cell. I was not to know that in 1979 I would watch that lighthouse blown to bits, to make way for a Cuban airport. The communist Prime Minister, Maurice Bishop, had his hand on the plunger, insisting for some reason that the edifice was a symbol of imperialism, communism's code name or buzzword for, mainly, America. In fact, that lighthouse merely served to save lives. It was the focus of years of evening walks my wife Colleen and I took, down the sandy lanes perforated by red crabs, past deserted inlets like little Trou-Jab, across to salt marshes where anyone could collect enough sea salt in an hour to last you a year. Our dogs gamboled with friends, while locals fished for snapper and couvalli, the horse-eyed jack lifted out of indigo water for a destiny of butter and almonds. It has all vanished now, and airport dredging killed the fishing. Nor was I to know that pictures of this little paradise were one day to be flashed about the TV screens of the world.

Celia reappeared on the *Starlight*'s salty deck. She had spruced herself up for arrival in the Carenage of St. George's, wearing two hats and mismatched shoes. The latter had been cut open at the sides, for comfort's sake. I knew I was going to like Grenada. What I didn't know was that I was going to spend the best part of my lifetime there.

Traffickers

I was struck by Celia's toothlessness, which prematurely aged so many of her kind – she told me she was but thirty-six (with seven children, outside and inside). As in the Yorkshire Dales or suspicious Welsh hills a century ago, country folk in Grenada simply ask for an ailing tooth to be yanked out. This has remained the case despite that now the churches (Baptists, Seventh Day Adventists) have sent down free dentists with good equipment. My first days in Grenada there was only one (government) dentist. He told me he *averaged* forty-five extractions a day; his record, when he took a chair and pedal drill to one of our island dependencies, was seventy-four. When I asked him if he could give my teeth a clean he suggested I buy a toothbrush. After the Bishop coup there was a lot of propaganda about the health services Cuba sent us down. Some still believe it. The two dentists who came were butchers, while their so-called doctors (or paramedics) had just discovered the circulation of blood.

Celia tugged my sleeve and pointed to a woman squatting nearby.

"She does sell everything she take."

She does also buy, I wanted to reply, noting a fancy cassette set, ghetto blaster or Third World portmanteau, perched on rotting yams between her knees. With weathered hands Celia gathered up her baskets.

These women were traffickers. They went down the islands, chiefly to Trinidad, to sell produce: cheap vegetables grown in Grenada's well-watered hills (Dominica, of course, actually sells water in quantity northwards), even sheep and goat (though not to strictly quarantined Barbados), and sea moss, a highly desirable product ripped off our reefs – Trinny has none.

Instead of helping these traffickers, Bishop did his best to stop them. Every month or so he could be heard fulminating on the radio against these old souls. The fact was, they were mothers whose sons were being herded into the PRA (People's Revolutionary Army) and they were going over to Port-of-Spain and telling the truth about what was happening in the new Mecca of Caribbean communism. Besides, it was all of a pattern; in the same way the Castro brothers had persecuted the black crones of Cárdenas who opposed the fishing collectives and the Ortega brothers the Misquito Indians. These market dames were labeled "counters" – counter-revolutionaries. They were.

During the Bishopric Trinidad instituted visas for all visiting Grenadians, a roadblock understandably set up against communist elements infiltrated into the island from the usurping New Jewel Movement (NJM); this requirement was removed after intervention and, in any case, the casual, trusting nature of inter-island traffic in this part of the world is still remarkable. Around our Carenage grave dames and graceful girls may be seen tossing packets to this deck or that, for northward delivery, within the dependencies.

It must be admitted that the anarchic nature of our sea traffic has made these smaller islands sieves for contraband. Rum smugglers, far from being bloodthirsty buccaneers like Morgan or Lolondais, were generally old fisherfolk in small and leaky craft incrementing a trip here and there with a case or so of "ex-bond." They were looked on with a relatively lenient eye by authorities; after all, they were sort of "self-employed." As a consequence, the price of spirits was kept risibly low. Even today it is not hard to get a case of red rum more cheaply than one of Coca-Cola, though it's as well to decant it before a party since someone in government might spot an unstamped bottle.

Unfortunately, the drug scene descending on us like a cloud from the north has injected new anxieties and pressures, with one out of forty teeners in New York on heroin, and a Scottsdale pusher grossing US$100 million annually on cocaine. Though marijuana, ganja, or "de weed" have been traditional for years in our neck of the Caribbean, the stuff may for that reason have been used with more circumspection than in the big cities north. The old-biddy traffickers don't touch it. Rastas think it sacred. Some weeks after the intervention I was given a Huey copter ride over Grenada's northern hills, when the pilot pointed down to a particularly green bit of bush.

"Jane," he said. "Boo."

"How do you know?" I asked him.

"Because it's so well tended," he replied.

Recently four tons of marijuana were seized by police on the tiny island of Anguilla. The authorities decided to burn it. Just as the pyre was being lit, however, Mr. Emile Gumbs, Chief Minister, saw the possibility of the entire island being overcome by giggles and visions. He ordered old tyres added to the blaze.

At about the same time a case on the Turks and Caicos concluded with government Ministers facing a grand jury in the US. Tony Field, son of a High Court Judge in Grenada, had got into the same can of worms, in his case quite innocently, some years before. Coke, coming up mostly from Colombia in our part of the world, is the curse of the peripatetic air traveler. Being searched down to one's socks makes one love the swinging drug culture.

I remember that the pilot then came aboard *Starlight* and, an old friend of Cap'n Williams, took not a smile but a grin of white.

"Him live up dere." Celia gestured to the north, gave a name I did not catch, then frowned at my thickness. "Where de water he weep ober de rock."

Did every Grenadian talk in metaphors?

"You stay at Ocean View, mister. Is best hotel in island."

Now from the Carenage, where dinghies nuzzled the wharves like puppies, a boat brought us the Immigration Officer. A cold youth in bureaucratic collar and dark tie, with the obligatory pen (or top of same) clipped in his breast pocket, he wore heavy shades and spoke in an accent of acquired precision. I completed my formalities and left him arguing with the Auntie with the ghetto blaster. I stepped onto the Carenage, where the conch horns were sounding, and found the Snug Corner restaurant rivaling the Happy Bar as a spot where I might wash myself and leave my bags. After which I set out to dig St. George's, then as now capital of Grenada.

City in the Sun

The core of St. George's is still mellow eighteenth-century brick, under fish-scale tiling (increasingly dismantled, alas). On a quiet morning such as that on which I first arrived the town seems decorous to the point of prim, framed in hillsides staked out with the usual tropical trees. Bell-pelmet windows were striped red and white. A taxi called UNCLE RAY offered me its services. A wooden bus called SWEET ROSES hammered by.

The businesses were coming alive, though not presumptuously so. Melancholy reverie prevailed within. On the *Starlight*, England being light hours ahead, I had heard the trickle of cricket commentary from Lord's, out of Auntie's player. And indeed St. George's had the gravitas of some cricket outfield, men moving like monks to their occupations. At the same time, a high-smile area. Grin at a Grenadian and he'd grin back. He still will. Even Bishop and his cronies could not eradicate that, though they tried to discourage cricket. A mistake.

From the Snug Corner I passed up shady steps to a street with faded shops where surely no one but relatives had entered for years: The Tip-Top Bookshop, Men's (Cashe) Shoppe, the Pitch-Pine Bar, Just-Step-In Boutique.

"Edrich on sixty," called a tall figure loping past me as if he'd known me all my life. "Boyce comin' on to bowl, man."

At intersections policemen went through balletic motions, wearing dark blue trousers sashed with scarlet and blancoed topees. Today, less the "colonial" puggarees which are reserved for ceremonial occasions (outside Government House or Parliament), they make the same stylized gestures except during a Test match involving the West Indies, when headphones can be seen under caps, or a transistor glued to one ear.

The Royal Grenadian Police Force was at one time extremely effective. It then became politicized and was virtually disbanded under Bishop's PRG (People's Revolutionary Government), when the PRA assumed its powers, including in its ranks boys of thirteen who would issue stern orders in falsetto voices, backed up by Kalashnikovs. A book by Hugh O'Shaughnessy published after the intervention assures its readers that under Bishop there was "better behavior from the army and police." As there was not an army, as such, under Eric Gairy, how could the PRA be "better"? Such police as remained were mostly confined to traffic duties and other formalities. The PRG followed Lenin's precept:

"There is only one way to prevent the restoration of the police, and that is to create a people's militia and to fuse it with the army." It was certainly one of the most difficult tasks for the incoming government, after intervention, to recreate a prideful island police force.

So from those cozy shops, not selling much and taking their time doing so, I descended into an open market. This was and is pure West Indian. Crones and girls, doubtless "great-grands," sold limes that might have been painted, breadfruit, sapodilla, soursop, sugar apples, avocadoes (called pears), small bananas (called figs), pumpkins, and that repertoire of root vegetables (dasheen, tanya, eddoes and bluggoes) which makes our diet so high in fiber. Sea moss, obviously, is rich in iodine. And Grenada, the spice island, sells those little brown acorns called nutmegs to the world – excluding Russia, for some reason. When Bishop wanted to settle some of his bills to Moscow he offered nutmegs, only to be declined, apparently Ivan doesn't use them, not having discovered, perhaps, that they can stiffen the alcoholic content of your vodka.

In the Market Square open wooden buses, left-hand-drive relics of postwar US Lend-Lease, stood parked about, their drivers chewing rotis. They had names like IN GOD WE TRUST, ACE YOU WIN. Sail-like tarps protect their passengers against the rain, some sporting stained glass panels by the windshield with religious motifs. Someone shouted with delight, "Ninety-three for fo-uh!"

The biggest store in the town was and is Jonas, Browne & Hubbard (all partners extant). It straddles the Carenage, over storage recesses, where big men wrestle bales, or pull down lumber or cement. If this wasn't Conradian enough to remind me of my Malayan youth there was one emporium full of bolts of cloth called Everybody's, where change for your purchase was run to the cashier on overhead wires. But to see the island I needed wheels.

By this time I had noticed a few white people. Today's cruise tourism was unknown then. But the riff-raff off the yachts have not changed much with the years: filthy, bearded, salt-and-sunburnt men searching for parts and their equally scruffy barefoot women (one centipede bite cures that insanitary habit in the tropics). Today, too, the ex-Brits have largely gone. At the time I'm describing the islands were cheap enough to make retirement for British ex-service and civil servant types attractive. You would see some craggy case, perhaps seventy or so, in bush shirt and Baden-Powell shorts, sporting a tennis visor, his wife beside him with fine rings on work-worn hands, low-heeled shoes, and queenly shantung dress, her hair in some twentyish style. Their breed has gone.

In the office of Momma Aird, the island's Volkswagen agent and now old friend, I found two girls, one attending to her nails, the other listening to the cricket scores. Both were pretty in a bun-faced way and I later had occasion to reflect that the advent of the mini-skirt must have meant little to the maidens of these islands, except that they had to shorten their slips.

I stated my request.

"Doreen, does we has a car free?"

"Yes, Pam, we has."

Doreen sighed and sorted papers, repairing to a ledger of a kind I had last seen in Army Nissen huts in World War Two.

"You be of age?"

"I be," I said.

"And has a license?"

"I has," I said.

"Riding or driving?"

This beat me. "Come again."

With a sigh at my ignorance Doreen explained. In the islands a license to drive a motorbike is called a riding license, and is apparently inherited by the entire male population at birth. To crash into a car is to "bounce" it.

Eventually I was issued with Hitler's original Volkswagen, it was push-started for me, and I was on my way to the Santa Maria

Hotel. I was told it was the best hotel in St. George's and in those days it had to be. It was the only one. The rest were "guesthouses," usually extensions of family dwellings.

The coast road ran past gray board shacks and walls of lime-washed stone. These homes of weathered wood, some with fretworked eaves, were raised on stilts, around which children played. A trade wind stirred the sea-grape and manchineel beside a sea like a slab of silk, where nets lagged. I soon learnt the local rules of the road: if you met a banana truck you took evasive action (only a few years ago the police were offering a course in Defensive Driving) and in Grenada a hand signal meant one thing – the driver had his window open.

The Santa Maria, which became The Islander and then Maurice Bishop's NJM headquarters and then a burnt-out wreck, was jalousied with demerara windows. Inside it punkahs whirred like stricken birds. I was at once treated with a courtesy forgotten as a natural way of life outside the Windwards, and a welcome punch brought me by an aproned maid who slapped shyly across the terrace boarding. I sat back in a wicker chair beside old copies of sewing magazines and religious calendars and watched the pelicans plunging for sprats.

Below me the legendary, faultless sands. Some of Captain Teach's treasure is said to be buried off these beaches and after my second or "next" punch I didn't doubt it. I saw green shallows tufted with weed and boys catching crabs. The atmosphere was of a sort of ragamuffin divinity and I felt I'd come home. I knew it would become easy to be a hedonist here. What I didn't know was that, while this might be an island God created from the rainbow, a young man called Maurice Bishop was cementing his communist ties in London and planning to hand it over to Cuba.

Getting There

No man is an island but I am an islomane. Over the years my wife

Colleen and I have sunk roots in many. For a while the affliction drove us Ulysses-like around the Mediterranean – Giglio, Rhodes, Corfu, Ibiza, Corsica – but always the mobs arrived and we fled what Matthew Arnold's scholar gypsy called "this strange disease of modern life / With its sick hurry, its divided aims." In his company we departed "indignantly." Their bloom was off and with their bloom went we. Today the east coast of Spain sees an annual influx of over a million Brits a year, all howling for their table d'hôte. At three a.m. the streets of Marbella are said to be more active than Piccadilly Circus. Tourism ranks as Spain's prime industry.

On the other hand, as I look across the bay to St. George's, past bluff after bluff of roughly hammered gold at sunset, my eye discerns no development of size in the past thirty years. A few hill villages have enlarged, from board to block house, but there are no high-rise hotels. We have no world-famous cathedrals nor three-star Michelin restaurants. Silk-soft beaches, yes, and the whisper of palms, and islands rising like murmurs around, and cricket-crazy boys fishing from rust-colored reefs. The Bishop communists failed to teach those boys that courtesy is servility, and Castro a Galahad.

In some respects the island has regressed. The population has declined though no strict census is available; the exodus under NJM told its own tale. Until 1984, when the American firm of Morrison-Knudsen repaired our roads under US AID, such had been untouched for twenty years, barring some patching by old "tatou" women smoking pipes. A recent book by three British Polytechnic teachers complains that the US forces left our roads "quagmires."[1] No. The Cubans left them quagmires thanks to their tracked vehicles, mostly Russian and seldom carried on transporters. M-K repaired our roads and left solid equipment behind for us.

Mail has not got faster. Sacks for Grenada have been found in a well in Barbados. The telephone "service," after the Bulgarians were invited to instal an elaborate eaves-dropping system, is slower than when my wife and I first came. Under Cuban occupation we went for two years without mains water, while their "construction" chaps washed down their Russian trucks daily. Electricity, known as "current" locally, was an on-off affair during the Bishop regime. Anyone who could afford to bought a generator.

Now control of the utilities is a communist principle and after intervention the machinery of our Power Station at Queen's Park was demonstrably sabotaged by ex-NJM elements there. Bishop openly boasted of his seizure of the services, in his "Line of March" speech of September 13, 1982:

> We must assume total control of all Public Utilities – electricity, telephone, water, National Transport Service. And here again, as comrades know, we already in fact control those four. The missing one for us now is Cable and Wireless and the Satellite Dish from the Soviet Union will be one aspect in the timing in relation to Cable and Wireless.[2]

To this inventory I might add that, thanks or not to the NJM, the two hospitals in the island, the St. George's General and the Prince Alice, are today rather worse than they have ever been (one X-ray machine between them at times). I speak from experience. Colleen, my Irish wife, spent time in the former after having been knifed ("chopped," locally) by an intruder across the face – twenty-three stitches, most subcutaneous. Today there are many more cruise ships around our islands but far less white permanencies, in the form of settlers and retirees, than there used to be. As I write, there is no theater, one cinema (non-stop kung-fu), no restaurants of any quality, and somehow or other we have to get by without Cronkite or Walters.

The main signs of islands hereabouts being dragged, kicking and screaming, into the twentieth century are the mushroom growths of television dishes by the palms. Television will of course insert new pressures into our tiny island communities. The first such program I caught in Grenada was a typical American newscast, hostessed by the usual well-groomed anchorwoman; its subjects highlighted the proliferation of AIDS rather than AID, a New York homosexual High School, and a black riot in South Africa which the bar limers beside me assumed to be taking place in America.

For a long time the difficulty or inconvenience of getting to these islands made for a visitor with persistence. I first landed at St. Vincent in a Grumman seaplane (after all, the first, wartime BOAC flight from Poole, Somerset, to Baltimore, Maryland, took five days). Even today, to get to St. Vincent or Dominica you must fly to Barbados (or Trinidad) and transfer to a small and uncomfortable Rolls-Royce Avro 748 turbo-prop of LIAT (Leeward Islands Air Transport) a line that has regularly lost luggage but nary a life, until 1986, when a craft carrying nineteen (including a Minister) went down without trace off St. Vincent.

To get to these islands you had to fly in before dark and on Grenada you landed at the now abandoned Pearls airport near Grenville on the east coast, one seized by Seals on intervention; it is, as I write, even more abandoned than ever, the rotting hulks of an old Aeroflot biplane and the Cubana derelict given to Bishop by Castro parked by the runway and speaking volumes. To get to St. George's the tired traveler had then to engage an expensive taxi over the top of the island to where the hotels were. Although Grenada is only twelve miles broad it is mountainous, and this trip took most of an hour in the dark, around spaghetti bends. The roads were appalling, patched by the old "tatou" women, named after the local armadillo whose tasty meat I have often eaten, and the ride over them bruised not only our tourists but our bananas, a tricky crop, one carried to England by the Geest Line, whose family has been so loyal to the Windwards.

By this time in life I have made most possible approaches to the islands, leaving it to US Rangers and 82nd Airborne to drop by parachute and to the Nazis of both breeds to venture in our waters by submarine. A German U-boat came in to St. George's harbor unharmed in the last war, while a submarine facility was being built for Russian use at Egmont Harbor on our east coast when the Americans interrupted it. The bathymetric characteristics of the Caribbean are ideal for deep-diving submarines, of which the Soviets are constructing a colossal fleet. Churchill was forever warning Roosevelt of the U-boat paradise in this area, whose deep waters (more than 1,500 fathoms in places) and overhanging inlets, like that at Egmont, make sonar detection very difficult; sonar transponder buoys dropped from the air are further impeded by the thermal layers of our warm waters. No access to Grenada was as cheap, though, as my *Starlight* whose deckfare from Trinny was, when I took it, EC$10³' and I even heard later that at a pinch (or smile?) Captain Williams would deliver you to the door of your hotel – in one of his dinghies.

Getting off Grenada during a general strike, however, was far more tedious, we found, than any arrival on it. No telephones, no "current," no water, no airline office open, no gas available, no shops, no banks ... you were stranded. Some simply went to Pearls and slept there till a plane came in. One or two sneaked out, expensively, on cruise liners. We ourselves, during that three-months general strike of 1974, walked onto a yacht. Yachts have marine radio. Ours called another in St. Vincent whose owner sent us down a charter plane and we were able to save the life of a local granny in urgent need of hospital attention in Barbados. There are freighters.

Over the years I have seen the following lines, operating under various flags of convenience, cease plying to these islands at all: Atlantic, Booker (the former "sugar barons" of Guyana), Booth, Harrison, Seaways. This lack makes it an uphill battle to get goods to the Windwards on any sort of schedule, especially if trans-shipment is involved, while chill cargo gets left in the sun dockside for days – forget about wines – and pilferage is high. These circumstances do not make the building of a house of any quality easy. Still and all, freighters have a warm place in my heart, thanks to having taken one from Brooklyn to Grenada with a skipper and crew of superb eccentricity.

In those days there were concessions on duty due if you accompanied the effects for your house or future residence. Taxis are not allowed on the Brooklyn waterfront, so Colleen and I unloaded at the gate and faced the prospect of a three-mile walk to the Booth-Line *Seabelle* with our baggage. Fortunately, a passing fork-lift operator took pity on us and delivered us to the scruffy-looking scow, its derricks already hauling up containers.

The boat had been built in Hamburg and ran under a Panamanian flag, to avoid US labor laws – we lost two galley Bajans in Bridgetown and others elsewhere. No women are taken on for freighter crew, as they are by yachts. This is understandable since more than one skipper has found himself with an infant on hand in full voyage. The tot is then extremely hard to unload since it lacks proper papers and a Flying-Dutchman situation ensues. What's more, freighter crews generally strip to the waist …

The *Seabelle*'s complement was polyglot. The skipper was a gritty little Liverpudlian in his late thirties, his First Engineer an ex(?)-Estonian, the Chief Officer a Gaelic-speaking Scot, the Mate a Greek who played cards incessantly called (yes) Nick, and so on; there was the customary complement of hands from the islands, who trolled for fish in the stern. There were but two passenger cabins, tiny compared with those on the Geest boats; our colleagues were a Baptist missionary and wife and lovely Indian daughter adopted from a South American posting. The ideal of these ship's officers was to take freight up the Amazon past Manaus, past the walls of foliage of Caicara and Tonantins on to Iquitos in northern Peru, where they seemed to have friends. It took them over three months and kept them out of the clutches of Head Office. In fact, the high point of our highly inebriated trip was the castration, or "cutting," of a little mona monkey they were taking as a present for the Bishop of Iquitos, South American gardens being rich, in my experience, in exotic pets.

From our long drinking sessions it soon transpired that Skipper Eric was petrified of the sea and, in particular, of its larger denizens. We have had but two shark fatalities off Grenada in a century, and that attack was provoked. However, there are whale shark around Trinidad, where shark meat is prominently barbecued on Maracas Bay. The whale shark is supposed to be harmless 'to man and one hears of skin divers boarding such without unduly bothering the fish. The lemon shark, preceded by its striped pilot and wearing a remora on its back, is a carnivore that can crunch up turtles without discomfort, possibly a quicker end than what overtakes our local baby turtles who stray from their sand nests after hatching, to be caught by ghost crabs and scraped out of their shells alive. Grenada has largely been cleared of reef fish since first I went there, and dived through shoals of gaudy wrasse, doctorfish, and grunt. The spear is said to be responsible for this. In fact, spear-fishing is disallowed off St. John, Bonaire, and Bermuda. All the same, I have a friend who was hit by a shark on Trinidad's Cocos Bay beach. He did not pause to analyze whether it was whale or lemon. Chatting with Eric in deck-chairs about such, I saw that his face had gone rigid, his lower jaw shaking like that of a cat watching a bird. It was when I mentioned burial at sea to him that the power of his phobia came through, and he turned a vivid verdigris in the moonlight.

Sea burial, only permitted in certain places, is surprisingly popular in the islands. Two such I attended proved disastrous. In the first case, that of a prominent St. George's businessman, so many plucked at the body's plastic wrapping for a last look that the corpse wouldn't sink and had to be reburied. In the second, that of a friend who wrote for *The Times* of London, dolphins played with his body on the way down. Myself, I have applied to be buried in a buoy, vertical, neither on land nor in the sea. My application appears to be permanently pending. Eric twitched at these anecdotes of his anima, the ocean. I soon learnt of his compensatory side – the man longed to be a surgeon.

Now, as mentioned, monkeys are kept as pets all over South America, particularly, for some reason, in Ecuador; in Brazil, at the Iguassù Falls, I had my room keys swallowed by the hotel ostrich. Introduced from West Africa, the mona is still legal eating in the islands; the meat makes a sweet stew akin to manicou (opossum) but I have never eaten it with relish, remembering the owner's little old-maid face coupled with the prehensile fingers of a child.

What is not legal, even in lawless Trinidad where bow-wow (pulverized puppy) may still appear on a Chinese menu, is to eat the live brains of a monkey in true gourmet fashion. For this the monkey is put in a special cage with head alone protruding, then placed under a special table through a hole in the top of which its cranium alone sticks out. The diners then crack its skull with a mallet and spoon out the hot brain. I am glad to say my father was partially responsible for outlawing this barbarity in Malaya, but Grenadian monkey is legally eaten today. A police chief called, of all names, Innocent Belmar, of whom more below, was shot to death by a Bishop supporter at our Birch Grove Bamboo Bar while he was washing down monkey with the head of the Grenada Nutmeg Co-operative, Robin Renwick. All the same, animated expectancy ran through the *Seabelle*, and a lot of hard stuff traveled down gullets, as Eric scheduled the operation on Milor' (as the monkey was called). It was considered that the animal might need a day or so's rest after the surgeon's ministrations.

I discovered that apparently freighter traffic is provided with some sort of hot line for medical emergencies; you get on the subscription frequency and ask for instructions as to what to do in the case of your bos'un's broken leg or whatever. I don't know if such advice runs down to root canal therapy, but Eric was clearly delighted to test the system.

Castration may not be a complicated procedure, but it is an emotional one for a male to watch. My dog book says to take some brandy along for the mutt afterwards, but generally I needed the brandy rather than the dog. But when Eric got onto his hot line for instructions on how to take the balls off a monkey, he was curtly told to sober up. The crew members who had volunteered to "scrub in" for the operation had long gone to such counsel, being squiffy, pie-eyed, or shot-away.

Nothing loath, our Eric proceeded to anesthetize Milor'. Assuming a monkey to be a dog he weighed it. No problem. Eric drew six cc of the best into his syringe, while the immense Estonian and one other held the puny monkey on its back. Milor' looked sourly from one to the other as Eric stuck him. No effect. Again the skipper-surgeon filled up and slid the needle under the coat, pressing home the plunger. Milor' looked wakeful. On the third shot Eric's hands shook as the liquid left the gradations of the cylinder. Then the monkey slumped. He was "down," in vet parlance. Estonian and buddy took hard hold. Eric reached for his sterilized knife. His day in court had come.

At which point the mona gave an eldritch screech, easily broke loose and started swinging wildly around the cabin. Huge men tumbled over each other trying to stop him – "Get 'is leg, Joe ... I'll have the booger next time round." And so forth. Milor' escaped from the cabin and the total crew gave chase all over the *Seabelle* at speed. Eventually they caught their prey. Eric injected again, put the poor animal out, and "cut." Years later he heard from the Bishop that the operation had been an immense success and that Milor' was thriving. It made Eric's day.

But his men held on to their appendices.

Caribbean Handout

Through the area we loosely call the Caribbean pass approximately two-thirds of America's oil, two-thirds of its imported strategic materials, and about half its other trade. The fact that it arrives seems to satisfy most Americans but, as Churchill repeatedly warned Roosevelt, one day it may not do so. The oil lanes we traveled on the *Seabelle* were highly hazardous in World War Two and will be so again, should Russia put in place its submarine navy here.

When I first went to Grenada it was, in common with most British possessions in the area, a Crown Colony. I had been brought up in one with exactly the same structure, from the Governor-General down, though the then-FMS (Federated Malay States) was as rich in natural resources as Grenada is poor. Some Caribbean islands have even seen indigenous movements of late actually to return to this "colonial" structure. But what particularly distinguishes Grenada, its economic glory, if you will, is that everyone seems to own some land. Our gardener has far more than us. In a recent book Grenada has been called "the strongest small-peasant agriculture in the eastern Caribbean."[4] Statistically it is so, as the three-months strike on independence showed us, nationals being in possession of land, and its crops, to a greater degree than anywhere else in the ex-British Caribbean, and in strong contrast to the next Windward up the line, St. Vincent. It was, indeed, this factor that made Grenada so resistant to communism.

To some extent this seems to have been a legacy of the past. Slavery was milder in Grenada than elsewhere locally, as attested by the fact that Indian and Chinese labor was undeterred to take the long journey shortly after British conquest. Large-plantation farming was uneconomic on Grenada. Large-scale cane cutting is what demanded slave labor and Grenada never knew the slavery of Barbados, let alone the horrors reported by John Stedman in Guyana, though Maurice Bishop borrowed both for his rewrite of our history. Of course, if you want to dig far enough back, almost everyone was enslaved at some time. Certainly England was under the Romans. Her Queen Boadicea killed herself after being publicly flogged, a fact that fails to make me ostracize Italian restaurants.

What Grenada got was refugee boat people from Barbados, the first stop from Africa in the ignoble trade. These became unindentured workers on small estates, some of which still exist in the same manner today, plots being farmed fairly casually. When the former Premier Sir Eric Gairy started a strike among farm laborers in 1985 I checked some figures. By far the lowest wages were being given by government (viz. the Blaize government, inheriting wage scales from NJM). As for the private estates there were hardly any left, the largest being of the order of a hundred acres or so. Our plantocrats packed up early, unlike the Punnetts and Abbots and Barnards of St. Vincent. This individual land ownership was of great importance psychologically when the communists took power in 1979. As the same book puts it, NJM waged "a class war on behalf of a class that did not exist in order to build a workers' state in a country in which, at least in the Marxist sense, there were few workers."5

After World War Two the Windwards proceeded to independence, via a number of preliminary groupings which showed their factionalism. Such is a penalty of insularity all over, and not exclusively Anglo-Saxon in heritage, Aruba initially declining to become an entity with Bonaire and Curacao. So there was the short-lived Federation of the West Indies, then the trade union called CARIFTA and after that the St. Vincent Treaty, with Premiers Mitchell of St. Vincent, Compton of St. Lucia, and Gairy of Grenada endeavoring to set up some sort of free union of goods and people. In 1987 the call for "one nation" south of Jamaica was heard again, but Antigua/Barbuda could not be persuaded of the idea.

So instead, the tariffs went up, visas were required. I watched the celebration of the strident St. George's Agreement of 1979, shortly after Maurice Bishop's accession to power. Every speech praised his revolution. Under this banner Maurice Bishop hoped to organize and drive forward Caribbean communism but it is a scrap of paper now, if that. I doubt whether many in the islands have ever heard of it. Inter-island bickering has recently been seen, too, in aborted attempts by Tobago to secede from Trinidad, Barbuda from Antigua. Grenada is presently the second smallest member of the UN but if Barbuda obtained independence it would have a UN vote off a population of seven hundred.

All the inter-island alliances failed. Clearly England wanted to rid itself of these embarrassing colonial deposits, running on deficits and difficult to defend, so that it blessed the secessions. Jamaica and Trinidad (with Tobago) went independent in 1962, Barbados and Guyana followed suit in 1966. The Windwards were then granted Associate Statehood, from which category Grenada was the first to free itself, under Eric Gairy, and become independent in 1974.

I watched this evening ceremony for which Washington sent down Cyrus Vance, Secretary of the Army in the Kennedy administration and of State under Carter. It took place in darkness, Jewel dissidents having blacked out the Power Station. Television coverage was virtually inoperative, though I saw shadowy replicas of it all later. The independence issue was scarcely at stake, but the blackout had psychological effect. Even though major Jewel leaders were under arrest at the time, to a West Indian populace Gairy's teeth looked drawn and he consistently lost power from this point on, scoring only a wobbly 9-6 victory for his GULP party in the hastily run elections of 1978, after his friend Errol Barrow had unexpectedly gone down to "Tom" Adams in Barbados (to pick himself up later, see below).

In sketching this background, fully covered in Archie Singham's *The Hero and the Crown*[6] (a book Gairy used to give visiting dignitaries despite the fact that it criticized him), I would add my strong impression that in the West Indies, certainly in the smaller islands, politics is merely power. It gives you no esteem with your peers. Chamber of Commerce businessmen openly despise the politicians, who seem unable to count change or run trade with their own efficiency (or legerdemain). Politicians are seen as necessary for the three Ps – Patronage, Permissions, Perks. Frankly, since I've known it, Grenada could have been operated more efficiently (and probably less corruptly) by its

Chamber of Commerce than by any existing government, most of which consisted of small shopkeepers, petty civil servants with enterprises on the side, commission men, and the like. People whose upward mobility resided in government appointments, concluding in the OBE (Obey Brass Eagerly). You don't meet politicos as parties in Grenada, outside those at Government House. Not a single politician belongs to the St. George's Club. Trinidad is much the same.

In these islands it was union strength that gave local aspirants to power a venue. And, as an outgoing colonist, you cannot hand over to a vacuum. Union votes are votes. Gairy collared a lot of them and faced down the British hegemony. To his credit this did not turn him anti-white, though to be so was in the mainstream of local emancipation, and it did not save him from being served up, almost daily on the radio, as a Fascist dictator by Bishop.

When he was nineteen Gairy went for work to Aruba, in common with many Grenadians of his age. He returned a few years later (thrown out, some say), at which point he organized both his union, the Grenada Manual and Mental Workers Union, and his political party GULP (Grenada United Labour Party). With the introduction of universal suffrage in 1951 he called a strike to establish a power base and won six out of seven seats on the Legislative Council. On and off he held power for approximately a quarter of a century. Recently he was in exile for four years (the Khomeini, of course, for thirteen). In 1984, after intervention and deposition of NJM, the discredited dictator returned to his homeland to win 36% of the vote in a scrupulously policed election, during which he barely bothered to go to the hustings.

From 1979 to 1983, as will be shown below, Grenada was effectively run by the Cuban Ambassador, Julian Enrique Torres Rizo, a close friend of Castro.[7] Previously head of the Cuban mission to the United Nations and a senior DA (Departamento América) officer, Rizo lived with a fiery American Weatherwoman, Gail Reed; she caused a lot of unnecessary trouble on intervention. The DA, a branch of the Cuban Communist Party, should not be confused, as it often is, with the DGI (Dirección General de Inteligencia) which was set up in 1961 and functions as a branch of the KGB; the DGI had several representatives on Grenada during the Bishop years.

After them the incumbent US administration felt prompted to accelerate some assistance southwards. The Carter group had given some aid but the Reagan formula, which came to be known as the CBI, or Caribbean Basin Initiative, was somewhat more organized, the idea being to give favorable exemptions for our regional exports, notably from the smaller islands, plus boosting economic aid in general (to more than US$379 million in 1986).

It didn't work, or hasn't yet. By the start of 1987 exports from our area had fallen by 23% since initiation of CBI. Inflation in the Dominican Republic has gone up by six times since 1983. Grenada, which contributed to the whole conception in that year, has shown scant economic recovery since intervention, though culturally we have seen a turn from a Eurocentric orientation in ways of life, which will be followed up below. Why so?

It is said that the US Congress emasculated much of Reagan's version of CBI before it could get going. It certainly attenuated some of the clauses (principally in the area of textiles), but the problem lies deeper. In local employment and taxation. For we are dealing here with child populations. Half Nicaragua is fifteen or under. *More than half Mexico* is under fifteen. Without benefit of census John Toland, a then Under-Secretary of State for Caribbean Affairs (and no relation to the war historian), published a demographic conspectus of the ex-British Caribbean from Jamaica to Guyana; he estimated 60% of this population to be under fifteen years of age.[8] Whatever the figure it is self-inflicted. Our maid has eight children, by various men; our gardener admits to eleven. That's nineteen mouths to feed without the beneficence of US Welfare of AFDC (Aid to Families with Dependent Children). In the United States Welfare daughters can get pregnant at sixteen and apply for AFDC on their own. Today more than half the babies born to black mothers in Great Britain are illegitimate.

In the Windwards, where contraception is considered unmanly, and a woman not a woman till she has "made" a baby, Planned Parenthood has barely made a dent. Nor is male abandonment merely lower-class. Respectable Grenadians, with white-collar jobs, have "outside" children, and I know at least one matron, running her own business, who simply does not know the father of one of her sons. Marriage is far from essential in the islands; indeed, many males see it as simply a restraint.

The pattern has always been with us and we have not infected the English-speaking democracies with it; promiscuity has. In the USA today one-half of all black females have a baby before they turn twenty (one-quarter have two), and over half of black marriages result in divorce. More than a million American teeners of all colors get pregnant annually, four out of five unmarried. Compare 1950 when fewer than 15% of teen births in America were non-connubial. According to a recent Johns Hopkins survey one out of five American fifteen-year-old girls now admit to intercourse. In both Washington, D.C., and Chicago more than half the children born are the offspring of unwed mothers; in the latter city *75% of black babies are born out of wedlock*. And then a Chicago University Sociologist passes on the truism that there is a dearth of black marriageable males. Why? "Unemployment, incarceration and an appalling rate of murder."[9]

Those are depressing statistics. I fear for those nineteen dependents of two worthy folk who work for us. Some will be subventioned by money sent back from that capitalist hyena called America, for the USA has programs and stipends to assist such mothers; the Caribbean has none. In 1986 the US INS (Immigration and Naturalization Service) turned back a million Mexican illegals from that country's 2,000-mile border with America. Tear-jerking stories in the weekly news magazines emphasized the awful fate of Juan or Angel obliged to return to his native land with eight or nine children, none of which we had asked him to have, of course. But one got lucky. Last year a Mexican mother gave birth to a girl in the back of a border patrol van escorting her back to her homeland. As born on American soil the infant became an American citizen, entitled to all US benefits, as will be her father and mother when the tot turns twenty-one.

With the marriage vow no longer the institution it was in England or America, then, family disintegration has to be judged by other norms. In Grenada child abandonment and/or the single-parent home are more the rule than the exception. It is simply a way of life, or living, but to force this into a communist mold our three Polytechnic professors ascribe such promiscuity to "a legacy of slavery where stable unions were discouraged."[10] What then, when stable unions are not only not discouraged, but encouraged (by the likes of Planned Parenthood), and promiscuity persists? Doubtless there is some Marxist rationalization available, to be laundered into our left press, alongside *Pravda*'s unemployment statistics about the Caribbean.

For normal standards of employment cannot be applied to the islands where many of our people are *by choice* occasional workers. In any event, the only regular, dependable employment about is in the civil service, places like banks, stores, the like. By US norms I would wager that well over half the Grenadian population is unemployed on any given day. When by work you mean constant employ, and the latter state is not the preferred one, you are, it seems to me, in the situation of assessing divorce rates where chastity is inexistent.

For at the root of the CBI failure, as of work attitudes in the region, lies the fact that there is no mass market any more for Caribbean goods. Who wants sugar or bananas these days? The Geest family are doing the Windwards a favor and everyone knows it. Finally, go-ahead Asian competition makes our productivity look silly. Talk to one of the major entrepreneurs in the islands, like the Minors brothers, who import widely. You will find out that even after CBI it is cheaper to import a shirt or pair of shoes from Taiwan, via America or Canada, than from neighboring Trinidad.

As in Jamaica local governments have been reluctant to give up statist perks inherited from predecessors. This has been especially widespread in the Eastern Caribbean, not to mention Guyana, a disaster economy dealt with below. In Grenada the post-intervention Blaize government inherited crippling price controls and import duties from Jewel, plus a vastly inflated civil service (largely composed of relatives and friends of NJM, or New Jewel Movement). Blaize axed a lot of these decorative, and usually impolite, chair-bashers but his incoming government retained control of all elements of tourism seized by the Bishop regime, often on extremely flimsy legal grounds.

In Jamaica Seaga did the same both with tourism and bauxite. Why not? Such politicians have to pay their bills. The tax structures of Hong-Kong, Taiwan, South Korea and Singapore are hospitable to entrepreneurism (as are those of Mauritius and Botswana). By contrast Seaga's Jamaica continues to tax incomes at a 57.5% marginal rate. As a result, about a third of Jamaica's managerial class left the country. More than that have left Trinidad and Guyana lately, and their respective economies stagnate.

In little Grenada, for the purpose of raising revenue, the Blaize government imposed, post-intervention, VAT of 20% on every-thing, including services (I today pay VAT of this amount on a car wash). At the same time it annulled income tax. This sounded good, but it was hardly a fair trade, since the last figure I could get of those paying income tax in the island was between two and three thousand out of approximately 85,000. Imported goods (and truly everything is imported into these islands for the purposes of daily living), have become astronomical in price. A year ago I imported from Germany a modest VW Golf runabout which would have cost me around US$6,500 Stateside. It was more than three times more expensive than that in Grenada, excluding freight services.

The statist economy can only exist off a rich state. It is said, for instance, that half the population of Puerto Rico is on food stamps and that 70% depend on the Federal government for food, housing, and medical supplies. It is well known, however, that welfare dependencies of this sort stultify initiative. And other than in the US territories state handouts are unlikely to succeed. The Dominican Republic has been signally handicapped by one of the region's largest and most ossified public sectors. Ours in Grenada has looked quicksilver by comparison. Presumably the failure of CBI will be blamed on America, though it is hard to see why. It was a helping hand in time of crisis and critics often fail to take into consideration the prime factor in its failure, namely the extreme volatility of our area.

This is far from theoretic. During the 1980 Jamaican elections over eight hundred people were killed (mostly by Trevor Munroe's Workers Party or WPJ, the island's main communist unit). In apparently peaceful Bermuda the Governor, Dick Sharples, a friend of wartime days, was cut down with his ADC as he strolled the grounds of Government House. A thriving Communist Party exists in Guadeloupe, its leader married to a Russian; such is not the case in Martinique where it is estimated that over 40% of the available work force is employed, directly or indirectly, by the French government, with attendant medical and pension benefits. On the island of Hispaniola the CBI could do little for Haiti, despite a viably low tax rate, on account of its ever-ready political radicalism.

It is through this glass, darkly, indeed, that one has to take an honest look at our Caribbean. What does a would-be investor see? Grenada and Suriname (and Union Island!) knocked over in coups by handfuls of armed citizens. If they can do it Qadhaffi can. Libya lurks around these perimeters. Despite media focus it is a fact that terrorist attacks on US corporate giants of the past three years of present writing were conducted more frequently by Hispanic groups than by those operating out of the Middle East.

We in the islands are much closer than we used to be (or might want to be) to South America these days. The Libyan People's Bureau in Panama functions as a terrorist hub for activities in Colombia and Venezuela, while Suriname has been frankly assisted by Libya in subversive activity in the region. At least, that is true of the Suriname of Bouterse.

It is more than this, more than mere opinion. Caribbean handouts are of no help, so long as you cannot tell what the rules are going to be tomorrow. "Fast Eddy" Seaga takes Jamaica from the Marxist Manley by fifty-one votes out of sixty. The pollsters tell us that were there to be a Jamaican election tomorrow, this count would be reversed. I personally don't doubt it. Nor its successor, a wild swing in the other direction. In Barbados the likeable "Tom" Adams carried all before him at intervention and organized what seemed like a prosperous community. When he died shortly afterwards, his successor (St. John) identified himself wholly with his predecessor's free-enterprise program – and lost to the (late) anti-American Errol Barrow by twenty-four seats to three. In neighboring Trinidad, Tobago's A.N. Robinson recently unseated the incumbent (Chambers) by thirty-three seats to three. I submit that these were not wins, but electoral massacres. And they certainly make crystal-balling about our Caribbean most risky.

Interlude in St. Vincent

Perhaps because Grenada is such a strong small-peasant agriculture, it has always been jealous of parting with its land. My 1775 Thomas Jefferys map of the island, the earliest ever made, notes: "The Dotted Line along the Coast denotes the Fifty Paces belonging to the King." You could rent from the Crown but it was hard to buy and after independence the right of Grenadians to their own land was jealously safeguarded. One could never imagine Grenada turning into Providence Island in the Bahamas, where locals can often only reach their beaches by trespassing through private property. Indeed, it was the case of Lord Brownlow interpreting his cadastral rights over-zealously that gave the New Jewel Movement its first *casus belli*.

When we put in our first application to buy land in Grenada the Alien Land-Holding Office was in the hands of good, kind Paul Scoon, now knighted and our Governor-General. It remained in his pending tray for many years. We only learnt the reason for this much later. At the time we had no way of knowing that the mild-looking lawyer who had put in our request was in fact a rabid Bishop supporter, currently organizing a strike against the Premier, a mistake when that figure was Sir Eric Gairy holding fourteen out of fifteen seats in our lower house. We turned elsewhere.

After Maurice Bishop's communist coup suspicions over work and residence permits and the holding of land became paranoid. Officious youths in paramilitary uniforms staffed our Immigration and Customs counters. I recall arriving at Pearls once and lining up behind a rather crusty old American and his wife.

"What is the nature of your business here?" asked the youth behind the Immigration desk, who might have been all of fourteen. "I'm taking a vacation," replied the American.

"From where you coming?"

"Kansas City."

"Is where?"

"America."

"You is employed there? How?"

"In a factory."

"You does work in the factory?"

"I own it."

"And what does the factory making?"

"Ball bearings."

"And these balls, they is made of what?"

"Steel."

"What kind of steel?"

"Sheet."

"What sort of sheet that being?"

After this had gone on for some more minutes the exasperated American snapped out, "Look, I'm a capitalist."

The Immigration youth nodded and stamped his passport.

The island's opthalmologist tried to import a tonometer under this dispensation. Although he had every explanation for the instrument's use it was examined warily, confiscated, and has not been seen to this day. The fact that my wife Colleen's father was a prominent British General was a strike against us in those days. We put down roots in another Windward, one which has not, to date, been used as a kind of communist laboratory.

Northward by three hundred isles, St. Vincent is quite comparable to Grenada in land size with a surface of 133 square miles to the latter's 120. The populations are about the same, though I suspect St. Vincent's to be rather larger now. The figure usually pulled out of the air by journalists for Grenada is 110,000 but it is almost certainly far less today (loan agencies will lend you more money if you're over 100,000). During his February 20, 1986, address at Queen's Park in St. George's President Reagan used, I noticed, the figure of 90,000. That's certainly more like it, though I would guess at even less after the exodus under the Bishop regime.

The last Grenadian census, in 1970, gave a figure from the Registrar General's office of 94,838. In 1981 the Jewel government started a new census. There was a lot of hoopla on the radio and census takers came around and had a good snoop. I co-operated, and awaited the result; but none came. Clearly it hadn't yielded the desiderated figures. The strategy is characteristically communist. It happened to Seaga's landslide victory in Jamaica. For weeks Radio Free Grenada (the word *free* occurring in Orwellian measure as we were less free) had been assuring us that Manley was a shoo-in. His defeat did not even make our air waves. This was especially silly since Grenadians could turn their dials to Barbados, Trinidad or Radio Antilles in Montserrat.

St. Vincent has mainly black sand beaches, but golden sands encase its lovely Grenadine appendages, such as Mustique and Palm. Neither has turned out to be a shangrila for recluses, however. Colin Tennent took a long lease on the former and created a resort where royalty disgorges, his wife being a friend of, sometime Lady-in-Waiting to, Princess Margaret. It was here that the French cruise ship *Antilles* foundered after a crazy run up inside the reefs past Grenada. Palm Island, renamed from Prune, was more modestly converted by an Australian couple called the Caldwells, with yacht charter business in Antigua; it presently has hordes of raucous cruise tourists dumped on it daily.

Bequia, pronounced *bek-wee*, a mail-boat hour from St. Vincent, also has fine white sand beaches, similar to those of fashionable Young Island, a few yards across from the St. Vincent Yacht Club. In this area, then, we bought not a house but the house – since Cane Hall was the only private house marked on the map of the island. It had its own water plus a series of rococo frontal arches, the work of the priest who designed the cathedral in Kingstown, the capital. We got an architect from Rhode Island to effect the restoration.

For the necessary permissions we hied ourselves to Chambers, a series of clapboard lawyers' offices off a pitch-pine corridor. Here everything went with surprising ease and alacrity, partly thanks to Alec Hughes, a man six foot eight inches tall, and Lawyer Nanton, a Dickensian figure, rotund and fussy, who wore a belt as well as braces. Some West Indians take no chances. Theirs is certainly a cautious semantic. Toss a cheery "How you this day, man?" at a Windwarder and you receive in return "All right up to now" or "Well for the present, please God." You never know when a thunderbolt might hit you.

At this time Milton Cato was Prime Minister of St. Vincent, a most approachable man and one who made the island so agreeable in many ways. I think of him (now retired) when Caribbean friends insist that local politicians must have charisma. Cato had none, yet was elected year after year. Lawyer Nanton used to speak to him over the telephone like an errant child. It was not the way you spoke to Eric Gairy (unknighted then). Nanton's secretary was a lovely leggy daughter with the usual lap-length apology for a skirt who dissolved into smiling shyness which I thought had gone from girlhood generations ago. If Lawyer Nanton, starched of collar and elastic of cuffguard, was out of Dickens, she was Tolstoy's Natasha, albeit with a sepia skin.

Finally, Paul Scoon told us we could get a land license in Grenada right away. So, with old Joshua ranting about slavery nightly in Kingstown, we sold Cane Hall and started building on Grenada. It seemed more stable in those days! And as the fantasies about our troubles seem unceasing, I should perhaps clear up a couple here. For one Caribbean newspaper, based in Brooklyn, informed the world that Sir Paul "was detained during the uprising".[11] This is rubbish, if "detained" means put in prison.

As clarified below, Paul and his wife Esmai, a fervent Catholic, were rescued from a surrounded Government House. US Marines (one badly wounded) managed to take them down to Queen's Park the back way, whence they were coptered to the *Guam*, the flagship of the Urgent Fury operation. From the *Guam*, as soon as things looked safe at Pointe Salines, the couple were flown to our house, where they spent three nights and days. They then were returned to Government House.

Sir Paul's stalwart presence in Government House throughout the Cuban occupation was all-important for Grenada and, as we shall see below, it made all the difference in what came to be called the Maurice Bishop murder trial, the longest and largest such in Caribbean history. Meanwhile it is understandable to ask why Bishop, railing against colonialism every five minutes, should have retained a Governor-General at all. It was not simply to trot him out as a figurehead on ceremonial occasions (as alleged by *Newsweek*). Indeed, to his honor, Sir Paul never attended the ridiculous rallies. No, the office was essential to island status in the Commonwealth, whose increasingly tatty shield came to extend over Bishop's atrocities as it had over Idi Amin's.

More important still, retention of the Governor-General meant that the question of official recognition of the revolutionary regime was not at issue. Independent Grenada recognizes Queen Elizabeth II as its head of state, and her representative, the Governor-General, as her legal surrogate, Sir Paul having been named to that position by Her Majesty in 1978 (viz. under Gairy). The situation differed from the relation of Suriname to Holland, from which in 1987 liberation groups connived at the ouster of Bishop's friend, Desi Bouterse. Scoon's role was specified in the Constitution of 1979. He made the Governor's role continuous and, ironically enough, thereby facilitated the sentencing of his own murderers in 1986.

AmEmbassy Barbados were frequently asked if America recognized the Bishop regime, imposed by coup d'état. The answer was that the United States was not in the business of re-recognizing anyone. Political power had changed hands on the island but the head of government, in the person of Sir Paul, had remained constant. Such was the fiction, at least. Sir Paul's personal fate under Jewel remains unwritten, but he was undoubtedly coerced. NJM minutes for April 20, 1983, for instance, report a decision that "periodic sessions should be held with him so that he would be in line."

So we bade farewell to St. Vincent, its windward coast a sort of Cornwall with sunshine. But no bronze weed decorates its black beaches. No amber reefs seduce the sunset cormorants. There is simply not the same diapason of sun and sea as in Grenada; this island, where we made our home, has been called "a state of mind".[12]

It is that, a way of life (one nearly taken from it for good by the communists) where the eccentric is the norm and you go into a liquor store to buy a dog collar, or rent a video cassette from an ex-Austrian butcher's bar, or get your photos developed in a shop selling kids' clothes ("Trimmings, Pompoms, Tassels"). The high-fiber diet is healthy while Grenadian sea moss has acquired a cult status as good for the libido, the local ginseng (wait until Estée Lauder bottles it). Bush medicine has deep roots since for long these islands lacked doctors and, comparatively speaking, they still do. The other day, concerned about a man who had once worked for us, I stopped at his village and asked him how he was doing. "A little bit much more better," was the answer. "I get a bit of bush and boil it." Our selenium-rich soil appears to make for remarkable longevity, during which you can sit under the fretworked eaves of Craftee Souvenirs or Veronica's Speciality Centre and play the games the children play, collecting the names of passing buses in a string: NEVER DESPAIR followed by A LITTLE PRAY FOR YOU, CHANCES ARE by IN GOD WE TRUST.

They say it's paradise if you can stand it.

We have stood it ever since and not regretted the choice, despite the alarms and excursions about. We have made many friends and accumulated the customary family of animals of such parts. Our first German shepherd we named Carl after a much-liked yachtsman of the islands, Carl Schuster, who took his boat *Zigzag* up to Antigua for refitting and never made it. He tied up in St. Vincent's Cumberland Bay overnight (one of the few places in the West Indies where I have found total hostility), was boarded by drug dealers, and chopped to death in the fight that ensued.

The Alsation or *pastor alemán* is used brutally by the police in Cuba with the result that Carl surprised us by the scares he gave Cuban workers wandering through our property. He had great fun treeing them. Thanks to constant break-ins, dogs are essential in the islands,   but until some recent pharmaceuticals made their appearance they were not easy to keep alive beyond five or six owing to the prevalence of heartworm; in the tropics we have a permanent mosquito population and the mosquito is the vector of this killing, spaghetti-like worm. Most vets sent down to us by agencies like WHO (World Health Organization) estimate that four out of five dogs on the island have heartworm. Furthermore, at 115 miles from South America we are susceptible to other animal diseases.

Among these is rabies. The Burmese mongoose introduced (from Jamaica) to kill our snakes carried rabies. Our locals get bounties for catching mongoose and may be seen lining up with their traps to collect them. We still have rabies fatalities and it is not a pleasant death. Two friends of ours returned from a late party to find a mongoose in their living room; the presence of such a shy and wary animal in a house is a sure sign it's rabid. Both were bitten around the ankles and had to have a series of painful injections.

Barbados has rid itself of rabies, chiefly thanks to the poisoning program of a government vet, the late eccentric Dr. Proverbs. Colleen found such to her cost. A cat-lover, she had bought a beauty at the Madison Square cat show and planned to bring it down alone, for cats are useful in the tropics (though they also kill lizards which are in your corner). Obtaining the necessary clearances from Bajan authorities in New York, she took a pleasantly empty Pan-Am down, with whiskery Sir Ferdinand (the Fur Person etc.) sleeping contentedly in a carrying case at her feet.

No sooner had the clipper come to a halt than two large plain-clothesmen from Barbados headquarters CID stepped into the cabin, asked for her to declare herself, and announced that on no account was the cat she was reputed to be carrying to be allowed on Bajan soil. She had to take it back with her to New York.

Panic button. The Pan-Am plane was indeed a shuttle, due to return to Kennedy in an hour. It looked horribly like an expensive day's outing by any tabby's standard. Colleen pleaded but to no avail. I was in Grenada. The officials were adamant. Finally, in tears, she begged to be allowed to leave the cat in its box on the plane and telephone the government vet.

Dr. Proverbs was ninety-four at this time and totally deaf.

Holding strain, in island terminology, Colleen crossed the tarmac and bellowed into a phone. Proverbs too was adamant at first but finally gave reluctant permission for Ferdinand to be carried, without touching Bajan soil, to an onward flight to Grenada. By this time the last LIAT flight had left and Colleen had to charter a Piper Cub of Tropic Air. Never had a cat had such treatment in the islands. Placidly yawning, he was seen onto the Tropic Air plane by two burly Immigration officers in full fig (topees and white jackets) and took a seat costing, even in those days, US$600. Colleen arrived at Pearls in a frazzle with an entirely nonchalant McFurson. He was a very poor mouser. I recommend local varieties for ratting. We came by one of these in an accidental and even more unusual manner.

As is well known, Carnival or Mas (Masque) is a deeply ingrained West Indian institution. There are some who live all year round for it, and one of the silliest things Maurice Bishop did was to try to politicize it (awards for anti-American floats and so forth). Mas is a bacchanal and you'd better believe it. The amount of rum downed could pickle a regiment, while the decibel level of the bands competing is comparable to a bombardment of heavy artillery. Yet Carnival has declined in the "lesser" Antilles of late.[13] Gone are the lavish costumes daughters spent a year embroidering. Obviously this is due to the increased technical expertise of nearby Trinidad's Mas, a tourist feature that now strives to vie with Rio's. Trinny makes a pretty penny out of its parade on the Savannah, with funded costumes and bands. We can't match that. However, if the tinsel and plumes have gone from Grenada, the Jab-Jab men remain.

So does Jouvet. Carnival is preceded by post-dawn Jouvet, a patois contraction of Jour Ouvert, open day for Mas, and a good moment for the sobersided to stay out of town. People carouse and dance or just plain visit all night long, then erupt into St. George's for a collective jump-up. You dress for Jouvet in your dirtiest dungarees since the Jab-Jab men dancing around cover their bodies with bituminous oil, drums of which are left roadside, so that when they brush against you (as drunkenly they do) they leave their tarry marks.

Tolerable for a human perhaps, but less so for a tiny terrified cat such as Colleen spotted being swung at the end of a cow chain by an inebriated Jab-Jab. Not only was the cat terrified to rigidity, it had been tarred too. In his free hand the man swinging it about carried a bottle of best Fernando's and was seemingly about to bash its brains to bits at any moment.

I am glad Colleen rescued the cat. She fought to her knees to get it free; it was no easy task to loose the mite from its chain, but fortunately some of the women in the crowd shared her concern and lent a hand. We took it home, clinging to Colleen's blouse like a crustacean, and cared for it. Yet it was a week before that cat would come out from behind some old packing cases where we had left milk. When it did so it was snowy white. It walks sedately beside us to the beach for our bathes to this day and, since it was a tabby rescued on Jab-Jab day, we had no hesitation in calling it Tab-Jab. All the same I keep it quiet in our household that the poet Thomas Hardy was found to have been keeping forty cats when he died.

To date Tab-Jab has not killed a mongoose, but worse pests were to come, in the form of Spanish-speaking primates. For if physically life in the out islands has changed relatively little over the years, psychologically the Cuban, and then Libyan, connection saw the most brutal intrusion of other mores the region has known, one which caused a questioning of what it is to be Caribbean.

Between Two Worlds

Reflecting on his upbringing in Trinidad V.S. Naipaul denies cultural identity to his part of the Caribbean: "Nothing bound us together except this common residence." Indeed, the area called

Caribbean is constantly redefining itself. Its tongues include English, French, Spanish and Dutch. Its population shows large deposits of Chinese and Indians beside African blacks. Is "common residence" island status? This does not seem a defining requisite – consider Belize, Guyana, Suriname. The last, whose population is half Asian perched on the edge of South America, calls itself Caribbean ... why? Presumably because of the shared Caribbean experience (a sugar-cane plantation colony). But this would be to stretch the defining factor all over Central and South America. In truth, countries call themselves Caribbean when it is politic to do so. Hearing that Venezuela had done so the late Prime Minister of Trinidad, Sir Eric Williams, fumed, "I expect to hear Tierra del Fuego called Caribbean next." And, in fact, purists would deny Trinidad Caribbean status as a mainland continuation!

The French element (Martinique, Guadeloupe, though not Haiti which is largely creole) has remained departmentally linked to the mainland, enjoying obvious social service advantages; the media (radio, TV, the press) can be seen to be Paris-oriented. The independence movement in Guadeloupe, though it breathes fire, is as fractionally tiny and insignificant as that in Puerto Rico; however, it appears to be Russian-orchestrated and Guadeloupe's Revolutionary Alliance has received covert Libyan funding.

In any event the French parent would seem to have been readier of tin towards its offspring than the outgoing British. At present writing 1985 is the latest year for publication of the relevant finances, when it would appear that UK aid to the seventeen ex-Brit Caribbean countries came to less than what was accorded Gibraltar. The latter Whitehall has evidently deemed a "defensible" property whereas, as will be shown below, Grenada clearly did not rank as such. The Falklands, which received 8.6 million sterling, are said by some to have been moving into a negotiably borderline status of defense, when the Argies jumped the gun.

But in the Caribbean black Albion went independent. In 1985 British financial aid for Jamaica was slightly more than half that given to Costa Rica, with which England has no cultural or ethnic ties at all. Millions more were given to Mozambique and Zimbabwe. Such support of the former should surely give any democrat pause for thought. Mozambique's ruling Communist Party is being courageously opposed by RENAMO. The press taints RENAMO with South African support, and the democracies cave in. The nominee for US Ambassador to Mozambique (Mrs. Melissa Wells) currently describes the anti-Communist forces as "bandits." The US State Department does its best to flush them down the sink as South African puppets.

Independence is a siren song, a cause no politician can oppose. Aruba initially refused to become a Dutch-protected entity with the other ABC islands (Aruba, Bonaire, Curaçao), but now seems to be reconsidering the decision. Factionalism, as mentioned, inhibited the ex-British West Indies from uniting, and their post-war federations and trading communities were short-lived. Jamaica and Trinidad/Tobago went independent in 1962, Barbados and Guyana following in 1966. The Windwards were granted Associate Statehood, from which category Grenada was the first to free itself in 1974. Montserrat has remained a Crown Colony, as has tiny Anguilla, but there have been mutterings about independence in the latter, which would in effect confer a UN vote on the employees of a luxury hotel complex.

A certain sociological shift became apparent to those of us living in the islands, particularly after the Grenada intervention. In general, the British left an authoritarian and hierarchical society behind them, one with which the average agricultural West Indian felt, and still feels, comfortable, perhaps partly due to the strong religious element bequeathed by the French; an island like Grenada is predominantly Catholic, the rest being colorful Baptist spin-offs and fringe religions. The schools are notoriously conservative, so much so that there have been cases of West Indians living in "liberal" London boroughs sending their children back to the islands for more disciplined schooling. Children must attend in uniform, paid for by their parents (usually mothers), and the cane is not uncommon; in fact, corporal punishments ("strokes") are often awarded in magistrates' courts, particularly in Trinidad where rapes are unpleasantly routine.

In November 1985 the sodomist of a woman in St. Lucia was ordered strokes publicly, not with the brutal "cat" as reported in the inflamed liberal press (always going on about birchings, of three strokes, in the Isle of Man), but with the traditional tammy, or tamarind limb. Thousands of St. Lucians came down to the capital, Castries, to witness the event, which was, however, modified, and the culprit thrashed in prison. It is also of interest that all the islands retained capital punishment when England abolished it in 1965. It came out clearly in the Maurice Bishop murder trial, dealt with below, that our death sentence is mandatory for a verdict of guilty of murder.

The result has been a standard of behavior, a code of manners, which is perhaps exemplified in cricket, a game followed with passion throughout the islands and at which West Indians excel. During his interregnum Bishop discouraged cricket in Grenada, importing Cuban boxers; he had little effect. Cricket is a grave and complex game that has not changed since I played it as a boy and at which some of my boyhood heroes could still excel today. It is rare that umpires' decisions are disputed. Cricket has no John McEnroe. When the Jamaican fast bowler Michael Holding jostled an umpire in a match against New Zealand he was sharply rebuked in the West Indian press. The Guyanese Clive Lloyd, who captained so many West Indian teams to victory, was a model of sportsmanship and personal conduct on the field.

There is no doubt but that all this feeds down into public conduct and behavior locally. Obscene language is disallowed and, outside the larger islands, little heard, certainly compared with the streets of Manhattan, while in Grenada beach nudity is not merely frowned on, it is illegal (I have known old biddies guarding goats to report sightings to the police). Set three West Indians to work for you in your garden and two will be calling the third "Sir" in five minutes.

This sort of grading is based on an innate respect. Religion hands down a vertical world. Everyone greets everyone else (except in the cities). This recognition of the individual, a real feature of life in the islands, was exemplified for me the other day when a market dame, standing beside her stall of vegetables, watched a Rasta, clearly high on "de weed," twitch past, giggling. "Him don't like himself," she said, the translation of which was that man is created in the image of God and such a creature had so debased that image he hated himself. Playing snooker in the St. George's Club (which has to be the most select in the world since there are only eighteen members, most from the judiciary) I have long since decided that senior West Indians are the last Englishmen left around. Now, thanks to geographical proximity, the global village, tourism, rapid transit and media influence, America has come into the picture. The vertical world meets the horizontal. It is a matter of tone, more than anything. You are no longer Sir or Madam, but a buddy.

In the former value system behavior was coded to a norm; as a result, nearly all white residents dressed conservatively. Tourists could wear what they liked; if they dressed sloppily (or, in the case of women, suggestively) then they couldn't think much of themselves.

In the past two decades, however, tourism to and settlement in the islands has shifted from British to American (and Canadian, which I call north North American). The EC dollar turned from its sterling link to the American dollar. Changes in American and, especially, Canadian immigration laws mean a warmer welcome for ex-colonials than in England, for which Windward Islanders needed no visa before independence. Whole unions in New York City, such as that involving nurses and hospital paramedics, are ex-Jamaican today. Miami is heavily Caribbean-serviced. Only 5% of legal immigrants into the United States came from Europe last year; 10% of the population of El Salvador today lives in California. The Bahamas are a prolongation of Florida – you can pass through US immigration at Nassau; so you now can in Aruba (will Haiti be next?). A headline in *The Economist* of March 10th, 1984, post-intervention, put this turn from Albion to America in a nutshell – "Say Something If Only Goodbye."

So a new white class has been structured into this slow-moving society. It is not based on social caste, however indigent such might be (I am thinking of the impoverished English retirees who used to put themselves out to grass in the islands), but on the privilege of cash. Americans give the appearance of coming and going rapidly, with ease. They do not always behave as expected of white people, often walking around braless and untidy, and using drugs. It could be said that yachtsfolk, equally dirty and barefoot, always offered the same spectacle, but one could add that the average West Indian hardly knew how to "place" them sociologically, either. Them too hate themselves.

Now, however, the local cane cutter or banana grower is adjured to encourage this element, since tourism is vital to these islands. During the season Barbados will get as many as eight hundred tourist arrivals a day, nearly all of them American. It would be bereft without tourism. So would Antigua. Both would be in sad shape if cut off by a war. For though the Caribbean has been dubbed America's back yard, it is strategically more like its front door. Managua is closer to Washington than is California. Today Jamaica claims to have more than a million US tourists annually (viz. half its own population). Such visitors declined to 386,000 in 1977, the height of Michael Manley's economic chaos and anti-Americanism. Jamaica was hard hit by the collapse of the world bauxite market in 1980 but now, via the relevant authorities, attributes its increase in tourists to "exposure in the United States."

From such it follows that the alien manners system introduced by American tourism carries pressures. The first dishes have sprouted in the islands, the video-cassette finding a ready outlet in a world sumptuously devoid of cinemas and theaters, and US TV shows the good life coming down from America, in what might be called spades. Not that West Indians had to be told this, so many having relatives in "the States." After all, quite a few Jamaicans are on food stamps and I have frequently stood in line at the bank in St. George's behind locals cashing their Social Security checks (larger than mine).

TV's pressures, being almost wholly geared to the American way, are bound to confuse and change the balance of life in the islands. Already Trinidad has complained of saturation by US programming, yet seems unable to substitute anything in its place. Beside the glossy lifestyle on offer, the British seem a drab and impoverished lot when those few who do come step off their cheapie cruise or airline tours (what's more, they're inferior at cricket). In fact, those English who have built houses for themselves in the region often tend to be rich absentee landlords, which only exacerbates the situation – take the story of Lord Brownlow in Grenada.

Furthermore, to the emigrating West Indian middle class, England looks absurdly vulnerable to the latest American trend or fad. Even under Maurice Bishop, who roared away about women's rights with the best of them, feminism never got a foothold in Grenada. Nor did the gay rights movement. In fact, the smaller islands are probably the least homosexual places in the world (with AIDS, aside from Trinidad, virtually unknown). But no sooner have some Yale students dedicated a shanty to Winnie Mandela than some London borough, like Islington or Hackney, will leap-frog them ideologically with glorification of an even more extreme and bloodthirsty revolutionary.

In England the GLC (Greater London Council), which boasted as official adviser on civil defense issues a left-wing journalist called Duncan Campbell, spent hundreds of thousands of pounds of tax-levy money on interlinking causes (for environmentalism, homosexuality, etc) in an endeavor to by-pass the elected government of the country. Mrs. Thatcher was able to put a timely end to it. President Reagan was not able to deal with an American equivalent in the LSC (Legal Services Corporation).

Just before he left office in 1974 President Nixon signed a bill creating the LSC. This eminently worthy idea, to provide poor people with free legal help, has been deviated, in all senses, into an acknowledged mission to socialize America and tax-fund social aberrance. *Destroying Democracy* by James T. Bennett and Thomas Di Lorenzo has shown the use of public dollars in suits to require State disability payments for homosexuals, to force States to pay for sex-change operations (under a National Health Law that would fund trans-sexualization under Medicaid), to give illegal aliens free education, require "Black English" in curricula and so forth – in short to make the abnormal normal.[14] One particularly pernicious suit argued that alcoholics should receive supplementary Social Security benefits.[15] After all, alcoholism is a choice, and therefore ought to be funded, even though doing so would increase alcoholism. Today LSC clients include extremely well-heeled groups like NAACP (National Association for the Advancement of Colored People). President Reagan made an attempt to eliminate LSC but ran head-on into the powerful lawyers' lobby.

The point of mentioning these repulsive pressures here is that the shift in cultural emphasis from England to America in the islands means a greater vulnerability to social absurdity. England possesses a few last buffers against nonsense. America, a more open society, will send down what is dramatic and colorful at speed, meaninglessly – I doubt if many in the Windwards are interested in homosexuality or, for that matter, have even heard of a transsexual. And the US taxpayers' pockets are much richer. By fiscal year 1981 LSC's surpluses were more than US$60 million. But listen to an Indiana University Law Professor who served (in 1982) as Chairman of the Board of LSC:

LSC is a political-corporate giant. In any situation, it can deal with the Congress, or the Reagan Administration and its appointees, as it might wish. In 1981 the *net income* of LSC was larger than General Motors Corporation. It had 2,000 lawyers more than the entire Department of Justice. In 1982, its *net income* was larger than every bank in the United States, except five ... In 1982, the net income of CBS ... was less than half of LSC's net income ... In my judgment, its political side operates the strongest political network in the U.S. today. It can directly affect every local election.[16]

But LSC is only one of such bodies that will influence, via tax-levy funding, transmission of American culture to the islands. The tax-supported PBS (Public Broadcasting Service) has shown pro-Soviet films on Guatemala alongside eulogies to Stalinists like Anna Louise Strong; the latter appears to have been something of an analog in female form to that gaitered buffoon Hewlett Johnson, Dean of Canterbury, who accused America of dropping infectious lepers behind the lines in North Korea.

To date feminism has hardly made a toehold in the Windwards. Even UWI (University of the West Indies), wild and woolly as it often is, has not to my knowledge scheduled a session on "Lesbian Nuns," as did the 1985 University of Washington National Women's Studies Convention. And what would an islander think of that feminist self-parody, in which misled Yankee ingenuity takes a trend to its end, so to speak, namely the lady founder of Aplex Corp. who wants to persuade women to stand up when urinating? She is even marketing a device (Le Funelle) for them to do so. What one notes here as particularly American is the market respectability instantly accorded to the idiocy; she has incorporated what most people in their senses would consider a put-on. Nothing succeeds like excess, and least of all in America.

For these extremes, of personal conduct and private behavior, simply serve to accompany and to further extreme radicalism in politics. It seems almost unbelievable but there is more than one Congressman who has expressed satisfaction with the Soviet occupation of Afghanistan e.g. Tim Wirth (Colorado): "In the long run, the Russian invasion of Afghanistan will turn out to be a stabilizing influence in the Middle East" (Boulder *Daily Camera*, January 18, 1980; Jane Fonda and Barbra Streisand contributed to Wirth's successful 1986 campaign for a seat in the Senate). That all these excitable extremes can be uttered at all, let alone given wide and serious circulation, makes America look like a very permissive society indeed to the average West Indian native. He may not respect it but he can get something out of it, the reverse of his attitude to England.

When Maurice Bishop took power in Grenada in 1979 the populace was subjected to what was obviously a carefully planned, non-stop vilification of America and/or capitalism (its Politburo code word), to say nothing of the filth hurled on "cowboy" Reagan. I listened to four and a half years of this at close hand. But despite the introduction of Marxist educational lackeys, like the English Alan Searle[17], the society as a whole, the schools and churches, remained surprisingly uncontaminated – for these very reasons: the islander does not respect Cuba and moreover knows perfectly well he can get nothing out of Castro. Decorative elements existed; children were made to chant revolutionary songs, attend the rallies, paint slogans, and so forth. Well and good (or bad), the full-blooded attack on authoritarianism, and the vertical society, really did not succeed.

For, despite the lure of unpunished truancy, our children deserted the rallies, until they stopped. Their parents left the island not for Africa, but for America, the Rastas' Babylon. So the anti-American rhetoric rebounded on itself; it drew attention to the United States as offering more handouts than England, let alone Cuba. After Bishop's murder the turn to America was intensified; it was respect for American feeling that made St. Vincent, to its honor, decline a US$65 million offer by Ferdinand Marcos for asylum.

In October 1985 the Queen paid Grenada a visit to open the first elected parliament since the coup. Admittedly it was pouring with rain but her visit did not, quite frankly, arouse much interest, certainly nothing like as much as had her first in 1966, when friends of ours put her up nearby. After the 1985 stop she went on to New Zealand, where eggs were thrown at her. In Grenada there was the expected smattering of civil servants about to receive their OBEs, but I saw more Stars and Stripes displayed by shop-keepers in the capital than the Union Jacks issued to them. One sign read: ENGLAND FORSAKED US AMERICA SAVED US. On February 20th, 1986, President Reagan paid us a similar visit and was met with rapturous applause by nearly half the island on our main cricket ground.

All the same, if the islands God made from the rainbow are today inhabited by children looking northwards to America as role model, then we can expect the worst as well as best of the American horizontal freedoms to infect them. The momentary popular embrace of Maurice Bishop in Grenada was, apart from fatigue with a long-time incumbent, not so much hatred of America as infatuation with the most extreme aspect of American socialism. Within five years Grenada had turned its back on its initial hopes for NJM. Rational diplomacy was not thereby made easier in the region.

The Old Jewel

The best political history of the post-war Eastern Caribbean remains Archie Singham's Yale dissertation of 1968, *The Hero and the Crowd*, already mentioned. To recapitulate: in 1958 the Federation of the West Indies was formed, under the Governor-Generalship of Lord Hailes. After various associations the islands then found independence too heady a draught to decline. Grenada's present Prime Minister, Herbert Blaize, was against independence at the time – though it should be remembered that he was acting as leader of the then opposition, and that the opposition consisted of one representative, himself. Blaize saw insufficient economic base to support this final flourish (who is to say that, fiscally, he was wrong?); in the event, given a little British subvention the island got her independence in 1974, the British flag being run down in the darkness of a general strike, organized by the New Jewelers.

During this postwar period a dynamic young Grenadian called Eric Matthew Gairy redefined the island's politics, using the universal suffrage introduced in 1951 and union power. With one interrruption he dominated Grenadian politics for a quarter of a century, calling for social justice, "land for the landless," better health services, roads, schools, whatever. He called himself Uncle[18] and secured real gains for his rural followers.

The simple story is that Gairy, like Guyana's Forbes Burnham, Trinidad's Eric Williams, and other local politicians, was in too long. West Indians have five-minute attention spans. Around longtime office-holders such as Burnham or Gairy there grow like weeds the vices of fiscal corruption, land seizures, patronage and brutality – though Gairy's Mongoose Gang was less brutal than the House of Israel in Guyana (see below), often carrying out personal vendettas Gairy himself knew little about. Ironically, the Mongoose Gang was led by Willie Bishop, cousin of Maurice, who was incarcerated in Richmond Hill prison from 1979 until 1986 (without charges). Jay Mandle describes the Gairy period aptly: "Politics in Grenada ran on two tracks: the electoral track in which Gairy was consistently successful, and the non-electoral one in which left intellectals increasingly were effective."[19]

When he left office in 1979 Gairy did not leave one political prisoner on the Hill (in prison). During his incumbency Bishop is estimated to have put anything up to a thousand there, at various times, including one American woman whose case was complicated and sexual and thus seldom mentioned, but whom it took AmEmbassy Bridgetown six months to spring.

In March 1979, then, Gairy was deposed in absentia, by the communist coup, to be succeeded by the same in Nicaragua and Suriname. The armchair London Polytechnic pundits tell us:

"There were few in Grenada who did not greet the news with enthusiasm."[20] The *Observer's* self-appointed expert, Hugh O'Shaughnessy, bubbles over about the happening: "the coup was enormously popular with Grenadians and it seemed as if the whole of the island was coming out in the streets to celebrate."[21]

That makes it appear as if O'Shaughnessy was there. He was not. I was. My own guess (and it is no more) is that Bishop would have won an election at that moment, though not by a landslide. He promised elections, and lied. Doubtless his Cuban masters were behind this decision. Yet despite the cheering on the air that morning of the coup Gairy still had a legacy of support. He proved it after intervention.

He also had a legacy of four-star, vitriol-pure hatred. Take this instance: in 1985 Leon "Bogo" Cornwall, Bishop's Ambassador to Cuba, in prison on charges of massacring his mentor, was found to be surreptitiously sneaking broadsheets out to the communist front press in America. I read some of these documents which consisted for the most part of relentless vituperation against Gairy who, at that moment, was politically powerless (one seat in our House), stripped of all his possessions, and going blind. Within the Chamber of Commerce hatred of Gairy became more than an article of faith; it became an obsession. Hatred does not make a polity. But the deuteragonist in the psychodrama, Maurice Bishop, made hay of it. The Polytechnic professors deride Reagan's "crude" anti-communism: in comparison, however, Bishop's anti-imperialism was little better than a prolongued animal howl.

Obsessions contain the seeds of their own destruction. In the blind hatred of Gairy that impelled the Scott Street boys to go Jewel (and thus ask to be liquidated) certain distinctions have been blurred. Gairy may have developed an increasingly ugly patriarchal style, as different from old Cato's as could be, but he respected parliamentary procedure. I watched him doing so, even when GULP held fourteen seats out of fifteen. He would have said that he couldn't have stopped people voting for him. And the elections appear to have been legal. Or were they, in fact, as fraudulent as Burnham's in Guyana? Large losers always cry fraud.

Nor was the country doing all that badly in the pre-Jewel period. Gairy had succeeded in hosting the new US Medical School, the OAS office, and a Holiday Inn. His opponents would retort that he milked all these investments. Nevertheless, under Bishop they dried to a trickle, as did tourism, invalidating Bishop's motive for the vast Pointe Salines airport.

Gairy did not trade on race, as he well might have (Malcolm X, or Little, was a Grenadian), and as Bishop did; nor was Uncle responsible for the castration of uncharged prisoners, as were the Cubans in Grenada. Though he often disliked it, Gairy did not directly muzzle the press, nor put any independent newspaper publisher in prison.

Before me lies the issue of *The Torchlight* (which Bishop was to suppress) at the moment of release of the Duffus Report, an investigation into governmental abuses. Its temper may be judged by the Guest Editorial at page one which calls Gairy "an unscrupulous paranoid schizophrenic who in his lust for power loosed on the country what the same Duffus Report calls an unlawfully constituted body of men who inflicted unspeakable atrocities on many of the citizens." Imagine what would have happened to anyone who wrote of Maurice Bishop in those terms during the Jewel era. A few pages further on, D.M. Patterson calls on Gairy to resign (an appeal he became immune to), concluding, "Onward, therefore, good Christian Grenadians, Victory is in the offing." So was Bishop and he meant business.

Though Gairy harassed *Torchlight*, somewhat understandably in view of the fact that they were calling him a lunatic, he did not formally close it down. It was closed by Bishop after it had reprinted a rather mild series on life in Cuba from *National Geographic*. Interestingly, in his tirade against the monster, D.M. Patterson denies that new elections would heal the wounds. Why not? Because Gairy stood to win them, that's why.[22]

These points are made not as a *plaidoyer* for Gairy, but to preserve certain distinctions. If Gairy was the Fascist dictator of NJM, what was Bishop? Mary Poppins? Gairy was a parliamentary patriarch rather than a *caudillo*, of whom there were plenty around. The *caudillo* tradition in the Caribbean and Central America is non-parliamentary. It could be characterized by the likes of Batista (Cuba), Somoza (Nicaragua), the Duvaliers (Haiti), and Burnham (Guyana) – for though Burnham had a parliament it wasn't in session much; moreover as President he could pick his own Premier and Cabinet.

Men like these were not Western leaders. Castro simply continues the *caudillo* code, one responsible only to itself. Carlos Franqui, propaganda chief of the Cuban July 26th Movement which overthrew Batista, says as much in his *Family Portrait with Fidel*: "A monster has been born. Its father was tripartite – militarism, *caudillismo*, and the total power of Fidel Castro. Its mother was the Soviet model .... Above, everything is different, while below it's the same old thing. In Cuba, we call this system *sociolismo*."[23]

Maurice Bishop was born in Dutch Aruba in 1944. Like Gairy, his father Rupert had gone there for work in the major refinery. Maurice grew up – to an impressive 6'3" – at Presentation College in St. George's, the island's leading Catholic school, and an excellent one to this day. It is run by lay brothers, which occasioned some pleonasms when New Jewelites insisted on calling everyone brother. Grenada is a religious country. Gairy's mystagogical side fitted in there (extra-terrestrial visitations). Bishop's speeches, which sounded like a mixture of Norman Vincent Peale and Adolf Hitler, were full of Biblical incremental repetition. So when Grenada's first Marxists arrived on the scene they did so drunk with dogma from their holy books, Marx a new testament for a zombie priesthood ministering to an inexistent entity called "the masses," and insisting on a weird sort of acolyte apprenticeship – for Jewel status you had first to be a Potential Applicant, then an Applicant, then a Candidate Member. After which you were canonized.

For it has been well said that Marxism is "the parasite of the Enlightenment and the ape of religion."[24] Bishop was a contemporary Ranter, issuing collective imperatives to an originally adoring, if rapidly diminishing audience. To watch the children brought to his early rallies was to witness an authentic case of possession. The chanting of anti-American slogans was the ritual liturgy, and I have no doubt but that such obtains in some of the new African states. Jeering at America in his rallies Bishop seemed high (until recently I could have indicated his cocaine supplier to anyone interested). His rhetoric filled the void, left in the hearts of a superstitious people by the absence of Gairy's pseudo-scientific interest in UFOs, with a starker cult – one that yet contained the characteristics of all religions, as defined by Julian Jaynes:

> a rational splendor that explains everything, a charismatic leader or succession of leaders who are highly visible and beyond criticism, a series of canonical texts which are somehow outside the usual arena of scientific criticism, certain gestures of idea and rituals of interpretation, and a requirement of total commitment.[25]

This world view the young Maurice found in London whither he went to read law (or at least to eat his dinners) at Gray's Inn. He fell in with an unsalubrious group of West Indian radicals, spin-off Stalinists, LSE (London School of Economics) dropouts, and American career trouble-makers, some of whom had been the heroes and heroines of campus riots, bravely burning library cards, trashing the offices of craven or bewildered Deans, and opening fire extinguishers on "reactionary" professors, while American soldiery was living it up in Nam.

For the first serious student riot of this era occurred at the University of California at Berkeley in December 1964, and a former student of mine was one of its standard-bearers. Nearly all these protesters were touched by the Black Power fetish, and Maurice's way was set, though he was to do some heavy concealment of it in the early days of his revo. From London he visited East Europe and Cuba and, after qualifying, married a Grenadian nurse called Angela Redhead. I met Angela once, tall and elegant, shortly before she deserted him and moved out of harm's way to Canada; she maintained some sort of proprietary interest in his corpse, though long before the end Maurice's affections had shifted to Jacqueline Creft.[26] Between 1966 and 1970 Bishop worked for the British Civil Service as a surtax collector, as well as for the radicalized Legal Aid Clinic in London's Notting Hill. In March, 1970, he returned to Grenada high on an overdose of Julius Nyerere, of whom more below, and Stokely Carmichael, whom George Garrett calls an "ivy-leaguer in blackface."[27] That mixture was all we needed. Gairy was playing into his hand, the Mongoose Gang carrying out more and more unordered beatings of personal enemies. Indeed, by the end of Gairy's reign it was unclear as to which beating was carried out by whom, Mongoose or Jewel. We were in danger of becoming Jamaica or Lebanon. In such circumstances Bishop couldn't help but become a Soul Brother.

Demonstrations started. Our lawyer helped organize a nurses' demo that gave Bishop and his bully boys an opportunity to attack the government on sympathetic grounds. They were arrested for inciting to riot. By this time Bishop's associates included names that were to ring round the world press. Kenrick Radix, a lawyer still at large in Grenada (despite nearly being lynched by an irate mob near Birch Grove after intervention), is currently fomenting trouble on the island as co-leader of the Cuba-Soviet funded MBPM (Maurice Bishop Patriotic Movement), which did not win a single seat at the post-intervention election. These associates of course also included Bernard Coard, to become Bishop's Deputy, a less attractive but tougher character than Maurice, to whom the latter was to play a Caribbean Trotsky. Coard and his wife Phyllis, a Jamaican Tia

Maria heiress, were both sentenced to death by hanging in the 1986 murder trial.

Not to over-encumber this text, one should add that five separate anti-Gairy factions coalesced into a party loosely started by Unison Whiteman in St. David's called JEWEL, or Joint Endeavour for the Welfare, Education and Liberation of the People. Jewel was officially founded in March, 1972, after elections had given Gairy a landslide. Bishop himself had at this moment just returned from spreading the good word among "progressive individuals" in Martinique, having previously, in 1970, attended a secret meeting of West Indian radicals in well-named Rat Island off St. Lucia – the name was apt if you believe, as does the present writer on evidence, that Bishop used to pimp West Indian girls in Notting Hill and had now determined to pimp his country to Cuba. So now he had his party. He needed support, a *casus belli*, and arms. He got all three in short order.

Blue-collar, as well as no-collar, support began to come in for the demonstrations. In 1973 the wealthy Lord Brownlow sealed off the beach at La Sagesse on our Windward coast, fencing in his property there. This was not only unwise but unlawful, public easements to all beaches being mandated in Grenada. I visited Brownlow's house on a number of occasions; it had a certain grace and is the only one in the Windwards modeled on a French chateau. It has now been kicked to bits by PRA occupation. As a result of Brownlow's action Jewel leaders drew local crowds who tore down the fences and opened up the beach. This won the new party popular support.

Directly support was obtained, the NJM appear to have been hell-bent on a revolution, or "overt'row." One of Maurice's cousins used to confide his belief in the same to me, melodramatically, in his cups. On November 4th, 1973, Jewel drew a large crowd and on the 18th had the bejesus beaten out of them by Gairy's police in Grenville, the major town on our Windward coast. The ringleaders' heads were shaved with broken bottles (afros and beards were *de rigueur* for Jewel). Bishop himself had to go over to Barbados for (much publicized) treatment for a fractured jaw.

After the coup, or "coop de tat," Bishop instituted this date as Bloody Sunday, marking it with revolutionary rallies and eventually putting a mock-up of the affair, complete with well-bloodstained clothing, in the St. George's National Museum. Some writers seem to imagine it is still there, but part of the exhibit was considered so fraudulent that the incoming government ordered it to be removed.

The Brownlow incident, with one other, decided Jewel for a full-blooded Marxist-Leninist approach, – an approach which had to be kept under wraps and which was therefore frequently denied. As Gregory Sandford and Richard Vigilante put it:

> the decision to transform the NJM into a Marxist-Leninist party was kept strictly secret from the party's constituents. Most Grenadians, especially the poorer rural peasants and workers, are Catholic, socially conservative, and virulently anti-communist.[28]

Teddy Victor, one of the founders of Jewel, (who nonetheless imprisoned him throughout their incumbency), maintains that Bishop had decided on a "military solution" well before 1976[29]. Even before that Bishop's notes show a Pol Pot list of police leaders, each marked with a black X, for elimination. Included was an X for Innocent Belmar, the police officer who had led the beatings of Jewel at Grenville, and who was shot to death on the porch of the Bamboo Bar near Birch Grove by a Jewel assassin, after having washed down some mona monkey alongside the Nutmeg King, Robin Renwich. When Gairy left the island in 1979 Bishop rapidly circulated the story that he had left behind orders for the assassination of the entire NJM leadership. This claim was taken at face value by the foreign press, yet there has never been any documentary evidence to support the rumor. Reciprocally, a police report of February 6th, 1974, made after a search of Bishop's house for guns, claimed that a plan to assassinate Gairy at his Evening Palace nightclub on Grande Anse had been found.[30]

From the first, Coard, who personally drafted the NJM Manifesto of 1973, was clearly eager to drive the new party Leninward. Two of its initial members. George Brizan and Lloyd Noel, saw the writing on the wall. A former teacher, Brizan opted out of Jewel and in 1984, after its demise, became the new Minister of Agriculture (our principal portfolio). In 1987 he left the ailing Blaize to form a party of his own. Noel became Bishop's Attorney-General, but not for long. He was soon found to be "reactionary" and sentenced to indefinite political detention, spending the duration "on the Hill." He is now a lawyer in St. George's, vociferously criticizing the Blaize government.

A last incident might be mentioned. By creating a martyr's day for his father Bishop sanctified the story that Rupert "was shot and killed by Gairy's police firing at point blank range."[31] I am far from convinced of this. A mild man, Rupert Bishop was participating in an anti-Gairy demo around the Carenage when the police, under some provocation, started firing in the air. According to one trusted friend, he and Rupert sheltered under an archway of the Cold Store (owned by a left-wing American who was throwing his weight about). Rupert received two bullets in the side, probably ricochets since they did not lodge deep. They were extracted in hospital, he was discharged, only to die days later of a heart attack.

The evidence of his wife "Ma" Bish, at the Coroner's Inquest on March 14th, 1975, is quite different, but it was entirely given through the representation of Kenrick Radix who had an obvious interest in making a martyr's death out of the affair. According to the story, Rupert and his wife and daughter took shelter in nearby Otway's house, where he was plugged once, able to get in a police car, and died in hospital, unrecorded there. Further confusions have been added by publicity-seeking "eye witnesses," and it is possible that a combination of the stories is closer to the truth. Mrs. Bishop personally recounted how her daughter, Maurice's sister, was stuck up for money at this moment by a Jewel man.[32]

However this may be, Jewel undoubtedly tried to rewrite history for the incident, in the usual communist manner. I listened to a falsified tape of it, purporting to give Rupert's end. Schoolchildren were heard screaming "The secret poh-lice," followed by the crackle of automatic gunfire. Neither the police nor the Mongoose Gang were locally referred to as the secret police and neither at that time had automatic weaponry at their disposal, only bolt-loading Lee-Enfields of World War Two vintage, the No. 4 Mark 1 on which I trained and which, chambered for 7.62 mm NATO ammunition, is still in service as a sniping rifle.

Now all Bishop needed was arms. He had made his play with Cuba and Guyana. Representatives of both supervized his coup, though took no direct part in it; they didn't have to, it was such a push-over, as we shall see. The 1980 overthrow of the Aaron Government in Suriname was accomplished with equal ease; Desi Bouterse took the country with fifteen soldiers, imprisoned its political leaders, and disbanded all political parties except the Communist.

In Grenada Gairy was over-confident. I listened to his Christmas 1978 address to the nation, in which he assured us he would not allow so much as the tips of his adversaries' heads to surface in the coming year, and wondered if he really believed himself. His tiny defense force, quartered in a shabby shed at True Blue and jeered at by Jewel as "green beasts," inspired no confidence in anyone. Press accounts of how they were "overthrown" were, for the most part, wildly exaggerated. So Bishop got his guns, both from Cuba and in the most amateur manner from America; two Howard University students, subsequently arrested in Washington, shipped the necessary hardware down in drums marked GREASE – I would hardly believe this Rube Goldberg doing, either, unless I had actually seen them.

March is one of our loveliest months, 28-29 Celsius with trade winds blowing, the reef seas furling, the fish rising. On the evening of Sunday March 11th 1979, Gairy played tennis at Tanteen. I was part of that four, and forty-eight hours later could not help comparing rival styles of government. Gairy drove himself down for our game from Government House in an open white Chevrolet convertible, without chauffeur or bodyguard. Bishop later addressed a gathering of Grenadians, telling them they were at last free, while Calibans in camouflage fatigues patrolled his podium with Russian automatics. Gairy left by LIAT for Barbados on the Monday afternoon following, there to confer with Frank Ortiz, then American Ambassador to the Eastern Caribbean.

Thus were the Ides of March upon us. It is important to establish that, despite the raggedy-andy appearance of Bishop's coup d'état, it was in fact part of a co-ordinated communist plan in the Caribbean and Central America. Bishop was going to prove the wild card in this game, "his death giving his people what his life had taken from them."[33]

All Honourable Men

"Our aim is to gain control of the two great treasure houses on which the West depends: the energy treasure house of the Persian Gulf and the mineral treasure house of central and southern America." The late Soviet leader Leonid Brezhnev said it. For the Politburo the destruction of capitalism, viz. the West, is a *jihad*, a ceaseless holy war. Faced with this gun at our heads, it is hard to understand the excuses made for Russian aggression by the "progressive" or Popular-Front Left. Would a similar threat against the USSR by an American President be greeted with pious excuses and forgiving smiles in Russia? The Soviet regime sanctimoniously stands up for its own people, while it is authoritatively assessed that it has killed sixty million of them since 1917. Brezhnev's comment was not merely an implication, it was a statement of intent. And only the dumbest calves select their butchers.

Recently in the Caribbean, however, the scales have been stripped from some well-intentioned eyes as regards surrogate Soviet intrusions, of which Grenada was one. After all, Ethiopia, Afghanistan, Chad, the Punjab are rather far away, even given TV. In Nicaragua, for instance, the KGB had by 1984 set up a 2,000-man Directorate of State Security; Asian security elements (Vietnamese, North Korean) have created terrorist training schools inside Nicaragua whose graduates are destined to be transferred to Mexico, thence to infiltrate into America; by the end of 1985 Nicaragua was openly hosting such terrorist groups as the PLO, the Red Army Faction (formerly Baader-Meinhoff), Italy's Red Brigades, M-19, Chile's MIR, Uruguay's Tupamaros, Argentina's Montoneros, and the Basque separatists from Spain.

As ringside spectators of these Trojan horses trotting onto the boards of local history, we have noted that the mask is always, on its first appearance, that of a reasonable man. Who could tell that Desi Bouterse, say, almost apologetic about his assumption of power in Suriname, would rapidly turn into a bloodstained bully? I met Castro (at Columbia University in 1959), Daniel Ortega (in Caracas for Jaime Lusinchi's inauguration), and Maurice Bishop (throughout his incumbency in Grenada). How affable their handshakes! Who could suspect such naturally modest figures of being ruthless communist clones, soon to be ordering execution and torture? Certainly not our Popular-Front Leftists in colleges and churches and Congress. No one likes being told he was not only dumb but stupid, and the second line of defense in the liberal mindset, indicted of lack of acumen, is that such strutting puppets were reluctantly driven into Soviet arms by American intransigence. In other words, *they* didn't commit their murders, *we* did. Since Maurice Bishop availed himself of this calumny repeatedly, it should perhaps be got out of the way here.

By this time an increasing number of high-level defectors have blown Fidel's apologia that America drove him to Moscow. The troika was unneeded. Carlos Franqui, Maurice Halperin, and other disillusioned Castrists who lived close to El Lider in the Sierra Maestra as well as Havana have put on record Castro's decision to go Soviet from the start. In *Family Portrait with Fidel* Franqui writes of the new communist *caudillo*: "He envisioned a new kind of government – a Russian structure, but with himself at the top."

Who else? Fidel was a "czar."[34] In fact, the Cuban Communist Party at first wanted to put the brakes on Castro's headlong rush into ill-advised Sovietization; some even took part in Batista's Cabinet, just as today there are more of Somoza's cut-throats in the Sandinista Watch Committees than in the poorly funded Contra resistance (many of which were barely ten when Somoza was ousted). The Russians were initially wary about adopting a new Latin swashbuckler, one apparently (after the botched Moncada assault) with more buckle than swash in his repertoire. When I met Castro in New York, in other words, he had already taken the Soviet-proxy route. His needling of Washington into a hostile stance was thus an act of policy, similar to Daniel Ortega's and Maurice Bishop's later, when they began to turn their countries into tropical Gulags for "security"'s sake.

In Nicaragua the Sandinista leaders *openly* proclaimed Castro's Cuba to be their model before accession to power. Carlos Fonseca, Silvio Mayorga, and Thomas Borge – present Minister of the Interior who boasts of having infiltrated the CIA, (no big trick given the present US Congress) – went to Cuba in 1961 and returned entranced with Castro's pro-Soviet ideals. Fonseca even wrote a book about the beauties of the Soviet Union. The Ortegas followed close behind, pushing on to Moscow and there receiving training in how to mount a totalitarian state long before they toppled drunken Somoza. That Borge, Arce, and the Ortega brothers carried out the Nicaraguan revolution is debatable; Eden Pastora and Alfonso Robelo and the senior Arturo Cruz probably contributed more to it.

The fact remains, however, that, with Somoza crumbling, Castro summoned the prevailing Sandinista brass to Havana and offered them arms and heavy aid if they would co-ordinate factions under the most Stalinist of them (Borge's). This left Pastora, Robelo, and Cruz Senior out in the cold. Borge and Moises Hassan (Construction Minister) at once purchased arms from North Korea and Vietnam.

In 1979, the year of Bishop's coup, the Sandinistas took power. At a vast celebration in Managua on June 20, 1981, they celebrated their links gratefully with the Libyan regime, most notably in a speech by Junta member Sergio Ramirez to which Ibrahim Mohammed Farhat, chief of the nearest People's Bureau of Libya, responded. But, of course, Colonel Qadhaffi had lent the Sandinistas aid well before they took power; Benito Escobar had proto-terrorist Sandinista units training in Libyan camps as early as 1969. Libyan arms deliveries to Nicaragua post-1979 were monitored, from America, as constant, but it was not until April, 1983, that four Libyan jet transports had to put down in Brazilian territory for technical reasons. Their shipment was manifested as "Medical Supplies" but sceptical Brazilian authorities found it to consist of military equipment. The Colonel brazened this out with a shrug. By this time he clearly felt confident in our area. Where was the opposition? In 1980 a Cuban MiG sank a Bahamian boat and strafed its sailors in the water. Despite diplomatic protests, Cuban helicopters then landed on Bahamian territory without apology – and nothing happened.

By this time Cuba had become an arsenal (with a quarter-million-man army) and an airstrip (with 197 fields, including thirty-three runways in excess of 2,400 meters). Today, even after the intervention and establishment of a regional defense force, Barbados and Trinidad have only one soldier per thousand of their population, compared to Cuba's one soldier for every 206. Bishop's PRA was based on the Cuban model and the aim of Sovietization was there from the start.

Now Bishop's "coop de tat" took place in the last year of President James Earl Carter's office with a weak incoming Presidential appointee (Sally Shelton) as US Ambassador to Barbados. As the documents captured have shown us, Bishop felt he could play fast and loose with this pretty young WASP feminist. It was not merely that things were running his way. Psychologically he could take far more liberties with America than had Castro or Ortega. America had no inbred guilt complex about Nicaragua. But in coming forward as another dark savior Bishop could pose as an African black confronting a white Southerner; moreover, he could, and did, usurp the notion of having freed his country from white colonialism (under Gairy!). The myth of Bro Bish as a closet democrat, dear to the Maurice Bishop Patriotic Movement at the moment, has to be abandoned forever in the light of the facts.

For he too, above all, had clearly planned out his path well before Cuba opened it up for him. There was the communist convention at Rat Island mentioned above, and then the regular visits to Havana. Furthermore in 1976 Jewel started the Grenada-Cuba Association and henceforth sent some of its young for military training to both Cuba and Guyana. Gairy's CID had thick files on all this. Well before the coup Oswaldo Cardenas, the Cuban Intelligence officer who was to become Cuban Ambassador to Suriname, was assigned to prepare the NJM to take power and to urge it along the right track. After this the senior DA officer Rizo, formerly in charge of the Cuban mission to the United Nations, was given Grenada to guide its fortunes.

Bishop himself was ready to front, as a mild "socialist," for the "Vanguard Leninist Praxis" to come. Despite the milk and honey of his first addresses it is now clear he always regarded liberal values about as warmly as they are regard in *Mein Kampf.* The mask of deception was ready at hand. Looking back later, Bishop tells us as much:

I can remember very well that the first set of names we announced for the ruling council was fourteen ... And these fourteen names were made up mainly (outside of the immediate leadership), of the petty-bourgeoisie, the upper petty-bourgeoisie and the national bourgeoisie ... And this was done deliberately so that imperialism won't get too excited.[35]

The fact that there was no "bourgeoisie" as such in Grenada didn't hinder him. In May, 1983, the KGB General Sazhenev arrived on the island and very likely despatched Bishop at the end of the month on his last Janus-faced begging-bowl trip to America. Daniel Ortega hardly had to bother with the mask any more. Desperate for cash Bishop went up to woo America, beneath the umbrella of front groups there, despite the fact that under his aegis Grenada had voted Soviet in 92% of the votes of the 1982 UN General Assembly. Until this point Bishop had not been considered more than a very low rent model in Russia, where the highest figure to meet him (unlike the case of Ortega) had been the ageing Boris Ponomarev, head of the Soviet International Department designed to further subversion in target countries.

It should perhaps be interjected that Ponomarev was not such a minor figure as my remarks may suggest. Born in 1905, and thus pushing eighty when Bishop met him, Ponomarev was "elected" to the Supreme Soviet in 1958, just after the founding of the Soviet International Department. This Department is an arm of the Foreign Ministry, assisting in disinformation, forgery, blackmail, and character assassinations (as in the *Der Spiegel* affair). The fact that Ponomarev, who has headed the Department for over thirty years, received Bishop at least twice suggests that Moscow wanted to ensure that the Caribbean leader followed Leninist requirements.[36]

But for men like Bishop even to go to Russia under such auspices was a feather in the cap. Let us not forget that sixty-five years ago an American newspaper reporter set the pattern for this starry-eyed adulation; returning from the Soviet Union, Lincoln Steffens wrote, "I have been over into the future and it works." I frequently heard Bishop declare that capitalism didn't "work." Kenrick Radix's brother Michael, a doctor, told me he was leaving the island (for Eire!) because he was certain that communism was going to sweep over the Caribbean.

Castro, Ortega, Bouterse, Bishop – all honourable men, as Shakespeare's Roman politician put it. All peace-loving democrats forced into the maws of the Russian bear. And here, as Dominica's Eugenia Charles has noted, a new animal gets into the back yard beside the bear; Libyan-Nicaraguan solidarity was cemented on September 1, 1984, when the belligerent Borge traveled to the fifteenth anniversary celebration of Qadhaffi's overthrow of King Idris, one ignored by all Arab leaders excepting the Vice-President of Syria. And as the Trinidadian *Daily Express* put it: "The trouble is that, left to Libya, the Caribbean would soon become not a 'zone of peace,' a phrase the militants of the left like to raise when it suits them, but a sea of blood."

1.   Anthony Payne, Paul Sutton, and Tony Thorndike, *Grenada: Revolution and Invasion*, London, Croom Helm, 1984.
2.   Grenada Occasional Papers – No. 1, United States Department of State, Washington, D.C., August, 1984, p. 8. Capitals and spelling sic. Referred to hereafter as "Line of March."
3.   The EC or East Caribbean dollar is, at my writing, worth US$2.69, buying. It was worth a bit more in the days I am here describing. The larger islands have their own currency but the Windwards go into the EC basket, specified as EC below. The unqualified $ is the US$.
4.   Gregory Sandford and Richard Vigilante, *Grenada: The Untold Story*, New York, Madison Books, 1984.
5.   *Ibid.*, pp. 77-78.
6.   A.W. Singham, *The Hero and the Crown in a Colonial Polity*, New Haven, Yale University Press, 1968.

7. Technically, Rizo should be referred to as Torres or Torres Rizo, just as the former President of Mexico should be called Lopez Portillo, Lopez being his father's family name. The usual English journalistic practice is followed here.

8. Writing a little earlier, John Groome, an old friend and former Charterhouse master, gives 70% of the Grenadian population as under seventeen (John Groome, *A Natural History of Grenada*, Trinidad; Caribbean Printers Ltd., 1970, p. 59). But I don't know how he arrived at this figure.

9. *Time*, December 9, 1985, p. 37.

10. Payne, Sutton and Thorndike, *cit.*, p. 29.

11. Caribbean American *National Review*, vol. I, no. 3 November, 1985, p. 6. This journal has nothing to do with William Buckley's of the same name.

12. Frances Kay, *This is Grenada*, St. George's, Grenada, Carenage Press, 1971, p. 9.

13. A delightful description of Carnival as it used to be in Grenada is given in Willy Redhead's memoirs: Wilfred Redhead, *A City on a Hill*, Barbados, Letchworth Press, 1985.

14. James T. Bennett and Thomas J. Di Lorenzo, *Destroying Democracy: How Government Funds Partisan Politics*, Washington, D.C., Cato Institute, 1985; Chapter XII (pp. 303 et seq.) is devoted to LSC "illegalities."

15. *Ibid.*, p. 305.

16. William F. Harvey,, "Legal Services Scandals," *The American Spectator*, January , 1987, p. 50.

17. Possibly to show his credentials Searle published, with a London Writers Co-op, a book entitled *Grenada: The Struggle Against Destabilization*, throughout which Bishop is depicted as a hero and the CIA responsible for dengue fever as well as conjunctivitis ("Barbardos eye," locally). Chargeless political detention Searle assumed to be proper. Unfortunately Bishop, to whom this book was clearly directed, was dead by the time it came out. All Searle could do was add a forlorn epitaph to We Leader.

18. This locution, common to most of the islands, is particularly charming and semantically convenient. A boy would call a man of my advanced years "sir," in normal circumstances; however, as he grows older, and more familiar with me, this is too formal, but yet

my first name is over-intimate for comfort. He then simply calls me Uncle Geoffrey. I join his family.

19. Jay R. Mandle, *Big Revolution, Small Country*, Lanham, Maryland, North-South Publishing Co., 1985, p. 14.
20. Payne, Sutton and Thorndike, *cit*, p. 16.
21. Hugh O'Shaughnessy, *Grenada: Revolution, Invasion, and Aftermath*, Sphere, 1984, p. 79.
22. *The Torchlight*, March 16, 1975, *passim*. NJM closed the paper down in October, 1979. Its nonagenarian director, Durston Cromwell, told me he knew he would have been detained but for his age.
23. Carlos Franqui, *Family Portrait with Fidel*, New York, Random House, 1984, p. 172. I have seen this passage quoted with *socialismo*, but of course Franqui is punning here on *socios* or associates.
24. Dennis J. O'Keeffe, "Swann-Song of Prejudice," *Encounter*, December, 1985, p. 71.
25. Julian Jaynes, *The Origin of Consciousness in the Breakdown of the Bicameral Mind*, Boston, Houghton Mifflin, 1976, p. 441.
26. "Bishop Trial Report," Barbados *Nation*, December 2, 1986, p. 43; of her late husband Angela is quoted as saying, "He made me into a strong woman in that he made me realise that life is not for you alone. Life encompasses more than you ..."
27. George Garrett, *Poison Pen*, Stuart Wright, 1986, p. 100.
28. Sandford and Vigilante, *cit.*, p. 39.
29. *Trinidad Express*, March 26, 1984.
30. Sandford and Vigilante, *cit.*, p. 45.
31. *Ibid.*, p. 37.
32. *The Torchlight*, March 26, 1975, pp. 2, 7.
33. Mayo L. Gray, *New York City Tribune*, January 21, 1985, p. 5B. Readers should not impute error to me in sometimes dropping the *City* from the title of this newspaper, below; the word was enjoined on the then *New York Tribune* by a harassment suit of the Paris *Herald Tribune*
34. Franqui, *cit.*, p. 103. Even sympathetic Tad Szulc's *Fidel: A Critical Portrait* admits that "from the outset, Castro went about turning Cuba into a Marxist-Leninist state."
35. "Line of March," p. 5. Compare Brutus' advice about conspiracy

in *Julius Caesar*, II, i: "Hide it in smiles and affability."

36. The Russian International Department, with its Active Measures and *Dezinformatsia*, from which we translate disinformation tactics, is well covered in: Chapman Pincher, *The Secret Offensive*, London, Sidgwick & Jackson, 1985.

PART TWO: DURING

2. DURING

Coop de Tat

On Tuesday, March 13th, 1979, Colleen and I woke up around six thirty, and I sleepily turned on the bedside radio. A stentorian voice, hoarse with excitement, poured from our local station: "This is the Third Bulletin of the People's Revolutionary Army __ we has just captured the Beaulieu police station __ any further resistance is useless __ support the revo, comrades bros sisters __ long live the revolution!"

Frankly we thought it a joke, the ghost of Evelyn Waugh. We knew the Beaulieu station to be a board shack housing a Corporal and his dog. We even knew the dog. But as more "revolutionary" bulletins came through, we were not so sure. Then a Minister went on the air, counseling co-operation with the new government. This looked like black mischief in earnest. We went down to our beach for a swim. Clouds of smoke arose from the area called True Blue, a mile or so from our home.

When we came back our gardener had arrived for work, in a state of some excitement. Living within a stone's throw of the defense force's "barracks," he had witnessed everything (he was later, in the firing round the Fort of 1983, to be hit twice in the leg). Apparently some thirty of the new PRA had surrounded the hut in which the men were sleeping, at about five a.m. Bishop himself got it all wrong when he came on the air later:

At 4.15 a.m. this morning, the People's Revolutionary Army

> seized control of the army barracks at True Blue. The barracks
> were burned to the ground. After half-an-hour struggle, the forces
> of Gairy's army were completely defeated, and surrendered.

There was no half-hour struggle. The arms of the dozy defense force were locked in another shed facing their own dormitory. Indeed, one unnecessary casualty was Lieutenant Brizan, cousin of the George Brizan mentioned, who was shot to death while reaching for the keys to this little armory – NJM elements said he was trying to pull a gun on them. There were other casualties, mostly walking wounded, but not many. Jewel adopted a replica of the Japanese flag, its rising sun symbolizing the drop of blood they had shed in assuming power; but I don't think many knew it was the Japanese flag.

I got my binoculars out and saw that across the bay, over the capital's Fort George (to be renamed Fort Rupert after Bishop's father), a policeman's white shirt was flying from the flagpole. More Ministers came on the air, counseling co-operation. They were followed by Cynthia Gairy, the deposed Premier's wife, in the same vein. It soon appeared that Uncle's entire government was in the hoosegow on Richmond Hill; this included senior police officers and the Deputy Prime Minister, Herbert Preudhomme, who only emerged years later, with a pronounced limp.

By the time I reached True Blue, leaving gardener, handguns, and two German Shepherds to keep my wife company, the area had been cordoned off; I lay no claims to having seen any Cubans or Guyanese around, though both elements are said to have been watching from the sidelines. Less than a month later, however, when Pointe Salines was being surveyed for the airport, and Cubans had been seen hobnobbing with our government brass, I did wander over to a group in a meadow opposite and endeavor to engage them in demotic Spanish. They looked at me blankly. I looked at them blankly. Suddenly I realized they were not Hispanics at all. I tried German, in which I am far more fluent, and got immediate response. These were East, or 'democratic', Germans.

So, having taken a so-called barracks in symmetry with the Moncada, Bishop could now accept the will of the people and become their Prime Minister. He did so at ten thirty a.m. in his "Bright New Dawn" speech, frequently reprinted.[1] In it he promised that "all democratic freedoms, including freedom of elections, religious and political opinion, will be restored to the people." No comment.

Fortunately, a friend put the whole of that first unbelievable day out of Radio Free Grenada on tape. Bishop had established power *in nomine Fidelis* and was going to use it. I do not propose to run down here a blow-by-blow description of those years of Jewel's solipsist hegemony.[2] Chasing lies only gives them legs and frankly I would rather forget them. Anatomies of our economy during this period are given in William C. Gilmore's *The Grenada Intervention*[3] and, in great detail, replete with tables, in Jay Mandle's *Big Revolution, Small Country*. Both are worthless. Why?

They are so because they are based on Jewel statistics and the NJM kept two sets of books. Such is confirmed in a leadership meeting during which Bishop proposed "that we use the Suriname and Cuban experience in keeping two sets of records in the banks." The banks were under severe government pressure, anyway, the new deposit law requiring them to lodge 20% of their funds with Jewel. Two moved out, one was taken over. Scotia and Barclay's, who stayed on for sentimental reasons as much as any, could do little to stop Jewel playing the piano with their books, not to mention the fast drying loans from Syria, Algeria, Libya. Buses with Arabic squiggles on their sides still ply our roads.

Another NJM meeting found Bishop even more dodgy, suggesting "technical assistance" from Cuba in book-cooking.[4] I thus find elaborate charts of NJM's "economics" supernumerary, and am satisfied with the overall characterization of R. Bruce

McColm of the Center for Caribbean and Central American Studies at Freedom House:

> Virtually all the institutions in Grenada were destroyed – the judiciary, the police, parliament. The interim government wanted to serve as caretakers but they couldn't, because the Treasury had been looted by New Jewel activities; there were chits signed to heads of the army, to Bernard and Phyllis Coard, to others. There were loans coming due that the government owed the local banks, something to the tune of $50 million. The short-fall in the national treasury meant that the entire government apparatus, what was left of it, would literally come to a halt.[5]

When it did, we were left looking at a debt of over US$150 million that could hobble us to the end of the century. Fortunately, much of it was to iron-curtain countries (it couldn't happen to a nicer group of guys). Meanwhile, the supposed wizard financier Bernard Coard was never near the ballpark with his budgets, chiefly because the airport, a Cuban project, was absorbing 40-50% of all investment funds. Coard's legerdemain was of course unknown to most of us on the island at the time. For Hugh O'Shaughnessy of *The Observer* Coard stood out as "a model of prudent caution at the finance ministry."

Jewel, in short, was opaque. We are not overburdened with intellectuals and philosophers in the islands and indeed, as for Cuba, Carlos Franqui only identified the malaise much later: "How did it happen? It happened because all power was concentrated in one man. Socialism became dictatorship, socialism became Stalin, Mao, Kim Il Sung, Brezhnev, Husák, Fidel Castro."

What, then, was life like under Jewel?

Caribbean Revo

For the first year of the regime, during which Bishop's task was to mollify world opinion and raise local consciousness (the buzz term for politicizing it), one could live a rational existence in Grenada, provided one had a sense of humor and tuned in to some other station than Radio Free for news. Orwell got it right: the Ministry of Truth was the Ministry of Lies. One who is truly free does not have to be told so all the time. In any case, our evening news was inscrutable to the body of the island. The cane-cutter was exhorted to adore his brothers in Zimbabwe and Namibia, of neither of which he had heard.

There was a lot of Bro-ing and Sis-ing and calling people Comrades, and it was momentarily exciting for the young to see the new fast cars, burdened with bodyguards trained in Cuba, escorting this or that tense representative of the people on some vital mission. Government trucks, mostly Land Rovers impounded from various Ministries, roared around, full of gun-toting young. For a few days Rastas, rather than uniformed police, controlled traffic in St. George's.

It looked like play-acting. Especially the rallies, where a thousand beards flourished. These gatherings, to which children were bussed gratis (plus free revo T-shirt), were the equivalent of the hate sessions in *1984*. Imperialism was derided in these jamborees which seemed to take place every three minutes at first. The bare-faced choreography of the screaming and yelling was too much even for liberal US TV commentators invited to witness them, like David Marash, then of CBS. *Forward ever, backward never!* was the national anthem, chanted ad nauseam.

If children found it fun to see another part of the island and sing "*A people united will never be defeated,*" adults soon had to be coerced into giving up their Sundays to listen to filth poured on America. Nor did they look kindly on being compelled to buy the new airport bonds, to paper their walls with. NJM growled away as fewer and fewer attended these rallies, absence from which was to be "viewed most seriously," according to Selwyn Strachan, Minister for National Mobilization, who mobilized for himself a neat abode, complete with swimming pool, not far from our own.

I was buying some foam rubber in a small factory employing about thirty men when PRA thugs swaggered in with their Akkas, as the Kalashnikovs came to be called; the proprietor was told that he and his work force would have to attend the next rally, or his place would be shut down. The employees replied with dead silence. They did not go to the rally and the shop was not shut down. When the kids who went to the rallies for "de lime" (to watch) began to fade away, the Central Committee decided at its December 1982 meeting that rallies and solidarity meetings would be restricted.

By this time the party was in any case fully occupied criticizing themselves. Bernard Coard had just resigned from the CC (Central Committee), after some "imaginative accountancy"; this prompted a purge in which Kenrick Radix was accused of "petty bourgeois opportunist attitudes" and forced to resign, while he himself attacked the CC for "left opportunism." Finally, a couple of rallies in St. George's produced zero attendance, and they were dropped. No one missed them.

The solidarity meetings or "collective ideological study" were another pain in the neck of the time, and a waste of man-hours. It was, for instance, impossible to get into the telephone company's offices on Friday mornings thanks to these compulsory indoctrination sessions. In these meetings, often addressed by Ministers, a rude past was concocted, full of Simon Legree slavedrivers, and Fascist dictators dreaming of UFOs. Under Gairy life had been Babylon, but we were now entering the "bright new dawn" of a progressive era. It was a child's coloring-book view of history and if anything was lacking, that was the fault of "cowboy" Reagan. Why, even cricket was "still being conducted without firm political control." You're telling me it was. I played for my local village, Kalliste, batting with one pad and no gloves.

Across the road from us at Pointe Salines huts were being put up to house the coming Cubans. When they arrived, and started blasting the hillsides about with ferocious molasses charges that cracked the walls of houses within miles, the new airport began to take shape. PRA lunks were very visible, readying to "pick up" anyone suspicious. One such was a charming American ornithological student, compiling a dissertation on bird life in the Windwards; he had to throw out nets in the bush, catch birds, tag their legs, and generally observe them. Unfortunately his bearded figure, hung about with binoculars and notebooks, prowling Pointe Salines was just about the perfect PRA caricature of a CIA spy, so that the hard-breathing PRA youngsters took him up again and again (even after he had secured a personal pass from Bishop) to Cuban Intelligence headquarters near our house. Apparently the Cubans treated the whole thing as it was, comic opera come true. No wonder they scribbled *infantilismo* on Bishop's last minutes.

Backstage, as it were, the revo began to eat its own children. Teddy Victor, a founder of Jewel (and its St. David's Commander in the coup), was picked up and put in prison on a baseless charge of having an Akka in his car – his detention order had been signed by Coard two days previously. He was held for two years for this – *habeas corpus* being designated an imperialist tool – then kept incommunicado for the duration, all his property, including a grocery business, confiscated. Next, Jewel's Attorney-General Lloyd Noel was put inside, and only released on intervention. Such men were considered "counters" (counter-revolutionaries) to be treated with "heavy manners," viz. lightless cells. If this sort of imprisonment were not bad enough consider the fate of inner-sanctum CC members guilty of "political timidity" who had to do a two-months' course in Marxism-Leninism taught by Coard and using as texts the works of J. Stalin!

For when the real Maurice Bishop stood up, he did so naked and unashamed. At the time we knew only little about these party arcana, no more than does the average Cuban about his. So when Bishop's "Line of March" speech came out after his murder it shattered many a myth:

> Just consider, comrades, how laws are made in this country. Laws are made in this country when Cabinet agrees and when I sign a document on behalf of Cabinet. And then that is what everybody in the country – like it or don't like it – has to follow. Or consider how people get detained in this country. We don't go out and call for no votes. You get detained when I sign an order after discussing it with the National Security Committee of the Party or with a higher Party body. Once I sign it – like it or don't like it – it's up the hill for them.

That's telling 'em. And if that were not plain enough, Bishop went on, "When they want to put out newspaper and we don't want that, we close it down. When they want freedom of expression to attack the Government or to link up with the CIA and we don't want that, we crush them and jail them. They are not part of the dictatorship ... When they want to picket Bata, that is good, but if Bata want to picket workers we jail Bata." Nothing could be clearer. It was the "politics" of the schoolroom bully. Indeed, Bishop went so far as to give his frank view of the state: "In the case of the Socialist State, the majority will crush, oppress and repress the recalcitrant minority."[6] It was Castro who put it of Bishop after the latter's murder, "It was impossible to imagine anyone more noble, modest and unselfish."[7]

The "Line of March" deception was unknown to most of us since Jewel went clandestinely about its business, first showing its real teeth in June, 1980, after a bomb, planted under the podium of the Queens Park Pavilion, had nearly elevated the entire People's Revolutionary Government leadership to its revolutionary Valhalla. I saw, and heard, the explosion from a distance. There were rumors that Bishop planted the bomb himself, but I know no hard evidence to that effect. It did give the regime the excuse it wanted to hunt down, imprison, and torture the Budhlall brothers, one of whom had been promised a Ministry then denied it, and also one of the innocent St. Bernard boys (who had a red-hot grater scraped across his ribs).

For the most part we subsisted on rumors, on the lies of Radio Free Grenada, and the flashes of light from independent stations like Radio Antilles (Montserrat), which Bishop particularly detested. For a while no cracks appeared in Jewel as Cuban arms and personnel began coming down from April 1979 onwards, first in a ship called the *Matanzas* and then in the Guyanese *Jaimito*, both of which could be seen unloading in port, under quartz lights at night, by the whole of St. George's (heavy guns were not boxed).

At first, while pots of paint were handed the young for "spontaneous" graffiti on island walls (THE REVOLUTION MUST BE RESPECTED), Bishop seemed to go from strength to strength. Reality had not begun to intrude. He gave one press interview in those early months of euphoria, and I think one only. During the course of it I heard him remark that he could not think of a single country where capitalism was successful; he did not mention that the Soviet Union and its Eastern European satellites are the only industrialized societies with *rising* infant mortality rate; nor did he mention that in the Soviet Union a third of male workers are chronically drunk, with life expectancy decreased by four years over the past two decades.

Speaking in East Germany in 1969 Leonid Brezhnev said, "The historical initiative belongs to socialism; it is on the offensive, and the future will belong to it, to socialism." His successor, Yuri Andropov, reiterated the call for a socialist offensive a decade later. He was echoed in Havana by Osvaldo Dorticos, a member of Cuba's Politburo, as by the Cuban Foreign Minister Isidorio Peoli ("The revolutionary awakening in Latin America and the Caribbean is an irreversible fact that is shaking the foundations of U.S. imperialism in the very area that it always considered its undisputed back yard").

For a moment everything seemed to be going this way. St. Lucia's John Compton had sent an appeal to the British government to do something about Jewel, but Whitehall ignored it; and no sooner had it done so than Compton was deposed by a radical Labour Party. In Dominica Patrick John was trying to overthrow the government of Eugenia Charles (he is still in prison in Roseau for the same). Daniel Ortega triumphed in Nicaragua and came over to attend one of Jewel's Pointe Salines rallies, wearing lots of medals. Bouterse took Suriname in 1980, a year in which Cuban espionage rings were uncovered in Trinidad and Venezuela, using pseudo-students. "Scores of Trinidadians," wrote the *Trinidad Guardian* in January, 1980, "are now undergoing training in terrorism, sabotage, and guerrilla warfare by Cubans in Grenada." Mexico was being afflicted by guerrillas who had "studied" either at Moscow's Patrice Lumumba University or in the terrorist-training camp outside Pyongyang in North Korea.

Bishop must have sensed the complete communist confidence of the day. Nothing much was being done about any of this. When the US Government showed pictures of Borge's chief aide helping load cocaine onto an aircraft bound for the United States, the American media (notably Dan Rather) scoffed. When Soviet Victor III-class submarines got into distress in American waters, rescue vessels from Cienfuegos base in Cuba helped them out of trouble. The Gorbachev generation had come of age, knowing no military inferiority to the United States and able to take risks unimaginable before.

It should be borne in mind that the great Cuban defection stories had not yet come out. Armando Valladares was still in prison, and Valladares' account of his appalling twenty-two years in Cuban jails briefly shook the liberal mindset in the West. An innocuous postal clerk who wrote poetry on the side, none of it hostile to Castro, Valladares was subjected to unbelievable cruel institutionalized sadism, being beaten to a cripple, burnt, and having excrement thrown over him daily.[8] No, Bishop felt himself riding the crest of a wave. In July 1979 he called his cronies to Grenada to sign the anti-imperialist Declaration of St. George's. I listened to their speeches, or screeches, from Queen's Park, which was staked out by PRA youths carrying placards reading CATO NEXT.

The declaration was signed by the Prime Minister of Grenada, Dominica, and St. Lucia. It prominently united Bishop's friends from the Rat Island meeting, the pro-Rasta George Odlum, then Deputy Prime Minister of St. Lucia, Dominica's Marxist Oliver Seraphin, Michael Pilgrim, Allan Louisy, and others of the ilk. Every speaker ended up, "Long live the revolution!" Michael Manley concluded, *"Viva la revolución!"* Bishop orated interminably. After all, his mentor Castro had been known to speak for seven hours at a stretch. Thus emboldened, Bishop went on to tell the Non-Aligned Movement in Havana that September that there was being built "a new Caribbean."[9]

Fifteen months later things were far less rosy. At home Jewel had to sweep under the carpet, as an allegedly inherited loss, a visible trade deficit of EC$34 million for 1980. It was imposing crippling taxes (many still with us). Take cement, a commodity much needed in the islands. The London Polytechnic professors claim that during the Cuban occupation "Cuban cement was purchased at below cost price."[10] This is absurd. Grenadians were forced to buy Cuban cement, which was inferior (solidifying quickly) at the inflated price of EC$18 a sack, or "bag" in local terms. A month after intervention we were able to buy superior Colombian cement on the open market at EC$12 a bag. I once told a Cuban official on the island that I considered EC$18 a bag an exorbitant price for their cement. He expressed some surprise, courteously worked his calculator, and told me they were landing that cement in St. George's for EC$5 a bag. It takes but one guess to know where the missing EC$13 was going.

Worse, throughout 1980 and 1981 Bishop's friends failed to get elected. St. Vincent went pro-American in December, 1979, re-electing first quiet Cato, then putting in "Son" Mitchell. In St.

Lucia Allan Louisy saw the same light and fell out with his fire-breathing Deputy Odlum (who is still around). In July 1980 Eugenia Charles, to prove a lady of mettle at intervention, easily won Dominica. In the same year pro-Western Vere Bird took Antigua, and at the end of it Michael Manley went down to stunning defeat in Jamaica.

Then Bishop fell out with Guyana, an ally in the coup. This is generally subscribed to the death of his friend, the communist "Dr." Walter Rodney, whom I heard speak on a number of occasions. It is a complicated story but, briefly, Bishop accused the late Forbes Burnham, known as Odo, of masterminding Rodney's death in Georgetown. There is another theory that has the learned doctor blown up by his own bomb. In any case, relations between the two countries were never again the same.

After that Tom Adams, jeered at by Bishop as "Uncle Tom,"[11] the man who had succeeded Errol Barrow in Barbados, started to strip-search NJM Ministers like Selwyn Strachan on their way through his airport, while Trinidad turned an increasingly cold shoulder on Jewel, Eric Williams refusing to open any communications from Bishop until he fulfilled his promise of free elections. (Trinidad had dealt fairly summarily with some of its homegrown guerrilla activity on the scaffold.) Clearly Bro Bish was not as dearly beloved of his brethren as he had thought. At Ochos Rios in Jamaica Grenada was very nearly thrown out of CARICOM, the inter-island trading organization. The St. George's Declaration quickly waned.

Yet at Bishop's back there was the pressure of his master's voice. Havana's Central American Bureau was announcing triumphs in the region. Speaking at a "Working Class Against Imperialism" conference in East Berlin Jesús Montané, foreign-relations head of Cuba's Central Committee, roundly declared: "The revolutionary victories in Nicaragua and Grenada are the most important events in Latin America since 1959."[12] Indeed, the implications of such pressures may well have speeded Bishop's end; Grenada was not keeping up with the rest in the march to Leninization.

For, though this was less known to us on the island, things were not going all that well for Castro at this juncture. After the UN Afghanistan resolution, in which all Caribbean countries *including Nicaragua* voted for withdrawal of Soviet troops, excepting Cuba and Grenada, so much egg was left on Fidel's beard that he lost the vacant Latin-American seat on the UN Security Council. In fact, there came a period when Cuba had very little diplomatic relationships in the region at all. In March 1981 Colombia cut such ties with Cuba, Costa Rica following suit in May. In October Seaga kicked the Cuban Ambassador out of Jamaica and severed all relations with Havana. In April, 1980, thousands of Cubans had sought sanctuary in the Peruvian Embassy there. Then came the Mariel exodus. Things looked downhill for the Cuban leader also.

One theory has it that Castro deliberately discarded any diplomatic approaches at this point, turning instead to the fomenting of revolution and terrorism as more productive. If so, he made several miscalculations here also. Thanks largely to Régis Debray (to be Mitterand's Caribbean adviser), Castro read most Latin-American military to be as ineffectual as Batista's corrupt forces. A mistake. The Peruvian army wiped out its guerrillas, at least for a while, and Bolivia captured Debray, having previously canceled the Argentinian adventurer, Che Guevara. Guatemalan guerrillas were taught some rude lessons. The crunch came when the communist parties of the larger countries in the area started to desert Castro, notably Venezuela. The Venezuelan Communist Party defected. Castro railed at them ("cowards, traitors, opportunists"). Next the Brazilian and Argentinian Communist Parties refused to attend Castro-led meetings of OLAS (Organisation for Latin-American Solidarity).

Of course, not all these events happened at once, but the chronology is there and they were cumulative in effect. The independence of Venezuela was particularly vexing to Bishop. This country, which can be seen from Trinidad, and whose many radio stations are heard on our island, was the domino that wouldn't go down. Castro's polemic reached new heights, or depths, against it, to the extent of even criticizing the USSR for failing to "deal with" an old oligarch like Campins. Venezuela was not impressed. It is well armed and has an extremely tough political police, DISIP. Also an up-to-date air force.

Uneasy lay the crown on Bishop's Afro. For a moment he appeared to be dancing a lonely tango there with Fidel. So the Cuban mini-Mussolini found he could put Grenada on his wait-list. This may well have provoked (1) the arrival of the Russians in order to speed things up, and (2) the massacre of Bishop and his minions by the pro-Soviet Leninist wing of Jewel led by his Deputy, Bernard Coard. The point seems to me that the setbacks to Cuba at this time occurred when, as Professor Erisman put it, "Cuba entered the 1980s with a reordered set of Third World priorities. Specifically it shifted its geographical focus from Africa and the Middle East to the Caribbean basin."[13]

Bishop must have felt that the time had come for Jewel to tighten reins, step up the paranoia; the former meant using internal terror and coercion, the latter was no problem. CIA plots were suddenly everywhere. Some prisoners were put on RFG Television to "confess" to one of these. Unfortunately for Bishop it was clumsily done, the NJM security chief, Liam "Owusu" James, being audible from behind a curtain prompting the confessions. The militia was increased, as were the phantom invasion scares (common to Nicaragua), together with the ludicrous maneuvers, many around our house. They may have looked ludicrous but the weaponry was for real, AK-47s, Soviet SA-9 Gaskin surface-to-air missiles, and quadruple-barreled TSU anti-aircraft guns. These last were to play a role in the intervention. They fired at about the pace of the Bofors of my youth (the only gun to be sold, from Sweden, to both sides). One blew off a hunk of bluff in front of our property.

So gradually, on Grenada, the masquerade grew thin. The fantasies became transparent as they ceased to achieve much reality for the fantasts (indeed, the final bloodbath may have been in the nature of some ghastly attempt to show Moscow that West Indians could be real, too). On the island itself it was difficult to keep manufacturing resentment against ... what?

In those first years there was little American hostility towards Bishop. The Payne/Sutton/Thorndike study takes at face value Bishop's claim that in 1980 the United States, through AID (Agency for International Development), deliberately blocked assistance to local banana and nutmeg growers after severe hurricane damage.[14] There was no hurricane damage in 1980. I was there throughout. What happened was that the PRG attempted to rustle up dollars from loan agencies on fictitious allegations of disaster conditions. The World Bank sent down two citrus experts. Robin Renwick lent them his car from the Nutmeg Co-operative. They drove around, found no damage, and departed. Bernard Coard was then mad as a monkey with Robin for not having at least faked up some damage, for a loan.

It is hard to tell, from the hindsight of today, how deeply the NJM version of events penetrated in Grenada. I do not think very far. I remember giving a young PRA conscript a ride down the Pointe Salines peninsular to his camp one night. He gave me the business – "Reagan comin'" and so forth. Finally I turned to him: "Do you seriously believe all that?" He clammed up at once and said no more. That the invasion, when it came, did so on appeal from his own people must have been profoundly unsettling to the dystopic mindset of a youth like that, nurtured on Bishop.

And, of course, one of the principal incantations of the new national purpose was extradition of Gairy, back from America where he was, to a kangaroo court in Grenada for crucifixion.

Wanted – Dead or Alive!

At this point it might be pertinent to pick up on Eric Gairy whom we left in Barbados preparing to depart for America. When Jewel commissioned the famous calypsonian Mighty Sparrow for the anti-Gairy song *Wanted: Dead or Alive* those of us on the island assumed the PRG were seeking urgent extradition of Sir Eric, and that their legitimate requests were being obfuscated by Washington. In fact, Jewel maintained this posture to the end, though Uncle tended to fade off their wave-length more and more. Since then extradition has been much in the air (Marcos, Duvalier) so that it might be appropriate to tidy up the facts about it here.

Stranded in America in March, 1979, Gairy seems to have behaved, as he did on his return, with considerable restraint, certainly not as the lunatic blood-stained Rosicrucian dear to the Chamber of Commerce. On March 20th he took up residence in San Diego, home of Marine boot camps and pornography publishers; he waived Secret Service protection despite Bishop's sabre-rattling vows to get him with hit men. Gairy's activities were monitored by the US government with regard to the Neutrality Act but the ex-Premier does not seem to have put a foot wrong in exile. Obviously he petitioned the UN, obviously he urged Washington to help him, but whether he tried to organize mercenaries I cannot say. He made one visit to Barbados, staying at the Holiday Inn, and was cheered by crowds (probably as an expression of anti-Bishop sentiment). He was asked to leave after two weeks by Tom Adams and he left.

Now, being a civilized country with legal standards, America does not permit you to extradite anyone you dislike from its shores. The new Jewel Attorney-General Kenrick Radix huffed and puffed about America's crime in sheltering Gairy but, like the Shah of Iran, he was in the United States legally, and properly unextraditable. Barbados Ambassadors Frank Ortiz and then Sally Shelton were fully apprised of the relevant laws to this effect, and conveyed them to Jewel who, when it came to push and shove, backed down rather quickly. Radix, a lawyer of sorts, initially claimed that there was no extradition treaty between the two nations. This must have been deliberate deception, rather than misinformation. Such a treaty was concluded between the US and Great Britain in 1931 and succeeded to by Grenada on independence.

The treaty bars extradition for an offense of a political nature – understandably enough. An extradition process is complex and time-consuming. The accused may mount a defense. Radix, however, speaking in a revealing moment to the UN on November 15th, 1979, considered the taking of US hostages in Iran to be justified and "that he would support the taking of US hostages in Grenada to pressure the United States to return Gairy." So much for those who later ridiculed the hostage threat on the island: in fact, during intervention a friend of ours, an old man living in a small beach house near us, was briefly held hostage by armed Cubans, as were two or three medical students.

On January 31st, 1980, the US government is on record as offering to send a Department of Justice extradition expert down to the island to discuss the Gairy case with PRG officials. The offer was accepted and on February 27th, a US government lawyer came down to meet Radix, and help explain legal procedures. He was not accorded a meeting. It is also on firm record that, despite what Bernard Coard told the *Trinidad Guardian* to the contrary, the US Department of Justice offered all possible assistance in meeting the requirements of this case, but the so-called "specific allegations" thrown up by PRG were never supported by any hard-nosed documentation. The PRG's sketchy extradition request did not include a copy of the 1973 Duffus Report, whatever charges might have been fermented out of that Commission's investigation into governmental wrong-doing; in any case, alleged offenses therein would have fallen foul of the US Statute of Limitations, since the actions codified within it were more than five years old.

The US Department of Justice described the PRG affidavits as "hearsay upon hearsay," and unlikely to persuade any Judge for extradition. In short, they were spurious, so amateurish as not to be taken seriously, *a request made so that it might be rejected*. For despite Jewel's bawling that they wanted Gairy back to hang, draw, and quarter him, they did not want Gairy back, for two reasons: so that they could go on charging the US with sheltering their enemy, and because Gairy still had a following in the island.

This became clear on intervention. When Jewel had immolated itself Gairy returned and, with everything short of forcible expulsion running against him put his party up in the election of December, 1984. After a half-hearted campaign Gairy's Grenada United Labour Party (GULP) won only one clear seat, yet it took 36% of the total vote (Gairy had only won 46% in the successful 1954 elections). Scanning the post-liberation results, one sees near misses by GULP all over. In St. Mark's Mitchell James, manager of the Victoria nutmeg-processing plant, lost by 180 votes. The St. John's GULP candidate lost by only 35 votes, the St. Andrew's South-East GULP man lost to a lady rival by 97 votes, and so on. These are far from overwhelming margins. Sir Eric himself continues to live modestly in St. George's. If he is still hated, it is less than before, the plantocracy learning that sheer hatred does not guarantee an intelligent analysis of society. As Professor Anthony Maingot put it: "The victors, all members of the New Jewel movement, promised a socialist revolution. They were confusing middle-class relief at getting rid of Eric Gairy with support for socialist changes."[15] By reacting to Uncle, rather than acting, Bishop went down in history as a protest leader, rather than as a social leader.

The Jewel Dims

By the end of 1980 Reagan was in the White House and a new strategy war beginning. In January, 1981, Jewel formed the PRAF or People's Revolutionary Armed Forces, a body composed of the army, the militia (locals given guns), the remaining police, prison officers, a cadet corps, and the like; this was put under the command of General Hudson Austin, a former prison guard of whom we shall hear more later. The proposed development of the PRAF would have given Grenada, in proportion to population, *the largest military force of any country in the world.*[16]

The press had been suppressed, first *Torchlight* then *The Grenadian Voice*, whose editors and owners languished in prison. This so shocked the free Caribbean that five Sunday newspapers in the region published identical front-page editorials condemning Bishop. *The Daily Gleaner* of Jamaica subsequently published an issue with the names of all political prisoners held incommunicado on Richmond Hill athwart its front page. The Roman Catholic Bishop of Grenada, Sydney Charles, sent out a pastoral letter on Jewel's abrogation of human rights. I once heard Maurice Bishop orating over the radio (upgraded to 75-kilowatts) to the effect that he did too have a free press; he had the *Free West Indian*, the government weekly that fed off the Cuban *Prensa Latina* and *Tass*, plus half a dozen other publications which, on inspection, turned out to be cyclostyled or roneoed broadsheets for various NJM organizations.

Then Grenada dropped its BBC tie-ups which, after all, were mild enough, Britain's stance being palliative in the extreme. Britain retained a High Commissioner on the island, responsible for visas, scholarships, cultural matters, so on. In 1982 Bob Willcock, who had fulfilled this office so genially, was replaced by John Kelly, soon to be nicknamed locally "Commie" Kelly. The copies of the *Daily Telegraph* which Bob used to bequeath to my club and pub began to be replaced by piles of *The Guardian*, refuge of the worst left-Labour riffraff.

By 1982 Bishop had about had it. The legends dispensed in various books, mostly British, about the cornucopia that was Grenada under Jewel are scarcely worth lingering over here.

Both O'Shaughnessy and the Payne/Sutton/Thorndike team report at face value NJM's claim of distribution of milk to needy mothers, together with free cooking oil and school uniforms. This claim is pure fiction: I have yet to find a mother whose children got free milk at school, outside of a tiny minority of mothers beloved of (or related to) the party.

Despite all the arms coming in, despite the consciousness-raising, despite seizing two hotels and ten thousand acres of allegedly "under-utilized" land by means of dicey People's Laws, Jewel was broke. Bishop kept failing on payments to his army of children, hiking taxes, and incurring debts around the world; Grenada had Embassies in Cuba, Libya, Algeria, North Korea, Syria, and (later) Russia. Bishop was no longer in charge. I was drinking one evening in the Cuban DGI house when one of their officers asked me if I would like to see a plan of the proposed air terminal at Pointe Salines. I at once observed on it that next to the Airport Manager's Office had been inked in: Counter-Intelligence Office. It was clear who was going to run the airport, and it wasn't Bro Bish.

Nor was it entirely the Cubans. In November 1981 a Soviet Embassy opened in a bungalow-style hotel stolen from a Dutchman. It started with a staff of thirty, under "Ambassador" Gennadi Sazhenev, a high-ranking General in the GRU or military intelligence branch of the KGB. Sazhenev, a good-looking man with a full head of white hair, had been director of Moscow's South American desk in the Argentine, a most important role. Prior to that he had been in Angola. The writing was on the wall. The Russian had come to pull rank, to apply the whip, chiefly to the dragging airport construction. He down-graded Rizo who up to that time had been running our affairs. You don't demote men like Sazhenev and it seemed clear that Grenada had at last found a place on the Kremlin's agenda. By intervention the Russians, almost unmentioned in the press, had grown to well over a hundred, including a number of bullet-headed Spetsnaz men, elite commandos.

The term Spetsnaz abbreviates *Spetsaznacheniya* or special designation. They go in groups to target countries like Grenada under Embassy cover. They hardly needed this fiction under Jewel's dispensation and for the size of the terrain were numerous. The chauffeur of Sazhenev's bullet-proof Mercedes limo, with whom I chatted on several occasions, was probably one of them, since he could speak perfect English, fluency in a host country's tongue being a requirement of Spetsnaz troops. Oleg Lyalin, a 1971 KGB defector, has given us gruesome accounts of the training of such special forces, with their detailed plans to flood the London Underground, to destroy the Fyling-dales early warning system in Yorkshire, and the like. Apparently they regularly practice assaults on mock-ups of No. 10 Downing Street. The 82nd had some initial trouble with these thugs, having repeatedly to return them to their compound, but they soon respected a show of real resolve. My wife and I were particularly happy to see them leave the island since our house was on one of Sazhenev's lists for take-over.

For a sort of Russian grid was to have been applied to Grenada. Those with up to fifty acres of land were "kulaks" and to be crushed. Eventually no one outside the government would own land at all. Agriculture would be carried out by the landless on collectivized state farms. This "solution" had already been advanced by the Leninist wing of NJM – in particular in a memo by Ewart "Headache" Layne – and it strengthens the theory that Coard had or was seeking Russian backing for the massacre. The Russians had also printed ration cards for us and a lot of uniform clothing for field workers was captured by the 82nd.

Property dispossession had taken place before they came, however. Don Street, a yachtsman of renown and author of books on sailing the Windwards, found access to his house blocked – it was too close to the new Calivigny terrorist-training camp for Cuban tastes. This sort of action, involving a publicist for the island, showed that Bishop wanted tourism like a hole in the head; he was completely in the hands of the Cubans in such matters. But Don Street finished up – as usual – ahead. His house was demolished in the rocket attack on Calivigny and rebuilt by Uncle Sam. But the Russians were going to be rougher and, with their arrival, Bishop had started his "Leninist" tumbrils rolling.

Vanguard Leninist Praxis

Maurice Bishop's notes, captured intact over two years, make it plain that he contemplated a Soviet Grenada from the start; throughout them, and increasingly in the minutes of the Central Committee, recurs the term Vanguard Leninist Praxis. I once made an attempt to explicate this elsewhere,[17] but suspect my interpretation fell on understandably deaf ears. For locally these are but whirling words, my Lord, meaningless gibberish to the average Grenadian, yet for Jewel the catchphrase carried some sort of hieroglyphic authority. Imagine how important you sounded, addressing the Water Commission men, say, or the telephone linesmen, with this kind of thing on your lips, not to mention as a verbal lapel button at NJM parties.

For obscurity conveys authority. Verbal disguises consistently further the Soviet cause. When the term Trotskyite Militant Tendency was adopted in England as a cover, communism was able to place "sleepers" in sensitive positions of defense, e.g. the Faslane nuclear submarine base, in a way they would not have been had its true identity been declared. We note that cells operating in the Ministry of Defence found themselves debarred from security posts if communists or Fascists, but not if Militants.

Now it is true that, along with his friend Engels in the Prussia of 1848, Marx advocated armed insurrection against the state; for this he was put on trial for treason, acquitted, sought refuge in France, only to be thrown out, spending much of the remainder of his days in the British Museum, an unattractive fate. But Marx was far from the agitator Lenin was to be and, indeed, the socialism of Marx and Ruge, stripped of its appanage of pseudo-economic scholastics, is closer today to that of Britain's Kinnock than to communism proper – if there is such a thing. I have three reasons for refraining from a dilation of Jewel's favorite catchphrase: (1) it does not apply to the Eastern Caribbean of the mid-nineteen eighties, (2) no one on Grenada knew what it meant, (3) Marx was wrong.

"No social order," Marx wrote in his *Preface to a Critique of Political Economy* (probably unread by the NJM hierarchy), "ever perishes before all the productive forces for which there is room in it have developed." In Marx's day this meant that a true revolution could only take place in the industrialized nations (especially England, France, Germany). Everything was incorrect, perhaps because Marx did not know what the world outside such nations was, or was to be. The monarchy was restored in England after the 1642-1649 revolution and has remained ever since. Today capitalist democracy is offering the individual the best chance to express and better himself, while communism came most forcibly and bloodily to the last feudal states of our time, Russia and China.[18]

In the notes he left behind him we can see Bishop wrestling with the irritation that Grenada had no industrial proletariat nor disenfranchised peasantry, the population being, in his words, of a "low cultural level." He added, "It is only under the leadership of the working class, led by a Marxist-Leninist vanguard Party that the process can be completed and we can go on to socialist construction."[19]

Frankly, it would not have mattered much if Bishop had found in Grenada the proper model for Vanguard Leninism, since Russia today considers itself the repository of true communism, just as yesterday it considered itself the *echt* or true Christianity, under Ivan the Terrible. The lack of "praxis" in a tiny, tatterdemalion Caribbean island forced Bishop to try to take up postures that would impress the Soviets; they remained unimpressed, referred to his revolution as a *gosudarstvennyi povorot* (or coup d'état), and sent minor figures to meet him – when not Ponomarev it was little Tikhonov. On the other hand, not only Daniel Ortega but Bishop's local rival Forbes Burnham both rated receptions by Andropov, after Brezhnev's death. Grenada's resident Ambassador to Cuba (where he couldn't get a telephone for two years), Richard Jacobs, was reassigned to Moscow without much impact on the Politburo.

If Marx was a monkish person, a man of libraries and letters, Lenin was cut from different cloth. Here was a man who, when faced with returning to Russia (from Zürich) in 1917, debated as to whether he should wear a woman's wig or pretend to be a deaf-mute (his wife counseled against the latter course, arguing that he would see mensheviks everywhere, shout at them, and so give himself away). This was your true Jewel Potential Applicant. Constantly dwelling on his brother's hanging for conspiracy to assassinate the Czar, Lenin turned into a far more able conspirator than Marx, postulating his Vanguard Party (or inner elite) as the instrument for seizing power from the working class, though ostensibly in its name. For Lenin seems to have been quite contemptuous of the libertarian mind – "this talk of feeding the starving is nothing but an expression of the saccharine-sweet sentimentality so characteristic of our intelligentsia." Cp. Bernard Coard: "the masses would have to be led to communism by a combination of force and fraud." Cp. Maurice Bishop: "When the revolution orders it must be obeyed." Cp. the Coard supporter quoted by O'Shaughnessy: "If the people won't accept it, the people will have to be made to accept it." This is straight, hip-shooting Vanguard politics.

Frankly, Lenin found the Marxist texts so much wallpaper and in 1918 decided, "We must organise everything, take everything into our hands." Power. It meant the single-party totalitarian tyranny continued as model by Stalin, it meant the Cheka, OGPU, or NKVD, and it meant the Terror during which millions of Russians died in the post-First World War purges. It also authenticated the axing in the back of Trotsky in a Mexican garden in the same dog-and-pony show that clearly overtook Bro Bish. He and his had been making up lists of small villagers who were "Petty Bourg," viz. hesitating elements like the provisional government of Kerensky. The Vanguard Party was, thus, a war waged against the Russian people in Russia, and against the Grenadian people in Grenada.

The vanguard Praxis saw the working class as an instrument to world conquest. In its crudest manifestations Vanguard Leninism turns its back on Marxism, and lets action dominate ideology. Hence Norman Mailer – "you created the revolution first and learned from it, learned of what your revolution might consist and where it might go out of the intimate truth of the way it presented itself to your experience."[20] This is Abbie Hoffman's "revolution for the hell of it." Blow up first, think later.

By conceding to Coard's Vanguard attitude Bishop became an ideological prisoner. His party, built on a mix of black-power radicals out of the American sixties and LSE (London School of Economics) dropouts, ended up urging more "ruthlessness" on We Leader. Phyllis Coard called him weak. Hudson Austin hoped that "his hand will now become a Marxist-Leninist-Stalinist hand." The island was under the gun but the cat was out of the bag. *The Grenadian Voice* may have been "crushed" by Jewel, but Grenadians were increasingly using independent eyes and ears. On the airstrip the first Soviet Antonov transport planes had been seen landing. Russian "cruise ships" put in with material. At a CC meeting a month before the murders Phyllis Coard denounced Bishop:

All programmes of the Revolution are in a very weak condition ...
The mass organizations are showing less participation in the political work ... The militia is non-existent, the army demoralized ... If this is allowed to continue the party will disintegrate in a matter of 5-6 months ... The Comrade Leader has not taken responsibility, not given the necessary guidance ...[21]

Bishop's satrapy was slipping from him. First, he could not stop a stream of truth about of what he was really doing leaking out to nationals in the US, despite reprisals taken against their families on the island. (One US TV documentary interviewed a small shop-owner in Brooklyn who had been threatened, in his own shop, by Radix with a gun. Secondly, there now went into this stream of truth a small but significant undercurrent of Cuban defection. In 1981 the most valuable turncoat of the era was Rizo's second-in-command Carlos Pedro Tariche Reina, who was promptly debriefed in Washington. In its May-June 1981 issue *National Defense* was able to rehearse in detail the hardware dumped to date on Grenada, including 3,000 stands of Akkas, far more than needed for its own defense. Eventually 10,000 such automatics were found, thousands of rocket launchers, fuses, tons of TNT, millions of rounds of ammunition, heavy communications gear, and cryptographic devices. It was also revealed that Coard had signed a secret treaty with Moscow granting landing rights for the TU-95, the Ilyushin Bear reconnaissance bomber, which requires a runway of seven thousand feet or more (depending on load).

Finally, it was clear by this time that Bishop would not win an election in Grenada, unless he was going to rely on an under-thirteen vote. With more and more Cubans coming down in 1983 intent on completing the runway (night work under lights was begun), Bishop was playing a zero-sum game with Havana. A thousand Cubans on Pointe Salines? A drop in the bucket for Castro who had at this time over 45,000 troops stationed far from its borders overseas, obedient to Fidel's principle, "The duty of a revolutionary is to make a revolution."

But even Castro had to be careful, with the Soviet hegemony on his back. He had pursued his dream into South America in the sixties and been rebuffed. Che had been killed. There came a point when for good order's sake Russia cut its petroleum shipments to Cuba (which depends on the USSR for 98% of such supplies), and made it toe the line.

It has done so ever since that point. As Professor Robert A. Pastor puts it: "No country in Latin America has so slavishly followed the international line of the United States in the 1970s as Cuba has that of the USSR."[22] Subventioned to the tune of US$3 billion a year, excluding free military hardware, Cuba can scarcely lay claim to much independence.

What was it like to live among its minions?

Semper Fidel: Life Among the Cubans

I can truthfully say that until 1979 the only Cuban I had met was Fidel Castro. That was on the steps of Columbia's Law Library in April 1959, during his first visit to America. I had just taught a class and some students told me, without much interest, "That's Castro."

In those days he didn't have the weight problem, nor so much facial fungus, nor the mouth running over with rhetoric. Yet we now know that Castro was soon to be sending out forces to topple neighboring governments, in Haiti, Panama, and the Dominican Republic (twice). And this was *prior to* any American hostility towards him. As Professor Pastor has put it, "It is hard to see how the Cuban revolution was made more secure by creating new foreign enemies."[23] There Fidel stood, in military fatigues, and accompanied by another *barbudo*, a man too tall to be Raúl, I think, and possibly José (Pepin) Bosch or Daniel Bacardí, the romanticists of the periodical *Revolución*, men who knew more about European surrealism than running a country, and most of whom are today in exile or prison, if not actually pushing up the daisies of some Cuban prison cemetery, for having failed to put Fidelity before legality. The new Cuban leader had no body-guards with him and he was not for once chomping a stogie, the now inevitable Upmann Four. There were no TV crews about. I held out my hand, got enveloped in a garlicky *abrazo*, and hastened on to Philosophy Hall, my mind full of Baudelaire and Joyce. For four and a half years Colleen and I lived cheek by jowl with Cubans on Pointe Salines and learnt quite a lot about communism.

The preconception that every *compañero* sent down, even in this select lot, was going to be an ardent Castrite and hard-line revolutionary was the first cliché to be jettisoned. The second, of Cuban machismo towards women, had to be instantly intensified. The Cubans behaved towards women like some male chauv parody out of Germaine Greer or Gloria Steinem. When their workers hit the beach it was as if they'd never seen a woman before. Any girl alone on Grande Anse simply got up and left. The apogee of this Cuban machismo in literature, if it can be dignified as such, is perhaps G. Cabrera Infante's *Infante's Inferno*, a novel of a young man in Havana masturbating through four hundred pages, and twice as many awful puns, over Cuban women, surprisingly few of whom are attained.[24]

Apart from this leering lechery over every woman in sight, our Cubans were colorless and boring. Indeed, they were so overworked they could scarcely be anything else. The Cuban worker enjoys no US labor protections, as regards hours for running a compressor or driving a bulldozer. The cadres sent down to Grenada rose at six a.m., breakfasted on bread and milk, and worked through to six p.m. with a half-hour break for lunch. Later, out to complete the airport for its March, 1984, opening, they had night shifts. It was hard to imagine how such night workers got any sleep in the daytime.

One particular irritant was that none of these Cubans seemed to have any idea of private property. Not only would they wander over into ours, urinate, take showers off standpipes in the garden, but more than once we found them felling precious royal palms behind our beach, a prison offense for a Grenadian. Nor were they doing this for sustenance – the water-nuts the kids climb for – but for fronds for one of their "cultural" evenings. A mile up the road from us an absentee Philadelphian had half an acre of his land bulldozed in a morning for an arms shed. I took polaroids of the activity for the owner, an old friend, but though he came down posthaste he never got his land back, nor any compensation. The Cuban attitude in real estate was one of puzzlement. Their officers assumed that the government owned everything. And, of course, they were about to do so.

The Cuban day workers had their *pan y leche* breakfast (paid for by Grenada) fortified with lashings of sugar in the *leche*. When the young Jamaican Colin Dennis trained in a terrorist school in Cuba he had the same meal, he tells us, of bread and "green tea," viz. bush leaves boiled into an infusion. In Grenada the Cubans early established a pig farm at Pointe Salines and Sundays they gloried in pork, rice, their own white rum, and aromatic cigars of some strength. Rastas supposedly decline pork, though I doubt if the prohibition is more than symbolic in most cases, with the result that Cuba returned some Jamaican Rastas coming to them for terrorist training, since they did not want to bother with catering for diverse dietary restrictions. It was *pan y leche* and like it.

Physically, due perhaps to their high sugar intake, the Cubans were an active lot, and I am not judging by the seven or eight hundred found on site at intervention. For this work force was rotated every two or three months, barring top-level supervisory engineers and the ubiquitous intelligence officers, so that during the 1979-1983 era I saw a fair cross-section of these so-called "internationalists," allowing for the fact that most tended to come from one province (Oriente).

These groups came on ships. Some of the senior were flown down, but so many defected when changing planes at St. Vincent that they were shipped down, too. They earned points, *puntas*, for such overseas assignments, whether in Grenada, Angola, Suriname or South Yemen. These points made them eligible for perks on return home, putting them at the head of the line for a toaster or whatever in the local supermarket. What the Cubans chiefly desired from us was electronic gadgetry, transistors, calculators, the like. They had to acquire these surreptitiously since they were policed by their DGI, with the result that local theft of such items went up by leaps and bounds. A Grenadian on a work party would sell a transistor or digital watch to a Cuban trucker returning to Havana the next day. Being para-military the Cuban avoided customs checks and could sell his loot in Cuba for five times as much as he'd paid for it with us.

By and large, though, they kept a low profile, totting up their points to buck the supermarket line back home. Even allowing for this, they seemed a cowed and glum lot. Grenadian friends who visited Cuba – and many did – came back with the same impression. If you can turn Havana into a tropical Moscow, and a *habañero* into the sort of torpid tractor driver I met on Pointe Salines, you can presumably do anything in the field of "human engineering."

The phenomenon of dependence induces this, plus, of course, the boringly predictable and hypertrophied style of their leader. Dependencies are demoralizing, as welfare programs show. The Cuban economy inhibits entrepreneurship, and if you can't get anywhere in your society you cease to use your mind inventively. We in Grenada were constantly exhorted to copy the Cuban economy, but they have no economy. Professor Antonio Jorge puts it well: "Cuba has no economic model *qua* 'economic model' to export. Eastern European societies have ended up looking like the Soviet Union economically; no society has ended up looking like Castro's Cuba economically."[25] Nicaragua is trying.

Supposedly a select lot, the Cubans I watched for nearly half a decade on Pointe Salines seemed to have lost all spirit. When you know your country is dependent on another for its existence, and direction, something dies within you. Castro complies with Russia. You comply with Castro. Professor Jorge calls Cuba "a totalitarian state of Stalinist filiation and *caudillo* sociohistorical ancestry." But it is the nature of the leader that is operative here, and Carlos Franqui limns it clearly:

What Fidel has done is to impose on Cuba all the punishments he suffered as a boy in his Jesuit school: censure, separation of the sexes, discipline, thought control, a Spartan mentality. He hates culture, liberty, and any kind of literary or scientific brilliance. All sensuality, of course, is anathema to him. We used to have one main prison, Isla de Pinos; now we have many. We used to have a few barracks; now we have many. We used to have many plantations, now we have only one, and it belongs to Fidel. Who enjoys the fruits of revolution, the houses of the rich, the luxuries of the rich? The Commandante and his court.[26]

I did not have enough Cuban to argue such ideas out with rough-and-ready bulldozer operators, but I had a try with the DGI officers. I met embarrassed shrugs. And if the Cubans' minds were warped, so were their physiques in contrast with the male West Indian norm of narrow waist, long legs, muscular arms. In Grenada Apollo works our fields. The Cubans were a very moderate lot, generally short and bandy of leg, paunchy and raunchy. And none of them could swim.

Their provenance was not complicated. They were what we in England in World War Two knew as REME (Royal Electrical and Mechanical Engineers), the corps I saw in Italy valiantly trying to throw Bailey bridges over the flooded Rapido and Garigliano rivers near Cassino. They may have been "B" Echelon troops, but a lot had had more bullets fired at them in anger than their colleagues in the line. And, as mentioned, Cuban military expansion (rather than diplomatic) was going great guns at this time. Castro sent his first troops to Angola in November, 1975, and by the end of the decade had some forty-five thousand of his countrymen out serving in thirty-seven distant countries. The dice was running his way and what he had to give was human capital. They, of course, had no vote in the matter.

We watched batch after batch of these military engineers

brought down to the Pointe Salines strip in Russian trucks off ships. After a while they grew so confident they did not even bother to erase the Soviet insignia off their vehicles. In army fatigues they jumped down to drill-sergeant commands, and doubled to the huts assigned them, where each had a foot locker plus an Akka taken over from another.

The matter of the military nature of the airport came to be a red herring, if one much debated in the press. During my years in Grenada I must have seen a dozen feasibility studies made for an international airport. They came to nothing because the government didn't have the cash to buy the land or because the owner of it (W.E. Julien) would not sell to his arch-enemy Gairy. In the event, Jewel simply took it, thousands of acres in all, from Julien's widow and Julien's cricket-star son Shane, by People's Law. The Cubans began moving earth in 1979, which suggested early planning of the seizure. The British firm of Plessey was called in for the electronics. Payne/Sutton/Thorndike write: "The non-military character of the project was subsequently confirmed by Plessey."[27]

This statement is naïve to the point of absurdity. The Thatcher Government had granted Plessey export credit guarantees for the contract, and the company did not want to lose them by being caught with their pants down helping on a Cuban base, one created under the smokescreen of tourism. Daily denouncing the United States (the main source of Caribbean tourists), Bishop wanted tourism like so much sody pop – the NJM 1973 Manifesto had been *against* a Pointe Salines runway. What Bishop wanted was money.

One could concede, with anxious Plessey, that the projected airport was not military if by such a term was meant an airport with wholly underground fuel tanks feeding apron hydrants, underground bomb-proof shelters and armories; but such standards apply to a very few such installations in the world, most around Moscow, and such were in any case impossible on the tough tiff (or *tufa*) of the Pointe Salines peninsula.

The military character was present in the enormous fuel farm set up (and now dismantled), parking lanes, safety areas each end, and the sheer length of the V-2 displaced threshold, one originally projected by 11,000 feet, today closed off at 9,800. It is pointless to object that Barbados has a runway as long. Grenada is not Barbados. Besides, one side of the Grantley Adams airport was wholly military during the intervention.

Furthermore, Plessey were constructing radar and radio apparatus *to Cuban specifications*. Indeed, they balked at lending their name to some of the shoddy Cuban material they were asked to use. The Plessey official in charge on the island, Mike Barnard, once told me that Pointe Salines was too "open" to be military. So was Port Stanley in the Falklands, kept operative, for Argentinian Pucaras at least, until the bitter end.

What came significantly to light when the terminal was started was the vast kitchen facility planned, obviously for heavy human traffic passing through (viz. on the way to Cuba's African bases), unless you were simple-minded enough to conceive that Grenada was anticipating six or seven hundred tourists a day on a hotel-bed capacity of a quarter of that number.

Grenadians worked alongside the Cubans, though seldom in the same truck, and always under NJM control, their supervisor being another of Bishop's cousins. Relations between the two groups grew cool since the DGI discouraged fraternization and finally stopped it with medical students.

Surreptitiously, the occasional Cuban worker would sell me fish he had caught (preferring cassette tapes to cash) and one chubby old bulldozer operator puffed up to our house asking for water. This was curious since the Cuban camp was abounding in mains water while we starved for it (in fact, got none for two whole years and had to buy). After this shy oldster had come up a few times on the same errand he unburdened himself. Having heard that I was a former literature professor, he pulled out of a pants pocket a piece of grimy paper and read me a poem full of *alma* and *corazón*. He then looked up hopefully: "So you see, professor, I'm not a bulldozer operator, I'm a poet. And you're going to take me back with you to America when you go." With Jewel going paranoid and calling any American in sight CIA, that would have been all I needed. Still, I hope old Pablo made it as a poet rather than a people's rusty bulldozer operator.

That the Cubans were giving Grenada anything was a myth. The manpower they sent down was paid for. The *matériel* also, excluding the arms. Their equipment was in any case antediluvian. At the end 82nd captured a few new Russian trucks, but the graders, bulldozers, steamrollers and suchlike brought down from Havana looked World War Two vintage to me, especially their motorcycle side-car combinations which might have come out of a film on Nazi Germany. US AID, on the other hand, left us with a fine bank of Chevvy trucks when they departed.

One of the first things the Cuban "internationalists" did was to be national, setting a series of white stones in the hillsides across from our house spelling out SIEMPRE 26, commemorating Castro's flubbed Moncada job. The Rangers dismantled these insignia on arrival. In their place they put up a sign which read: THIS IS AS FAR AS THE BASTARDS ARE GOING.

The Terrorist Future

It must be remembered, even if it cannot still be "felt," how strongly fortune seemed to be favouring Castro at the time of Bishop's coup. This sense was daily intensified over the air by RFG. Doctors, lawyers, accountants started leaving Grenada (since the end of World War Two more than 4.3 million natives of the Caribbean have emigrated, nearly all to the USA or Canada). In May, 1979, Castro visited Mexico for the first time since he had set out from his exile base there on the *Granma*. He was met with open arms by Lopez Portillo, as was to be Maurice Bishop, to whom the Mexican leader gave a promise of aid in developing our petroleum resources (there are none).[28] Puerto Rican terrorists, united under the Los Macheteros movement, were being extensively trained in Cuba.[29] On July 17, 1979, the Sandinistas took power, and both Cuba and Mexico sent immediate aid. Guerrillas were running riot in El Salvador. Bouterse toppled the Aaron Government in Suriname. Castro was crowing like a bantam cock and Bishop crowed back, calling Cuba "the best example in the world of what a small country under socialism can achieve."[30]

On Morne Jaloux ridge, high over St. George's, a Cuban Embassy was established by Osvaldo Cardenas, Chief of the Caribbean Section of the Central Committee of the Cuban Communist Party. It at once sprouted eighty-five "diplomats," a vast number for a tiny island (Venezuela still only has two or three), and included among them was Carlos Diaz of the Cuban Americas Department. As already identified, Julian Torres Rizo took over this Embassy, controlling the island alongside his mistress, the American Weatherwoman Gail Reed. Their affairs, like Castro's were looked after in the States by the liberal lawyer Leonard Boudin, whom I met when he was staying with neighbors on Pointe Saline, and possibly wondering how to lighten the fate of his daughter Kathy, facing a stiff sentence for cop-killing. But she was not allowed any bail she might have jumped.

So for Castro these were salad days. The Grenadian economy still ticked over on previous agreements, and the St. George's Medical School, then large, was pouring hard currency into the Exchequer. "Nicaragua and Grenada are the most important events in Latin America since 1959,"[31] to quote again Jesús Montané's battle cry.

Did nobody oppose this drift in Grenada? The press muzzled, Constitution and Parliament suppressed, citizens imprisoned without charges, tortured with electrodes by Cuban "neurologists," houses searched, communications censored, hit lists drawn up, whole communities demarked *Counter* – and no one raised a finger?

To Grenada's credit a thousand or so did, that being approximately the number of detainees put in prison at one time or another during Bishop's incumbency. Considering the population, and its components, it is a respectable number: for we had nothing to fight with. Bishop early called in all firearms, though by some quirk (a friend in the force) we were allowed to keep ours. At the end Bishop clearly anticipated trouble, since in both Butler House (which the PRA's magnesium rounds failed to incinerate) and in the main St. George's Police Station a large number of crowd-control weapons were found, including two thousand riot sticks.

The populace was gradually intimidated. Any dissenter went "up the Hill" there to receive "heavy manners." The 1981 closure of *The Grenadian Voice*, with proprietors and editors imprisoned or deported, had a depressant effect, particularly since these "CIA agents" included the Manager of the Royal Bank of Canada, who was given one afternoon to leave, with the shirt on his back, and his bank made no intercession for him. The internationally known journalist Alister Hughes was put under house arrest, his car and telephone confiscated. The newspaper's sin was to be found in its Editorial: "We have no axe to grind except the axe of the people who want a medium for free expression." Rizo unleashed overkill.

Apart from those quixotic attempts to object Grenadians endured or ran for cover; as in all cases of occupation there were some collaborators. The director of one company went with Bishop on his May/June 1983 visit to America, standing shoulder to shoulder beside him on various podia, extolling the glories of Jewel; however, it was rumored that he was taken up more or less at gunpoint. A fair analysis of this touchy situation is presented by an observer as follows:

One problem in Grenada today is that some of the leading members of the private sector were on such amiable terms with the reputedly charming Soviet and Cuban "ambassadors" and were so accomodating to the PRG ... Call them pragmatists or misguided optimists, they co-operated with the regime in ways reminiscent of German Jews at the dawn of the Third Reich, on the presumption that they were indispensable. Ironically, the private sector was destined to be phased out.[32]

On numerous occasions I was invited to visit Cuba gratis, a normal ploy in the circumstances. When I pointed out that my US passport did not permit such a visit, the answer was *"No hay problema."* Precisely. This is what the governments of Trinidad and Barbados had been strongly protesting. Their dissident youth was being lured into terrorist training in Cuba. Ostensibly they would cross to Bishop's Grenada to visit Auntie. Once on Grenada they were given passes and a free flight on Air Cubana, which began a weekly service to Grenada in 1981. Nothing appeared on their passports. When they returned home after two or three months learning "construction skills" at Cape Matanzas (Carlos' alma mater) or the Isle of Youth (opened in 1977 for 26,000 children), they simply said they had been staying in Grenada all that while.

Air Cubana's first flight from Barbados exploded in mid-air in 1976, killing some of the country's major athletes (Venezuela later acquitted the four charged with planting a bomb on the plane.) Cuba did not resume the connection but for a while the line was allowed a counter at Trinidad's Piarcos airport and, when passing through its mall of shops, I was invariably astonished at the mountains of copies of *Granma* brought down gratis, far outnumbering all the other newspapers put together. But eventually, before he died, Eric Williams tired of being host to insurrection. There is no Air Cubana desk there now.

The kind of terrorist training, even down to booby-trapping children's toys, which a West Indian could expect in Cuba, is described by Jamaican Colin Dennis in his *The Road Not Taken: Memoirs of a Reluctant Guerrilla.* The impression his account gives is of a gray prison-like boredom; this coincides with the pictures of drabness I got from Grenadian friends who visited Cuba during the Jewel era. One expects East Germans to be dour but not Cubans. Surely they used to exhibit a certain *alegría*. No longer. Pretty Gillian Thompson, who headed one of our tourism delegations to Cuba, reported great interest by groups of women in her jeans, which I must say she wears snug as gloves. The ladies ooohed and aaahed over the rear-end designer tag which they had not seen before; neither, I'll bet, had the men, who were more interested in how they were filled. Jeans seem to be excessively *de rigueur* in communist countries. An American student living recently in Moscow writes: "Labels are very important now in denim-conscious Moscow. I have several times been drawn into debates on the merits of Wrangler versus Levis."[33]

Colin Dennis' terrorist training in Cuba took place in 1980 when Manley's Jamaica was dissolving into a little Lebanon, out of which "Fast Eddie" Seaga urged to victory (though not without being shot at on his way to the polls). In the camp Dennis went to especial esteem was given by the Cuban trainers to "Rankings," namely cadre Jamaicans who had actually killed human beings. His group was particularly schooled in how to assault barracks – the Moncada syndrome. "In one class we were required to explain how we would set about mounting an attack on the Jamaican Defence Force (JDF) barracks."[34]

In Grenada the Cubans soon established a terrorist training camp and intelligence-collection facility on a tongue of land running out of the Windward coast called Calivigny, while Calivigny Island, off this point, was used for firing ranges. Calivigny Island was a Shangri-La, all rustling palm, reef seas, and sweeping beaches. On the coup Bishop confiscated the island "in the people's interest" from a Grenadian who was planning to start an hotel there. Colleen and I were the last to sail there. We were sitting down to a beach picnic with our guest, the New York lawyer settling poor Carl Schuster's estate, when bursts of Kalashnikov fire rattled the trees and gashed the leaves. We hit the dirt. Which was precisely what the grinning squad of young Grenadians, and their Cuban trainer, emerging from the bush in camourflage fatigues, wanted. They told us they had expended six hundred rounds in shooting down coconuts. Calivigny was put off limits and boats approaching were shot at.

The Calivigny peninsula itself was also sealed off. It soon grew a barracks and assault course of the type described in Cuba by Dennis: obstacle hurdles for the improvement of crawl techniques (so as not to set off mines), house scaling, so on. It was, in fact, modeled on a Brigadista training camp in Michael Manley's Jamaica where, until Seaga dissolved them, Brigadistas were killing children in their beds.[35] The Control Rizo held over the island was exemplified to me one evening when a large shipment of arms for Calivigny was trucked through South St. George's. I was enjoying a mild-and-bitter in a roadside pub called The Red Crab when Bernard Coard drove in and took a table, about six bodyguards prowling around in best vaudeville manner. To conceal his shipment Rizo threw the switches and the entire southern section of the island was plunged into darkness. Coard ducked under the table – he didn't have far to go – and the bodyguards went ape. It was evident he had not been apprised of Rizo's blackout and was most irritated not to have been. I was able to slip out a back way to Pointe Salines, and our home, but the guests and staff of the Crab were immured there till four a.m. The bar did excellently.

I revisited Calivigny Camp shortly after it had been taken out by US A-7 Corsairs. I suspect that American intelligence wanted this compound preserved for the record but that a lot of fire was coming up and so, after warning passes had been ignored, the place had to be destroyed. Yet the high wall the terrorist cadets had constructed, complete with fake windows, remained for all to see, plus scaling apparatus, a monument to much mindless inhumanity to come. For in order to continue to draw headlines terrorists have to be increasingly outrageous. The black Muslim leader, Louis Farrakhan, circling the Caribbean after accepting a

$5 million loan from Libya, was asked whether he thought Muammar Qadhaffi a terrorist and replied, "Hell no. Terrorism like beauty is in the eye of the beholder."[36]

Finally, to attract our jaded TV cameras, terrorism has to turn into psychosis, constantly reviling the United States for its own sickness. The mental health of the Symbionese Liberation leader Donald DeFreeze was probably about on a par with the Baader-Meinhof's Patients Socialist Collective which recruited from mental hospitals – note that the PRA gave guns to the Grenadian insane in the fighting on Richmond Hill. For by definition terrorism is insanity. The guerrilla, give or take a bit, still operates in a quasi-military environment. But the targets of the PLO included, in the last month of 1985, cruise passengers in the Mediterranean, one a 69-year-old wheelchair case tossed overboard, three civilians on a yacht off Cyprus (one a woman), a couple backpacking near Jerusalem, and an 11-year-old girl in Rome airport. These were incidents with no end. By contrast, the Israelis responded with an attack on the command center of such operations, illegally established in Tunisia. The targeted buildings were leveled, as at Calivigny, but no civilians were lined up against a wall and shot. That twelve Tunisians were killed in the Israeli attack was regrettable but, as William McGurn of the *Wall Street Journal* put it, "Placing a command structure within civilian populations is the terrorist equivalent of hiding behind a woman's skirts."[37]

Cowardice hardly comes into the equation when you are a beserk suicide bomber of the kind with which the Middle East is seething, and which Cuba and Libya export in droves. Retaliation is not enough, being usually accomplished within civilized norms (e.g. Entebbe). For the trained terrorist there is no ethical fighting. Gone are even those last rags of chivalry I was introduced to in the Western Desert of my youth, when German units returned prisoners to us since they had not been properly captured.

The modern terrorist follows the Hoffman-Mailer track,

bombing first and thinking later, if at all. After all, the enlisting of the insane on behalf of terrorist activities does not seem so crazy when you listen to someone like the psychoanalyst R.D. Laing, darling of the sixties' rebels, informing a 1985 conference that schizophrenics are really "brave victims who are defying a cruel culture."[38] The new church is not far behind, William Sloane Coffin telling his New York Riverside Church congregation, in a parody of John Kennedy, "It is not enough to resist with confession, we must confess with resistance."[39]

Were the Cubans we lived with on Pointe Salines the new men the Bolsheviks boasted of creating? "Soviet man is a cog-wheel," said Stalin. Khrushchev echoed him, giving Michel Heller the title for his brilliant book *La Machine et les rouages*. When your system turns into a disaster, as Castro's has, you "create" a man compelled publicly to admire it. I met one or two such in Grenada.

But my final impression of life among the Cubans was that Cuba is possibly a tougher communism to live under than the Russian version, certainly in the latter's rural provinces. Castro is more *el máximo líder*, bigger a brother than Andropov, Chernyenko, Gorbachev, men of whom the West knows merely photos.

Castro's Cuba was born in the post-Stalinist period and mood, one which regarded any freedom of thought as a bourgeois convention. Fortunately, Grenada was not a holistic society on which you could at once apply the Stalinist grid. I suspect Castro knew this and that Bishop, ironically, did not. Hence his announced desire to "crush" everything, to steam-roller every sphere of our lives into the Marxist mold for the future. Our future was a terrorist's dream. The trouble is that Marx, like God, created the world from outside; nor did he send down his son to see what it was like living it from within – as those Cubans I watched had to every day.

A Cultural Evening

During the four and one half years of Cuban occupation of Grenada I often had cause to cross a country road from our house on the Pointe Salines peninsula to the Headquarters of the DGI (Dirección General de Intelligencia)[40] to complain about the noise. Would they please turn down the *altavoz* or speaker system beaming Castro's speeches at the empty West Indian countryside? The furious squawks of the Cuban dictator, aimlessly amplified into the velvety dark, seemed an apt symbol of communism's folly and failure, for even the Cuban workers didn't listen, being so hard-worked they bunked down early; but it was interfering with our Mozart. Besides, the medical students who rented rooms nearby couldn't study against such sound. I led a delegation of them to the DGI house. I, in fact, knew it better than the Cubans did.

We were met with cautious courtesy and made our pitch. For a moment I couldn't help comparing the clean-shaven, short-haired Cuban intelligence men with the hirsute hoboes I had seen leading student demonstrations in the sixties in America. Señor dell'Osa was sitting at his desk behind which hung one of José Martí's more impenetrable slogans: "Culture brings freedom." By this time I had learnt that the Cuban macho despised most art as feminine, sissy, the preserve of degenerates like homosexuals, and had not Castro once boasted, "In our country there are no homosexuals"? Martí's *boutade* seems to have been elastically interpreted in Cuba. Shortly before Castro suppressed it, *Lunes*, a supplement of *Revolución* that soon went the way of our *Torchlight* (not to mention *Revolución*), banner-headlined *Culture brings Freedom* over pictures of Marx, Sartre, Faulkner (!), and that most arrant of social Snobs Virginia Woolf.

Dell'Osa told us that his Cubans, to each batch of whom an agent was assigned, were enjoying a cultural evening, *una nocha cultural*. If so, I reflected, they were doing so to snores, to be heard coming out of the barrack huts about. In the event, it seemed neither advisable nor possible to arrest His Master's Voice, bleating like Conrad's Kurtz's into the blackness, and we departed, the students disconsolate, myself the richer for a new translation.

For the term *cultural* seems to be communist code for yet another Orwellian opposite, since propaganda can never be art. It can supply art with pabulum, as in Eisenstein's *Potemkin* film, but that director's *Ivan the Terrible*, which rode roughshod over historical fact, showing Ivan as a progressive ruler, highlights the dilemma. Pictorially infatuated with church imagery, even Eisenstein could not organize it into political oppression. His subsequent effort to rid himself of the Party man-on-his-back in a sequel is singularly pathetic. It was banned and, despite a cringing confession of "ideological errors", Eisenstein never lived to complete it. Producing, often at pistol point, a monthly series under the cultural Commissarship of Zhdanov entitled *Victory Will Be Ours* could be guaranteed to turn even a Candide into an "agent of the opposition". So in Grenada, an island without art, *una noche cultural* had to make do. The "cultural revolution" announced by Maurice Bishop wasn't one: "I want to emphasize three main points – the spreading of the socialist ideology, the wiping out of illiteracy and the building of a new patriotic and revolutionary-democratic intelligentsia".[41]

It is conceivable that the internal diversity of a Windward Island saved the sanity of Grenada from this sort of bushwhacking. Looking back on his life in Trinidad, V.S. Naipaul reflects: "There was an occasional racial protest, but that aroused no deep feelings, for it represented only a small part of the truth. Everyone was an individual, fighting for his place in the community. Yet there was no community. We were of various races, religions, sets and cliques; and we had somehow found ourselves on the same small island."[42]

In Grenada there was no profound anti-imperialist feeling until Maurice Bishop tried to manufacture it. To follow the book, he was forced to come up with some sort of local cultural palingenesis. He couldn't get close. The rallies were being deserted, turning into circuses without bread. We were much too porous for Radio Free Grenada to conduct the kind of ideological disinformation of the authentic Fourth-World satellite, although we soon had the usual pro-Soviet pantheon down visiting.

Apart from the Ortegas, Samora Machel came, as did Sis Mugabe, Michael Manley, the CIA-traitor Philip Agee (given a Grenadian passport by Bro Bish), Ramsey Clark, Angela Davis, and so on. Apart from Manley, all these much-heralded figures were blanks to the average Grenadian. Machel's visit was perhaps the greatest fiasco of all. He left Grenada to empty country roads which our radio told us the next day were thronged with cheering crowds. That did not prevent Machel's unshaven face from decorating our Pearls airport for years, just as Raúl Castro's adorned our Post Office.

Desi Bouterse of Suriname was to honor us with a cultural visit, but canceled after his massacre of fifty or so prominent civilians (a body count given as fourteen in the *New York Times*), including the country's leading soccer player. Refugees from this slaughter, which took place immediately after a visit by Bishop, who had flown to Paramaribo from Havana, told me that after public exposure the bodies of those killed were returned to relatives with most bones broken. RFG called it an heroic action.

So the steady diet of "cultural" lies became unceasing under Bishop in Grenada. All the same, I had to confess to surprise at the crudity of the Cubans in this respect. After all, Cuba aspires to some sophistication in other ways. It numbers Castro's friend Gabriel García Marquez, the man who dismissed the agonized Vietnamese boat people as so many "currency smugglers" before receiving his Nobel Prize for literature. Cuba has some good guitar music, rotten painting, and worse ballet under the aegis of the ageless Alicia Alonso, another intimate of Castro's whom Juan Blanco called "The Menopauseless Giselle." Perhaps what Cuba sent down to us in Grenada by way of culture indicated their estimate of our intelligence. For instance, we got their astronaut Tamayo telling us that the American space program was aimed to destroy all life on earth, and this would presumably include its own. We heard a Cuban "doctor" back from Africa (dos Santos' Angola), dilating on the barbarous practice of female circumcision which was, he explained, a CIA scheme to keep all women in Africa subservient.

These absurd fables – they scarcely attained the status of passingly entertaining fabrication – meant as little to Grenadians as they seemed to merit to on-site Cuban *compañeros* who had of necessity amputated part of their minds, to survive under communism. However, I suspect that Bishop may have asked Havana to cool this kind of cultural input to us, since by the end we did not hear so many of these crass inventions, RFG preferring to cite Soviet-serving stories that had been respectably laundered in the left-wing London press.

"Nothing was created in the British West Indies," writes V.S. Naipaul, "no civilization as in Spanish America, no great revolution as in Haiti."[43] If culture is identity we lack it, one of the pleasures of life in the islands being the task of getting by somehow without Norman Mailer, Duran Duran, the Harvey Milk homosexual High School, journals devoted to Black lesbians and Chicano surrealists, and the rest of such packs bought off by the national endowments.[44]

BeeWee culture is social rather than esthetic. Bishop came to take his line here from the liberal American and British colleges alert to send him down fodder, as well as from people like George Lamming, an indifferent novelist who looks like a Bajan bear after having lost a tussle with a lawn-mower. I was once introduced to a black girl from the States who, I was told in awed terms, had won a number of NJM prizes for her paintings; it transpired that these were hate-America signs daubed on walls around the island. This teenybopper Rembrandt was last seen cheering wildly at the felling of a Cobra copter by the PRA.

Apart from such artificial imports Grenada has no folk art like

Haiti. Despite Bishop's efforts it showed no yearning for
Negritude, Africanity, the like. We have no theater and one
cinema, running non-stop kung-fu. The video cassette loan
business is today flourishing in the islands, now that functioning
television has come to stay. But reggae, what of that? Surely that
is indigenous? It is to Jamaica. Reggae – a contraction of ragged
and everyday – was launched as a national anthem of Rastafarianism when Haile Selassie I was crowned on November 30th, 1930,
Ras Tafari, King of Kings, Lord of Lords, Marcus Garvey's
second Christ and first black Messiah – though, of course, St
Augustine was a black from Numidia. Reggae came out of Ska
and, before that, Mento (home-made drums, reeds, so forth).
Despite its political braggadocio, and commercial success in the
hands of Ansel Collins and Bob Marley (who died of lung cancer
due to chain-smoking reefers in 1981), reggae can hardly merit
being called music. It is a sort of audible itch, one that makes it
impossible for anyone in the vicinity to get any sleep. With its
steady sequence of Messiahs, each presuming to be Moses and/or
John the Baptist (Garvey, Leonard Howell, Claudius Henry, two
of whom were convicted of fraud), Rastafarianism would scarcely
exist had it not received such starry-eyed academic attention, and
respect.

Maureen Stone, a Bajan teacher in Britain (where Rastafarianism is now institutionalized), calls it "the only indigenous
religion, faith and sect in the Caribbean."[45] Not long after I read
that I gave a Rastaman a ride down Pointe Salines. He was the
real McCoy or, should I say, Dreadlock, red of eye and reeking of
ganja. I asked him what he thought of the brutal treatment of
Haile Selassie's daughters, then penned in a tiny room without
toilet facilities outside Addis Ababa, one dying of cancer.

"Who dat?"

He had not the slightest idea who Haile Selassie was, any more
than he knew that the woolly mob cap he wore bore the colors of
the Hohenzollern Empire, or any more than he knew that Castro
committed troops to Ethiopia at the end of 1977.

But, after all, Haile Selassie was the progenitor of this creed, God himself in human form (although also claiming to be descended from Solomon and Sheba). Yet another tenet of the elastic Rastafarian religion has it that "Haile Selassie is the reincarnation of Christ." A versatile gent. Yet when that punctiliously dressed and pro-American mini-monarch actually visited Jamaica he virtually ran from the group of filthy Rastas assembled to meet him. My rider should have been pining to repair to the paradise of Ethiopia for "Jamaica is literally Hell for the black man, just as Ethiopia is literally Heaven."[46]

Bishop's flirtation with Rasta was instructive. At the start he wooed them. But since Rastas are orthodox dissidents they increasingly deserted Jewel as it became Establishment, declining to join his rag-tag-and-bobtail army. Eventually Jewel itself turned into Babylon and Rastas started knocking off PRA boys in our north-east, near Tivoli. At this point Bishop rounded up three hundred of them, and set them to work under the gun on Hope Vale estate. Those peace-loving people did not like that one bit. It is said Bishop chopped off the locks of some, in a mirror action of what Belmar had done to him, and that later he proposed rubbing out the lot, only to be restrained by Havana (viz. Rizo). Whatever, it seems certain our Rastas would have ended up like the Miskito Indians in Nicaragua. Indeed, Jamaican Rastas taken to Cuba for terrorist training were required to shear off their dreadlocks first.[47]

The half-Ghanian, half-Scottish ex-policeman, and now British MP, Paul Boateng, has lauded Rastafarianism on the BBC as an article of faith, filled with peace, love, and the rest, of the preposterous Marcus Garvey's Back to Africa movement. One does not today see the crowds making for that continent. Some British schools with over-developed guilty consciences teach Jamaican Rasta as a language, the ludicrous results of which can be seen in Shiva Naipaul's essay on "The Rise of the Rastaman." In fact, the patois or local slang of St. Lucia and Grenada (where a village called Permontemps may nestle next to one called

Woburn) is as much dialect French as English.

Most Grenadians make strict and pious parents. To dredge the gutters of inner cities for drug addicts and petty thieves and hold up the result for emulation as something called Black Culture is the height of condescension. We do not adulate the lowest elements of our northern cities as White Culture. There have even been cases of West Indian parents in England sending their children back to school in the islands, in order to obtain more disciplined instruction. But the virus of social masochism in education certainly seems to have come home to roost with a vengeance in England, at least judging by the 1985 Swann Report.[48] Sponsored by the British government, and costing its tax-payer half a million pounds, this document asserts that the English are ineluctably racist, and that such racism can only be white. The anti-capitalist curricula of English county schools thus carry the weapon of race alongside instruction. Most Grenadian parents I know want no part of this, nor of the ideology of hatred accompanying such contributions to our "culture."

If, in America, Rastafarianism continues to *épater* ambitious assistant professors, in politics it takes us into the jungle, to the racial insanity of Hitler. God is black and chose the black race. For their presumption to the contrary, the Jews have been well punished. The Pope is head of the Ku Klux Klan. *Una noche cultural* of this sort of thing must be enough to send anyone round the bend, without benefit of "de weed." Blackness becomes an instrument for mental suicide, a caricature of a delirium, a brew into which anything may be stirred. As the late Shiva Naipaul put it: "No theology is more fluid, more elusive. There is no church; there are no scriptures; there is no ordained leadership. Each Rastafarian has his own version of the thing. You become a Rastaman by declaring yourself to be such."[49]

But to be so permanently impermanent is scarcely to exist. Marcus Garvey no longer does so, yet is constantly recreated by the likes of Boateng. All Garvey's absurd disasters with his Black Star Line for repatriating Jamaicans to Africa, his fantasies of a

Negro Empire, were forgotton in 1965 when his remains were reverently disinterred and returned from England to Jamaica. To many he remains a holy hero. So does Maurice Bishop. After one BBC interview Shiva taxed his interlocutor as to whether she really considered herself black. She replied that she did not, but that it was the right term to use in England "to get the grants."[50] Shiva's brother, V.S., bears him out, citing the counsel of a Jamaican in the RAF to his compatriots: "Whenever they was in any real trouble I used to tell them, 'Boy, your only hope is to start bawling colour prejudice.'"[51]

Grenadian schools do not teach this. Nor do they teach sexual politics, whereas Rastafarianism offers the girl a wholly subordinate position ("It is a sin for a black woman to straighten her hair," etc.). So Bishop began encouraging the idea of school as Babylon, indoctrinating teachers and freeing children Fridays to go see some Jewel project, if not democracy at work in Richmond Hill prison. Needless to say, this simply turned into legalized truancy. A steady curriculum of reggae, African basket-weaving, *Reader's Digest* anthropology and hair-braiding is precisely what the average West Indian mother does *not* want for her children.

Hair-braiding, presumably to give an improved self-image for the displaced Caribbean girl, is surely one of the most ridiculous and redundant, of offerings in an already Mickey Mouse curriculum. Maureen Stone responds to it as follows:

> Why should schools have to teach young women how to look after their hair? I have been such a girl with "African" hair, looks and skin colour. I was educated in the Caribbean by completely black teachers; nobody from outside my family ever thought it necessary to teach me how to "comb hair."[52]

A House Mother at a Senior Girls Community Home School in England apparently thinks it necessary, reporting on a pupil with pleasure: "I know Cheryl is settling in all right as she was having her hair braided by Donna when I last saw her upstairs."[53] So if you fail to get an A for braided hair you are, it seems in a pretty desperate situation in Islington. And what about the British working-class kids in the same school agonizing over whether to braid or not to braid?

The NJM Deputy Premier Bernard Coard, sentenced to death by hanging in 1986, began his climb to fame with a book on this sort of errand entitled *How the West Indian Child is Made Educationally Subnormal in the British School System*. It is still given credence by relevant authorities in England. Coard set up a check of "cultural knowledge," consisting of forty questions for children of West Indian heritage. Of the fifty-eight children tested *none* had heard of Toussaint L'Ouverture; only four had heard of Garvey.

In short, Bishop imported his "culture," alongside his heroes and martyrs. The white-hats like Machel and Bouterse were lined up against the devil figures of Pinochet and Botha (Duvalier and Marcos slinking out of the scene). Above all, he eulogized as ancestor Julian Fédon who was, in fact, an extremely well-to-do French planter living in Grenada, who read the revolution in his own home country as an apposite moment for a rising against the occupying British. For Bishop his chief claim to fame was that he brutally executed most of his prisoners. Ironically, Bishop named the PRA training camp where his own mortal remains were to be interred Camp Fédon.

No-one in Grenada truly believes that Fédon was revolutionary; to be frank about it nobody had ever heard of him. How many in the class know where Rwanda, Burundi, and Sahel are, let alone that they have been the sites of vast tribal massacres? Nor did the average Grenadian countryman know much about the African butchers of millions: Idi Amin in Uganda, Mengistu in Ethiopia, Francisco Macías Ngeuma in Equatorial Guinea (a third of his own population eliminated), Bokassa in the Central African Republic. Fortunately, Grenada had not yet developed the civil rights movement with its liberation ideology, according to which European regimes just kicked out owed their successors instant financial subventions.[54] But since liberal hyperbole about the glories of Africa were heard repetitively in our island during the Jewel years, it could be logical to look at the phenomenon.

"The African Way of Doing Things"

The myth of Africa as "one huge village" (*pace* Professor Ali A. Mazrui) attained an apogee at the international airing of the BBC-made (though US-funded) television series called *The Africans*, an extension of the fiction *The Color Purple* by Alice Walker, a visitor at the time to Russia and Cuba.

Richard Grenier has called this kind of infatuation, into which Maurice Bishop encouraged little Grenada, *Turtle Bay Africanism*, an entity created, that is, in the corridors of the UN, a world where Colonel Qadhaffi is a saint, America Satan, and every non-Moslem responsible for every world misery. Various Moslem shops shot up in our Market Square in St. George's, only to disappear rapidly after intervention. Professor Mazrui, it might be added, lectures in Nigeria, site of bloody hecatombs and over a million dead in the Biafra revolt. As Bruce Anderson put it in *The Spectator* of London, "Black Africa has become a theatre of barbarism and exported political sentimentality. Throughout the continent, 'governments' are robbing, oppressing, incarcerating, flogging, torturing and murdering their subjects – but no one in the West gives a damn."

From and outside Africa itself we find assent to the worst elements of the continent given by the priesthood. One thinks of the Reverend Joseph Lowery, head of the Southern Christian Leadership Conference, singing *We Shall Overcome* with Yasir Arafat in his Beirut bunker; of the Reverend Jesse Jackson pushing PUSH (People United to Save Humanity) into indicting Begin as racist; of the Nobel-laureated Bishop Tutu; of the

Reverend Hosea Williams of the Christian Conference voyaging to Libya, there to confer "the Decoration of Martin Luther King" on Qadhaffi, just as the latter's troops invaded Chad. Hosea (of the new kind) assured us: "Brother Qadhaffi and the Libyan people expressed a great desire to ally with the black American in eliminating racism and Zionism internationally."[55]

All this sanctimoniousness while over 85% of black Africa was disenfranchised by its own. A roll-call of its unelected regimes, denied any popular accountability, would encumber these pages with a number of Russian clients: Benin, Burkina Faso, Burundi, Cameroon, Cape Verde, Central African Republic, Comoros, and on through the alphabet to Uganda, Zaire, Zambia.[56]

The flame of hatred against South Africa was kept brightly burning through the Jewel period in Grenada, of course. In fact, it was scarcely ever off the air. Sanctions against that country (opposed even by Alan Paton and Laurens van der Post) were deemed to make a moral gesture, which came down to the morality of denying US airports to South African Airways while keeping them open to Aeroflot, in a stance that meant eventual starvation for millions of black Africans. Of such sanctions Pat Buchanan made this analogy:

> Suppose, during the Great Depression, Britain declared she would lead a worldwide boycott of American steel and coal until President Roosevelt desegregated the South and moved American to one-man, one-vote. Would the destitute American workers have welcomed this as the act of a trusted and reliable friend?

The Reagan administration's opposition to South African sanctions was due to the fact that the so-called Lugar legislation involved approved extremist groups in that country, led by men like Nelson Mandela, Govan Mbeki, and Walter Sisulu, whom even Amnesty International did not credit as prisoners of conscience, men who refused to foreswear terrorism. At least one of the above openly lauded the infamous "necklace killings" of blacks in South Africa, while Oliver Tambo, leader of the African National Congress, supported such violence in his 1987 visit to the United States.

Apart from the massacres of Africans by Africans in Africa, the average Windward Islander knew even less about the monumental corruption by which their supposed blood-brothers were roundly duped, when not eradicated, by their own kind. Ghana, originally the Gold Coast, was the first new African nation after the war, and Kwame Nkrumah a fervent proponent of what he termed "the African way of doing things." This certainly turned out to be lavish, as he built palaces for himself, ships and stadia, even allowing one favorite to import a golden bed from London.

I attended a dinner given by the Mayor of New York for Nkrumah at the height of American infatuation with his "Africanism." I still have the menu somewhere. The food was appalling but the adulation of that flamboyant figure, to die in Bucharest, knew no limits, surpassing even the liberal love of Lumumba, hopelessly humiliated and cut off in the prime of his anti-imperialist endeavors. But Nkrumah's appeal has endured, the Reverend Jesse Jackson telling us in April, 1976, that " I believe we should look to the Third World for an answer."[57] Thinking the same, Nkrumah put a black star on his flag in sympathy with Garvey, socialized everything in sight, and had Ghana bankrupt in ten years.

That proved small beer. In Zaire "the African way of doing things" in the hands of Sese Seko Mobutu was an even more spectacular disaster, the foreign debt of that country rising to $3 billion by 1979, quite a bit of it owed to Walter Wriston's Citibank which finally abandoned the chase to throw good money after bad. Nkrumah's clarion call, *Africa Must Unite*, became sadly compromised as vast extravagances by the new African leaders continued, Anthony Sampson claiming that "about half the annual exports of diamonds, copper, coffee or cobalt were now reckoned to go to Mobutu's family and friends."[58] He was then reputed to be one of the wealthiest men in the world. At present writing, oil-rich Nigeria's foreign debt stands at US$22 billion. Since 1957 there have been over a hundred heads of state in Africa; more than ninety had to be removed by force.

Naturally, the massive and brutal expulsions of blacks by blacks in Africa through the seventies and eighties went unmentioned in Maurice Bishop's dialog to Africanize our culture, e.g. the expulsion by the Ivory Coast of 16,000 Beninese, by Zambia of 150,000 "aliens" in 1969, by Uganda of 50,000 Asians in 1972 (not including as many Banyarwandas shortly thereafter). Then Kenya expelled tens of thousands of refugees throughout the seventies, in a way that would have aroused rage if it had happened in America, while in May 1984 Ethiopian soldiers forced 50,000 starving citizens to leave the Ibnet camp (to which supplies were rushed by America) and then set the camp on fire, the refugees having to settle in Gondar. It is estimated that three million "foreigners" were forced to leave Nigeria in 1983. As Professor Wolfson writes, "Nothing South Africa has ever done is as horrible as Ethiopia's Stalin-like policy of mass starvation."[59] Even *Rolling Stone* magazine conceded there was a deliberate policy of starvation in the provinces of Tigre, Eritrea, and Wollo. Eight million Ethiopians faced death by starvation. Where were the Rastas?

The Ethiopian story belongs here because of them, and it has become better known than most largely thanks to a compilation by *The Economist* of London, which accords that country the lowest human-rights rating in the world. The tiny, fragile old Emperor Haile Selassie, darling of the Rastas, is overthrown, taken from his palace in a battered blue Volkswagen to be smothered to death with a pillow. A year later dictator Mengistu declares all agricultural land the property of the state. Forcible starvation is used to quell resistance. There follows the compulsory relocation of millions, farmers and their families packed into cattle trucks (after having been softened up by torture and starvation). The picture darkens further as the country becomes the customary Soviet client state, the dictator shoring himself up with Soviet arms, for which he presently owes USSR $5 billion. In return, Mengistu lends his vast army to replace the Cuban African legion; it can be paid in grain instead of money. Angola has been paying $500 million a year for its Cuban mercenaries. So these Ethiopians cost next to nothing – and besides, being black Africans, they are far less visible on the front pages of the world. Mengistu is even said to have started a black KGB, for use not only in Ethiopia but around the continent. With Ethiopia and South Yemen in its pocket Russia has the strategic Horn of Africa by the jugular.[60]

In fact, Ethiopians are already engaged in defending another Soviet flashpoint, the Beira corridor: this gives Mugabe's Zimbabwe access to the Indian Ocean through Mozambique, which has changed from being a Portuguese to a Soviet colony. Here Afonso Dlakama's Renamo guerrillas are engaged in an apparently fairly successful attempt to turn back Soviet imperialism. They were somewhat assisted in this by the death in a plane crash of the virulently anti-American President of the country, and Maurice Bishop's friend, Moises Machel. They are considerably handicapped by the fact that Washington continues to give millions of dollars to the Marxist Frelimo government in Mozambique – and not Washington only. Bemused by propaganda in the left press – that South Africa is assisting Renamo, which it currently is not, the Scandinavian countries, France and Britain are also assisting red Mozambique.[61]

Where were the Rastas with their red calypsoes?

Where, indeed, was Amnesty?

My wife and I were charter members of that organization when it was started by a rich and handsome Englishman, Ivan Morris, then Chairman of Columbia's Asiatic Department, and his lovely young Japanese wife. We noted, however, that Amnesty came to Grenada *after* Jewel, so professed ignorance of torture by Cubans. According to Amnesty, torture by "dipping the body in hot oil," or by "inserting a bottle or heated iron bar into the vagina or anus" is common in Ethiopia. Torture is allowed under the constitution of Angola, while in Mozambique public floggings are permitted, under Law Number 5/83, for political offense. In Uganda, where 600,000 were killed between 1971 and 1985 (and an unknown number since), torture is "widespread and systematic," according to a 1985 Amnesty report. In the Central African Republic Bokassa liked to murder political prisoners with his own hands. In Zaire torture is common. If this, then, is "the African way of doing things," pace Nkrumah, no wonder American blacks stay away from it.

For not to criticize these barbaric tyrants is itself a condescension. Why should we not demand that black people enjoy the same rights under black governments that we insist they enjoy under white governments? In light of the brutal regimes of most of Africa, Amnesty's sudden interest in the plight of the poor Coards *after 1983* was a parody of its purpose. Both Coards were sentenced to death by hanging for the murders of Maurice Bishop et al.

One side-effect of "the African way of doing things" was the creation of US AID by John Kennedy, and the Peace Corps by his brother-in-law, Sargent Shriver. These beneficent agencies, urged on by the World Council of Churches, only came to Grenada long after the intervention, not during Cuban occupation. Similarly, the AIDs virus was alleged (by Soviet news sources) to have been dispensed throughout the Caribbean at this time by the American Army's biological warfare headquarters (at Fort Detrick, in Maryland), using the results of experiments by the Nazi Josef Mengele.

Many of us were indignant to discover, post-intervention, of the appointment of leading Jewel elements to positions in the new government. They were said to be "rehabilitated." One sinister wall-eyed skinhead in the PRA, who had lorded it over Pointe Salines under Bishop's cousin, was suddenly put in charge of the new Airport Authority. My objections were met with the argument that if we did not employ former Jewel elements like this it would further disaffiliate and embitter them. Certainly, however, Bishop's imported white pre-fab "African" culturalists quickly bade farewell to the isle of spice at intervention, including Chris Searle, a radical Brit who had done a teaching stint in Mozambique.

No book to date has done justice to the solid decency of leading Grenadian citizens who stood firm in the public eye, and set an example of behavior, like the lawyer (and cricket total recalls-man) Carol Bristol, now a Senior Silk, or the Sandhurst-trained eye-doctor Tony Buxo, or Gordon "Knocky" Steele who ran a truly co-operative bank under pressure, or, perhaps the most important and toughest of all resisters, Robin Renwick of our nutmeg OPEC. Jewel was reluctant to take on men like this. But in 1984 the Russians would have.

There remains the calypso. Is it "cultural"? It is Trinidadian, as narcissistic reggae is Jamaican, though the most famous calypso-nian of all, Mighty Sparrow (Slinger Francisco), was born in Grenada, as was "Boogsie" Sharp, the world's number one steel band pannist. V.S. Naipaul tells us that "It is only in the calypso that the Trinidadian touches reality. The calypso is a purely local form."[62] He suggests that it has now degenerated into a nightclub act. And who is to deny him his reasoning? To start with, its monody cannot be called music. Most calypsos sound the same. Still and all, they are verbal, and so partake of topical social satire, none of which seems to last too long. The University of the West Indies' Institute of Social and Economic Research has an ongoing "Calypso Research Project." To my knowledge this has never answered the charge of ephemerality in the form, being chiefly concerned with internal bickerings, as to whether East Indians influenced calypso (a loud No!) or whether the lyrics are prejudicial to women (a loud Yes!). In a recent Port-of-Spain seminar featuring calypsonians like Roaring Lion (Raphael de Leon), Chalkdust (Horace Liverpool), and Shortpants (Llewellyn MacIntosh), together with an unidentified character called (doubtless with reason) Black Stalin, one panel was devoted to "Women and Calypso." This was hosted by "teacher-activist" Merle Hodge from the UWI Women's Study Group who loudly complained that calypsonians have denigrated women in their songs.[63] Trinidadian Merle Hodge was invited to Grenada by Bishop to back up Chris Searle's educational reforms.

After the coup, and during the supposed hunt for Gairy, Bishop asked Sparrow for a calypso and got one. Like Antigua's King Short-Shirt our Sparrow can be counted on to be routinely revolutionary. The result was *Gairy, Dead or Alive* played incessantly over RFG. Where is it now? I have never succeeded in acquiring a tape or plate of it anywhere. In a few years' time Trinidadians will be asking who Gairy was. Great satire is universal.

Then, Sparrow being notoriously extra-insular, Bishop organized an indigenous pro-Jewel calypso. This erupted from our Flying Turkey, Cecil Belfon, a PRA office related to a Minister of Tourism who got passed on to the "free" government. (Several of Bishop's Ministers published appallingly bad poems in the *Free West Indian*.) Flying Turkey's view was the following:

> People want to hear you come out in defence of the Revolution, people want to hear you come out and rage hostility upon Reagan, and American interventionist attitudes ... "The Lion" from Carriacou, he came out and he blaze imperialism.[64]

So Turkey concluded his lyrics with the reprise:

> *Let them come, let them come,*
> *We will bury them in the sea.*

Schoolchildren were made to chant this. It even got airtime over WBAI-FM in America. Yet another which went the rounds after intervention was entitled *Guadalajara*; it derided Cubans who claimed to have come to Grenada merely to kill cockroaches. When Reagan spoke at our Queen's Park on February 20th, 1986, he was greeted by a calypso from Scaramouche that mimicked the rat-tat-tat of firing and the "music" of intervention. *Time* magazine called it "the country's most popular ballad." I doubt if many remembered it or if you could buy any of these songs anywhere today, least of all in Grenada. No way is art as fugitive as this.

During the sixties, as we all now know, bemused Presidents and craven Deans of American colleges, terrified of being dubbed "racist," put Black Culture into their curricula, as regularly quoted by Searle in *Race and Class*, XXV: 1 (1983), p. 58. So do today the new clerics into their sermons, both feeling thereby absolved. I suffered under this dispensation. It rides roughshod over human individualities. I know a West Indian who looks completely Chinese, eats Chinese, is a fervent Catholic and cricket-lover, sends his son to accountancy school in England; is he considered by such Deans and dons as "Asiatic" or "black"? On April Fool's Day, 1987, the tax-funded Chancellor of the City University of New York gave an address in which he lamented that while in 1980 only 6% of all graduate students were black, today only 4.5% are. "There were no black doctorates," he declared, "in all of New York State last year – not a single one – in architecture, business, computer sciences, or mathematics." His conclusion, for one of his rank, was astonishing – despite all the educational assistance given to blacks, these figures represented deliberately racist deprivation: "Don't let anyone tell you that racism in New York exists only in the working-class precincts of Howard Beach and Jamaica [New York]." Perhaps those of us who find the whole topic faintly disgusting can take comfort from the story of the eighth-grade teacher of American history who asked a girl of obviously African descent her preference as to being dubbed black or Afro-American. "Sharon," she asked, "what do you prefer to be called?" The kid thought a moment.

Then, "Sharon," she replied. We can also take some faint heart from the fact that a reasonable percentage of New York City's Tammany Hall, at least, seem to end up in jail.

Yet unfortunately Shiva's interviewer was right. Blackness is useful "to get the grants." At one time during my teaching stint at the City College of New York I had several friendly student moles, all black, with part-time jobs in our college Financial Aid Office. Such told me how risibly easy it was for one of their skin colour to obtain Federal or State assistance. Just walk in. Black accomplices gave you forms to fill out in triplicate, even helped you do so, and you enjoyed a certain feeling of achievement doing so, forging your absentee father's Income Tax 1040 return. After that you received a goodly sum from BEOG (Basic Educational Opportunity Grant), which in turn made you eligible for SEOG from the State, and so on. Some of those kids were milking the taxpayer of enough to put them through Princeton free, had they been able to qualify. When I wrote a book exposing this boondoggle the Chairman of my Department tried to have me declared mentally incompetent. When a year ago Sidney Hook looked over a survey of grants for educational research awarded by leading educational foundations in America from 1975 to 1987, he found that not a single grant had been made for a study of the disruptions in American academic life, despite the billions lavished on other subjects. So University Centers for Rational Alternatives, calling on distinguished scholars, some recipients of grants from such foundations, submitted a proposal for such an inquiry. They received no answers.

All the same, it is sad to learn that England, where I was educated without bias, has also now capitulated to the same pigmentary prejudices, the loony Left translating something called West Indian culture into a new version of the three Rs – Reggae, Rasta, Revolution. This is what every West Indian parent in the real world of the islands hopes will not be taught his to children.

Rather than running down to Grenada for a day's visit (like Flora Lewis of the *New York Times* or the Congressional Black Caucus), such bodies should see a Sunday morning there. They would find ninety percent of the adult population at church, in Sunday best. No quickie sermons here, to the liberal chumminess of Riverside's Coffin (who advised young Americans to burn their draft cards), but a dozen full-throated hymns, and a lot of the back of the Book used too. Next, visit our schools and see our uniformed children, their well-pressed trousers and tunics all paid for by indigent mothers. Why, they even get "licks" if they misbehave. Shocking, ain't it?

Before he retired in 1985 Bishop's mentor Julius Nyerere admitted that African socialism or *ujamaa* had failed, saddling his country, Tanzania, with $3.5 billion in foreign debt.

"Peter Island Offers Nothing" runs an ad for a resort in the British Virgins. High culture attracts tourism. The Windwards don't have it. Yet, despite local politicians who yearn to see a wall-to-wall Miami everywhere, the Peter Island ad is right on. Our islands offer solitude, still, in superb natural surroundings. They appeal to the last scholar gypsies among us.

The Jewel Splits: Ten Days That Shook the Caribbean

The center could not hold. Throughout Jewel's last year most of us on the island were subsisting on rumors, some of which got respectably rococo, as the Central Committee met behind guarded doors. There have been various accounts of Jewel's last days, feeding off the prodigious haul of documents captured by 82nd and issued, as edited for the State Department by Michael Ledeen and Herbert Romerstein, in the form of a veritable brick of a book, *Grenada Documents: An Overview and Selection.* The Chief of XVIII Corps' Intelligence Production Section characterized this document bonanza as follows:

by rapidly over-running the former communist-led Grenadian government we were presented with truck-loads of documents providing everything from precise PRA manning (by name) to international military agreements. This, coupled with over 600 co-operative and talkative Cuban prisoners and an almost totally supportive Grenadian population, led to probably the single most prolific intelligence windfall since the conclusion of World War II.[65]

Not only were documents captured in the DGI house opposite our own, but nearby five million US dollars were secreted in suitcases in the bush; tending his goats, our gardener's son found them (and got a US$3,000 bounty for reporting them to 82nd). Cuban intelligence officers don't travel poor.

But at the time few of us on the island suspected the speed of the final split in Jewel's ranks. We of course knew of the arms build-up. I jogged almost daily past a warehouse stacked with Soviet Rocket-Propelled Grenades. We also knew the air was thick with plots and charges of "right-wing opportunism." The latter, however, appear to be par for this kind of course, a communist tic or St. Vitus' dance; in Guyana this charge is forever on the Marxist Cheddi Jagan's lips, only to be given back to him by the equally Marxist WPA (Working People's Alliance). There had been the Queen's Park bomb plot, the priests' plot (by "CIA priests" in Trinidad), the "Buck" Budhlall plot near Tivoli, the plot of American Grenadians allegedly fueled by Howard University Professor Stanley Cyrus, and so on.

We also knew that reprisals had got harsher, torture more frequent.[66] Deputy Police Commissioner "Luckey" (sic) Bernard, a most civilized individual who had been kindness personified to us after the knifing of my wife, was shot by PRA men. He recovered, only to die of poisoning later. His son took the name of Iman Abdullah and, as we shall see, played a principal part in the Fort Rupert slaughter. He too was sentenced to death by hanging.

Bishop returned from his summer 1983 visit to America claiming to have been rebuffed – "not the President, the Vice-President, a secretary or even a fortieth secretary." He was lying again. It is true Reagan did not see him – why should he have, being described as "an eater of babies" in Bishop's own paper? But in Washington Bishop was accorded a high-level meeting with Judge William Clark (then National Security Adviser to the President) and Kenneth W. Dam (Deputy Secretary of State). If Bishop's approach at this meeting was conciliatory it was so on Cuban counseling, and in the search for money. We now know he took to America with him a letter from Gail Reed ("Señora" Rizo, as it were) to Sanchez Parodi, Chief of the Cuban Interests Section in Washington, asking for Bishop to be briefed before any top-level interview. And if, on return, Bishop continued to see conspiracies everywhere he was, for once, right. Even the Rastas were being accused of links with the CIA.

It was a jittery time on the Isle of Spice, with support for the government ebbing fast. A Bolivar Day rally brought out ten participants. The party machinery was desperately cranking out what it believed to be Vanguard Leninism in a parody of what I used to hear being debated between Alcove One and Alcove Two of the City College cafeteria in the sixties. But this discussion group was armed.

Brother Coard, we may recall, had resigned from the Central Committee in October, 1982, in a letter which apparently took two weeks to get from one end of St. George's to the other. Kenrick Radix had been removed from office, and Bishop reprimanded ("too much humanitarianism"); if he declined the idea of joint leadership with Coard he would be guilty of "onemanship." Sandford and Vigilante put it well:

Although Bishop was not himself removed, he would hereafter be surrounded by Coard's staunchest allies, not only in the Central

Committee, but in the Political Bureau as well. Through them, Coard could continue to influence policy while avoiding any personal responsibility for the mounting difficulties confronting the party in the months ahead. When conditions once again reached a crisis, there would be only one man at the top to blame – and only one alternative to replace him.[67]

Cultism, onemanship – more whirling words. I do not propose to burden the reader here with all the names and biographies of what was, in effect, a South Bronx street gang trying to dress up in a purloined rhetoric, one which today most Grenadians slip their eyes over on the way to the cricket scores.[68] They spoke as no one *in power* had spoken in the ex-British Caribbean before; but their language was compromised to absurdity by their actions. The USIA papers cite the articles of power. The NJM Central Committee Minutes show a frantic effort to define what that power was for: destruction of "the corbeau of imperialism" and its "eater of babies" Ronald Reagan, plus the installation of hard-core Leninism, euphemized as "inner-party democracy".

At this point one must draw pause before the tergiversations of the inner party or fast-lane bloodshed boys ("We have to be coldblooded and cast all emotions aside .... The situation demands Bolshevik staunchness"). After Bishop's begging-bowl trip to America Coard left in August, 1983, in another direction – for Suriname. On return, according to George Louison, he became fairly frantic, advocating that what the Party really needed was a psychiatrist; Maurice Bishop had "lost his mind." By implication Coard had kept his.

As Jewel approached its self-destruct button, it went into a frenetic tizzy of self-criticism. In the last week of its existence it spent six and a half days of marathon meetings, *fifty-five hours* in all, calling each other names. No wonder the Cuban Intelligence readers added contemptuous marginalia to their copies of the minutes (these were blacks, remember, and Cubans didn't see themselves as such). The internal rancor attained a kind of genius. No matter that Major Einstein T. Louison returned from six months at Russia's Vystrel Military Academy the darling of Marshal N.V. Ogarkov,[69] Soviet First Deputy Minister and Commander-in-Chief, Warsaw Pact: he is notwithstanding "suspended and confined for his opposition and petty bourgeois behavior," to be followed by his brother George, a Bishop supporter who called Coard "shit." Both brothers, sons of an old friend of ours at Concord, are today back in Grenada, agitating hard.

The important membership meeting of September 25th, 1983, in which George Louison opposed the idea of a shared leadership concluded with Bishop being indicted of "petty bourgeois behavior," and the singing of the Internationale. The next day Bishop left for Hungary and Czechoslovakia (where George Louison joined him). This was ostensibly and principally another begging-bowl trip. Friends saw Bishop laying a wreath in Budapest and he might have been, as effectively he was, under prison guard.

Again and again in these last days Jewel parodied itself, until it ended in madness. Subconsciously, I much doubt they wanted to be understood, even by themselves. For to be understood would be to be found out, since the membership scarcely comprehended the mouthwash it gargled out. But the rhetoric claimed that paranormal power which has so often swayed West Indians.

It therefore manipulated a meaningless vocabulary, calling anyone who got in its way (including their leader) Petty Bourg. The Grenada Papers show us some sleepy village of a handful of inhabitants divided into *Economic Objectives, Military Objectives, Enemy Forces, Our Forces.* Thus *Economic Objectives* might comprise some small rum shop whose owner was rude when you didn't pay your bill, or a one-pump gas station ("bowser"), while *Enemy Forces* would be enumerated, all three of them, as "Petty Bourg – Dangerous." An attitude of indulgence here (of children playing with Marxism) is extremely patronizing. Jewel sponsored policies that distinctly damaged blacks.

The confrontations with power rivals continued apace. One Vincent Noel confronts "Chaulky" (sic) Ventour: "I asked him how things were going on at the level of the CC as things were beginning to get rough on the ground. I mentioned the rumors. Chaulky said, 'What rumors that? Is the chief that starts that shit.'" Ventour then told Vince that "Maurice was a psychopath." To which Vince retorted "I told Chaulky that he was mad." So was Vince. He's also dead.

Take the handles. It is true that Windward islanders go in for nicknames, many of which terminate in the suffix -*man*. But it struck 82nd's interrogation team on intervention that their Grenadian prisoners invariably gave their nicknames first. Leon Cornwall was *Bogo*, Radolph Callender *Baboo*, Fitzroy Williams *Mashie*. Then there were *Kamau* McBarnette, *Kojo* de Riggs, *Owusu* James (whom Bishop referred to as O), *Headache* Layne, *Goat* Redhead, *Porgie* Cherebin, *Ram* Folkes, and so on. These were members of a secret circle, a kind of Klan in reverse. Cross-examination at the trial repeatedly brought out that this or that witness was known only by his nickname. We were introduced to nameless individuals like *Edgy*, or *Inculcate*, or *Baba* (The Calivigny cook who cried when he saw the bodies to be interred "frying like eggs"). There was also "a fella called Rugs."

A number of them had studied at the Esbec Military School in Cuba, where they had probably got one word in ten. When they returned characters like *Brat* and *Pumphead* and *Big Dog* needed a rhetoric to prevent them from thinking. After all, Jewel's Ambassador to the UN, Caldwell Taylor (who had later to be forcibly removed from his seat), was accused by the Central Committee of "mysticism-deviation," a new one even on the Kremlin, I'd think. For by this point the Marxist charade had become confusion worse confounded. With Bishop off in America Headache Layne had obtained meteoric military promotion (the PRA was becoming an army of Generals, anyway), gained some sort of control of the army, and was advocating "the Afghan solution." In his last moments at the Fort Bishop referred to Layne as "a bloodthirsty maniac," one who had asked for his Prime Minister to be courtmartialed (as, in effect, he was).

A rumor circulated that the two Coards, plus Strachan and Cornwall, were out to assassinate Bishop. The latter certainly seems to have believed this and had for some time been sleeping around in various houses, to frustrate an attempt on his life. His bodyguard Cletus St Paul was carrying around a letter from Bishop to O, expressing such apprehensions. On October 8th Bishop returned from East Europe and his welcome committee told its own tale, consisting of only one man, a suspicious Selwyn Strachan in T-shirt and slippers.

For word had got out that Bishop had made an unscheduled stop in Cuba and consulted Castro at Cienfuegos. The Coard faction obviously suspected that Bishop, now their enemy in the power struggle, might have got some new support from Fidel. The latter liked Bishop, indeed ordained three full days of mourning for his death, more than for most Soviet dignitaries. It is true that Castro later denied taking any sides in Jewel's death throes (in a 1985 interview with US Congressman Mervyn Dymally) but evidence exists from prisoner interrogation that the Cubans on site were planning to rescue Bishop from his subsequent house arrest. Rizo spoke to Bishop by phone at the Fort minutes before he was executed.

With Jewel's Central Committee in almost permanent emergency session now island life was grinding to a standstill. To the emergency session of Monday October 10th Bishop sent St. Paul, complaining that "attempts were being made to marginalise him." St. Paul came back advising Bishop "to kill them or arrest them." Meanwhile Coard was telling his cronies, "Blow them up before they do it to us." It was a case of do unto them as they would unto you, only do it first, and it did not augur a prosperous future for We Leader. By this time push had come to shove and Bishop knew his Coards, especially Phyllis, of whom Shiva

Naipaul's words describing Janet Jagan, Cheddi's wife, might well have been written: "She was held to be an almost Mephistophelean force, forever urging her husband on to new acts of extremism. She was the dark power behind his Communist throne, the hardest of hard-line ideologues, a creature in thrall to the Kremlin."[70]

Relieved of his Makarov pistol, Bishop's bodyguard St. Paul was then sent "up the Hill" (in fact, put in custody at Camp Fédon first), soon to be joined there by another bodyguard, Errol George, who confessed to spreading what was in all probability a true rumor for once. Trial evidence suggested it was so. Then, in response to the general situation, Bishop supporters raided an armory in St. David's; this was put down, its main leader Brat Bullen being shot (but not killed – killed later at the Fort). The hard-line Abdullah Bernard was recalled by radio hotline from duty on the little island of Carriacou; he, Major Chris Stroude, Captain Lester Redhead, and Lieutenant Cecil Prime (all subsequently sentenced to hang) were to be the principal dramatis personae attending Bishop's last moments, a Marxist Greek chorus clawing down the central star.

Come Thursday, island life was at a standstill. Bishop was summoned to appear at still another interminable meeting – "All those evenings," as Oscar Wilde replied when asked what he thought about socialism – and this time was told directly to explain how stories about the assassination threat had circulated. Some members moved that Bishop be court-martialed, to be met by a motion (from George Louison) that they themselves should be court-martialed first. Chaulky Ventour pulled a gun. George Louison was voted out of the Central Committee. Fitzroy Bain, former General Secretary of the Agricultural Workers' Union who was to die most slowly of all at the Fort, said there was "too much Marxist-Leninist jargon" going on and that he was about to vomit. He then came up with the quote of the era, "we are going to end up with a revolution without the people." After which he burst into tears.[71]

The Central Committee then demanded Bishop make a pacifying speech to a shaky Grenada over the air. This he did at midnight of the 13th, talking in unusually querulous tones, and asserting that all rumors circulating about him were rumors. Grenada knew better. Bishop was then taken by Abdullah to his Mount Wheldale home, where he spent the period from the 13th to the 19th manacled to a bed in his underclothes. His mistress Jackie Creft, by whom he had had one child and who was carrying another, voluntarily joined him, and was strapped to a bed in another room.

Chaos was come again. Life began to imitate television. I cannot claim to have seen all the various demonstrations, riots, and marches that took place in our version of Cloud Cuckoo-Land. If, as was said, three thousand crowded into Market Square at one point, then you would not have been able to squeeze in one single titiri, our succulent freshwater whitebait. I remain chary of such figures, which are generally pure guesswork.

It was the case, however, that on the 14th Selwyn Strachan went down to St. George's, apparently to get the feel of things and, if possible, announce that Coard was the new Prime Minister. He was manhandled by a mob shouting "We Gairy than Coard" and "Go home" (directed at Coard's Jamaican wife). Strachan beat a hasty retreat. Journalist Alister Hughes had by now put all this on the wire services. Unison Whiteman, a mild-faced Jewel founder up in New York attending a UN debate, rushed back, ignoring a friendly warning (which would have saved his life) to stay in Barbados by Tom Adams.

Schools and shops started closing. Flights from Pearls were delayed by demos. Later in the day Coard resigned (from a post he had never held) and shortly before midnight General Hudson Austin came on the air announcing himself head of an entity entitled the Revolutionary Military Council. This was martial law. In a long address he told us that Bishop had refused to accord his old colleague Coard part-Premiership, and had thus been expelled from the Party by vote. Further attaint of spreading false rumors, he had been put under house arrest. Bishop stood guilty of "objectivist-theorist deviation," another new one on me and, of course, locally meaningless. The weekend of the 15th – 16th began.

On the Saturday Kenrick Radix, doubtless emboldened by the return of ally Whiteman, led a demonstration through St. George's demanding Bishop's release. Radix, the Falstaff of New Jewel, ended up in Market Square by noon and in Richmond Hill Prison by nightfall. Throughout the day RFG interspersed reggae music with increasingly hostile, and confusing, news releases directed against Bishop. We were told, for instance, that Coard had resigned as Minister of Finance, "Nazim" Burke supplanting him. Then, no, Coard had not resigned and anyone spreading rumors, etc.... But by this time we knew that Allister Hughes, the journalist, had been put in prison, to be followed there for no reason by his brother Leonard, another member of the giant Hughes family mentioned (what a basketball team they could field!) and a businessman of integrity known to be apolitical.

Sunday was quiet. On Monday slogans appeared on walls like NO BISHOP NO WORK. RFG denounced the former leader more and more stridently. But by this time no one was listening to RFG any more, tuning in to Barbados, Trinidad, and other regional stations. That evening the Big RA, Radio Antilles, told us out of Montserrat that a number of Ministers had resigned, including Whiteman, Lydon Ramdhany, Norris Bain, and George Louison (most today deceased).

October 18th was another day of anxious unrest, with the shops in St. George's shut and more anti-Bishop imprecations going out over the air. *Quis custodiet ipsos custodes?* Mediation visits were exchanged between the rival factions. Meanwhile, the Cubans were awaiting orders from Rizo who was awaiting orders from Havana; as stated, US intelligence-gathering via prisoner inter-rogation suggests fairly convincingly that Castro was gearing up for a rescue attempt of Bishop by his men on site. They were all armed. And Castro was revered by Bishop. He was not by Coard. The end came quickly.

"Some Fell Slow and Some Fell Fast"

By Wednesday October 19th, the situation had seriously deteriorated. All schools, banks, and businesses closed. Children began demonstrating against the Coardites. In the course of the morning a large crowd gathered in Market Square in the capital. Payne, Sutton and Thorndike give a figure of "up to 15,000," but this is sheer fantasy, physically quite impossible. Of this crowd Whiteman led five hundred to a thousand up the hill to Bishop's house. There Abdullah's praetorian guard of about a hundred fired warning shots into the air. Undeterred, the crowd broke down the gates and, led by a GBSS (Grenada Boys Secondary School) lad who knew the place well, effected entrance from the rear. Secured to their beds in underclothing, both Bishop and his paramour were weak, notably the former who had refused food in case it might be poisoned.[72] In green underpants the Prime Minister was lent a jersey and helped into a vehicle, muttering "The masses .... the masses." Truly, if Maurice hadn't existed, Evelyn Waugh would have had to invent him; as a matter of fact, in a couple of books he more or less did so.

The idea had been to take him down the steep one-way Market Hill to the square, for an address to the crowd, but he was too weak. It was thus decided to escort him on to Fort Rupert (named after his father) on the bluff above the town, where a public-address system could be fixed up and medical assistance obtained for him from the nearby hospital (as it was). Clearly, even in his weakened condition, he could sense the crowd going his way, especially when joined by loyal Ministers up from the expectant square. Together with his men (Lala, Kasha etc.) he tried for a last hurrah.

Padding into the so-called Ops Room of the old police fort, Bishop appointed Einstein Louison head of his phantom army, got some Kalashnikovs distributed from the confused armory, and sent out orders for the arrest of Coard, Headache and the rest to – of all people! – Goat Redhead, the hardest of hard-core Coardites who was to slit Bishop's throat and slice off a ring finger after the man had been riddled senseless with bullets. Some of the now thoroughly confused PRA at the Fort laid down their arms at Bishop's request, though the Fort Commander present, Major Christopher Stroude, 25, later claimed he was deceived into this surrender by Fitzroy Bain, who told him a number of Coard's supporters had given up to the mob. Stroude called up Headache in Fort Frederick. By this time there was pretty much everything going on bar a flaming cross.

From the heights of Fort Frederick the prevailing Central Committee brass had seen the milling procession wind up to Fort Rupert long before Stroude called for advice and assistance. Layne, also age 25, had now been made up to Lieutenant-Colonel. Stroude told him the crowd were beating up some women soldiers (as was the case). Bishop was helped to the upper storey of the main police block in the Fort and paced up and down, chain-smoking. His appointment of Einstein Louison, a graduate of Moscow's Vystrel Academy, to replace the thoroughly disliked and absentee General – or was it by now Field-Marshall? – Hudson Austin was cheered by the crowd.

At this point someone on the heights decided to unleash three armored personnel carriers to recapture Bishop's new headquarters and forestall any government not their own – and a subsequent jury of Grenadians were in no doubt as to the culprits. These were squat Soviet BTR-60P carriers of the kind we had seen increasingly roaring round the roads on the island. "If there was resistance," Layne ordered, "then them was to battle it out and the leaders were to be liquidated." Abdullah drove the lead vehicle (though he referred to it as second in line in his evidence) and it was from these carriers that the large-scale crowd casualties came, either by direct fire or grenades into the throng. The convoy crashed down pretty Church Street, firing in panic at random and needlessly killing women and children. Abdullah tossed out a grenade and pieces of bodies splattered about. One carrier misfired a rocket into a stationary car and set it alight, pouring black smoke over the scene; Vincent Noel, a Jewel Union organizer, lost both legs; he was carried to an upper level of the Fort and died. Hearing the crackle of the Akkas, and seeing the casualties sprout amongst them, the crowd tried to disperse. However, those who had clambered to the Fort's eighteenth-century surround had little choice; to escape the gunfire they had to do a second Sauteurs, and jump down ninety feet. Witnesses describe seeing the blood gush out of the skulls of some who did so. This leap was recorded on film, albeit fuzzily, and until recently could still be seen in the St. George's USIS offices.

The precise number of civilian casualties will never be known; some people are simply missing to this day. Our gardener received two bullets in the leg at this time. Inside the Fort now the executions were drawing closer. Abdullah recounts: "we had instructions that Maurice Bishop and other members of the party with him were to be executed by gunfire. I knew that they were to be executed before I left Fort Frederick ... Lt. Col. Headache Layne told me that the decision was to execute Bishop and the people with him."[73]

A red flare (for death) was sent up from Fort Frederick. As the crowd stumbled and ran out of the compound, often over the bodies of those already killed, the Old Jewel leadership, including Bishop, Creft, Whiteman, and Norris Bain were stopped and drawn to one side, with others. "Is execution time," Goat gloated at them. "Cool," added Major Stroude. Andy Mitchell's jeer at We Leader was "No fucking Prime Minister at this time."

Those to die were taken through a tunnel (through which I had once passed to get a gun license from Abdullah's father, Luckey

Bernard) and to one wall of a rough police basketball court. Here, with that grotesque self-caricature that seems to dog world communism, had been scrawled TOWARDS HIGHER DISCIPLINE IN THE PRA.[74] They were told to face this wall and, except for Creft, to take off their shirts. Stroude and Redhead stood by behind machine-guns mounted on stands, while Abdullah and others put their M3s on "rock'n'roll" (full automatic). There were two other machine-gunners in attendance, Vincent Joseph and Andy Mitchell (not to be confused with a sometime Comptroller of Inland Revenue of the same name). Jackie Creft made a pathetic attempt to postpone the slaughter, pleading her pregnancy. She received only obscenities – "No fucking pregnant woman at this time," etc. From Joseph, "Is bullet for you."

Fire was opened on Abdullah's order. Bishop was hit first, and finished off as he writhed on the ground. As Abdullah said in evidence, "Some fell slow and some fell fast." Creft was bludgeoned to death with gun butts. The recumbent bodies were then overkilled; firing went on, it is reported, for ten to fifteen minutes into the corpses, until some were unrecognizable. It was at this point that Goat Redhead slit Bishop's throat. "In bits and blood" the bodies were put in blankets for incineration at the Calivigny terrorist training camp. During the trial a girl PRA soldier entrusted with wrapping up Maurice's meat-like remains was asked by the DPP (Director of Public Prosecutions Velma Hylton), "What did he look like?" She pondered for some time before responding, "Dead." With the others, his mortal remains were taken to Camp Fédon and incinerated. Rumors to the contrary can be forgotten. I talked to the men of the 82nd who exhumed these corpses.

The Fire Brigade hosed down the bloody court. A white flare was sent up (mission accomplished). Abdullah shouted, "Long live the revolution!" Gunner Vin Joseph repaired to the canteen for a Coke.

Maurice Bishop had been marginalized.

The Curfew

As thick black smoke billowed up from Fort Rupert after the killings (actually from two cars blown up nearby) sporadic bursts of gunfire could be heard about the town. By 3 p.m. General Hudson Austin announced a 16-man Revolutionary Military Council to rule the island. This "brutal group of leftist thugs," as President Reagan was to term the RMC, included the unlovely Headache Layne.

At 11.00 p.m. Austin came on the air after a two-hour delay. He gave out Bishop's death in a fudged form, fulfilling the comment of Jewel's co-founder, Teddy Victor, that "the NJM was born in deception and died in deception." Austin imposed a four-day twenty-four-hour curfew, lasting until 6.00 a.m. of the coming Monday, though he seemed to have some difficulty pronouncing the word. He told people without light, telephone, or water, "No one is to leave their house. Anyone violating this curfew will be shot on sight. All schools are closed, and workplaces."[75]

The situation, with some seven hundred American medical students in dormitories or rented homes, was certainly critical. The curfew was lifted for four hours on Friday, October 21st, so that some provisions could be bought, but it was vigorously reimposed. Not until much later did I learn of the real venom with which the RMG went about rounding up supposed critics at this time, sometimes taking in whole families to the prison (where baffled children were found wandering vaguely about at intervention).

The following overview of this period, by writers not present at the time, is worth considering:

All inter-island boat traffic had ceased and passenger flights into Pearls airport had been very strictly controlled. However, the curfew was lifted for employees in essential services who were issued with passes and travelled under escort. In the country, peasants and others could obtain water from neighbourhood standpipes and could feed those of their animals close to their house. In some instances, PRA patrols helped them, anxious to restore good relations. But mothers of newly born babies had to fend for themselves and those who died at home were left unburied.[76]

Not only is most of the above completely untrue, it reveals a lack of knowledge of life on a Windward Island. Local standpipes only give water when mains water is pumped into them electrically. If there is no "current" there is no water in them, and there wasn't during the curfew. Flights into Pearls had not been "controlled," they had been stopped. OECS and CARICOM quarantined Grenada. While RFG played ceaseless reggae, interspersed with terse bulletins from the RMC, Grenada became a ghost state, the lifting of the curfew for shopping periods only increasing anxiety as housewives swapped stories of those picked up and/or killed. The list lengthened.

After endless insults and prevarications from RMG, AmEmbassy Barbados only succeeded in getting two men into Pearls on Saturday the 22nd and they couldn't find any government. Instead of peasants being helped by patrols, as per the Polytechnic professors, they saw the PRA dementedly rushing around in the twenty armored carriers given to Grenada by Russia, and loosing off their Akkas at all and sundry. The notion of their providing passes is absurd. I know a local whose chicken farm, his entire livelihood, was "liberated" by PRA soldiery, who took every bird they could lay their hands on. At the top end of the economic spectrum handsome Angus Minors, head of the firm of Bryden and Minors, was taken by PRA soldiers to his Lagoon Road warehouse under the gun and looted of EC$1 1/2 million, unrecoverable thanks to the act-of-war clause in most insurance policies. He "travelled under escort" indeed.

The curfew had two purposes. First, it allowed the army to dispose of incriminating evidence, especially the bodies of those they had killed and mutilated (there were said to be sixty corpses around the Fort after the massacre).[77] Most of these were loaded into dump trucks, taken to Calivigny, there burnt and buried. Others in the Jewel hierarchy were filled with Akka lead and thrown into the sea.[78] I spoke with US officers present at the exhumation of Bishop and his Minister and the remains were said to be completely unrecognizable. One story went the rounds that Creft had been disinterred elsewhere, only recognizable by her feet and the bottom of her jeans which had not been burnt. This touched a chord, whatever its veracity, since in the Western Desert in World War Two it was a fact that "brewed" (or burnt-up) tank crews were often identified by their feet.

Apart from keeping the population cowed during these horrors, the curfew served another purpose for the PRA, namely that of going after Bishop supporters or any sign of resistance. The prison was by now bursting at its seams, supposed opponents being kept in lightless cells (from which they later staggered out, having lost all depth perception), and George Louison and Radix being told they were to be executed. For two days there was no food or water. Leslie Pierre (editor of *The Grenadian Voice*) and Lloyd Noel (Jewel's bourgeois-opportunist Attorney General) have written movingly of these days of standing-room-only cells.

But let us keep the Cuban situation in front of us. In the midst of wholesale ostracism by a horrified Caribbean, the Soviet Union alone supported the butchers. Castro seemed shocked by the murders (his own head one day on the block?) and called for the perpetrators to be brought to justice.[79] The heavily reinforced workers on site encouraged PRA elements to rescue Bishop *before* the bloodbath. A letter on a captured Cuban "Internationalist" reads: "on the 19th I was selected to go on a rescue mission of Bishop but when we were prepared the news arrived that they had shot him along with his companions."[80] Let us not forget that in the period when Norman Mailer was calling Fidel

Castro "the first and greatest hero to appear in the world since the Second World War," and Susan Sontag glorified Cuba as "high on some beneficial kind of speed," Armando Valladores was undergoing some of the most vicious and humiliating torture imaginable in a Cuban prison in which Castro himself had been treated leniently.[81]

But in case anyone is in doubt as to Castro's intentions for Grenada, he sent down Colonel Pedro Tortolo Comas, a bottle-scarred (sorry, battle-scared) veteran of the Moncada, to stabilize the situation. It was Tortolo who organized the final resistance, such as it was, against 82nd and ordered the absurd charge against the Rangers around Hardy Bay, the results of which so polluted the air at that moment.

Either way, Sazhenev or Castro, it would have meant total repression for Grenada, and the idea that somehow or other the Grenadian people would have risen against their oppressors (as advanced in various articles) is perfectly preposterous. Freedom fighters were not able to do so in uprisings in Hungary or Poland, nor in Afghanistan. Hugh O'Shaughnessy of *The Observer* assures us that "It would have been only a matter of time before the Leninist aspirations of Coard and Austin were swept away by Grenadians themselves."

Armed with what? Nutmegs? Mace? Old copies of *El Capital*?

One should add that the medical students, living under the shadow of Teheran, were restless, and with reason (we knew many of them at the time). Several had been harassed by the PRA. Many had wives and children with them. O'Shaughnessy tells us that only a "small minority of medical students" opted to quit the island at this moment. That is what might be called a terminological inexactitude – the first vote at the school gave over 65% desiring to leave, the second over 70%. It may well be that Medical School Chancellor Modica (in New York) "repeated that his students were in no danger," for the purposes of general reassurance, but on being apprised of the facts later he modified his opinion. O'Shaughnessy did not modify his.

The Polytechnic team take another tack. They too assess no danger to the medical students (not having been there at the time) and dismiss President Reagan's argument that you don't wait around for hostages to be taken until you have a hostage problem. The St. George's Medical School did not want an evacuation situation on their hands during the curfew since there was no way to get the students off, the RMC disallowing even small charter flights in or out. We are told that "the regime had gone out of its way to inform the Medical School in particular of its good wishes."[82] As if any credence could be given to the RMC killers, most of whom were convicted of murder later by a jury of their peers, and sentenced to hang. Our absentee authors add: "the prospect of further chaos in Grenada which Reagan felt it necessary to forestall was not likely. In fact, after the killings of Bishop and the others on 19 October, the strict curfew had effectively put a stop to further outbreaks of disorder."[83] Sure, put the whole of Grenada into Richmond Hill prison and you'd have no "outbreaks of disorder" at all. This miserable reasoning, entirely ignoring the disorder spread by the RMG during the curfew, amounts to: Leave ill alone.

The good news was that our Governor-General was still in place, though under house arrest in Government House with his wife Esmai. The PRA guard put over him was, in fact, to fire on and wound US Seals dropped into the garden of the residence, while three BTR-60 armored carriers, *manned by Cubans*, fired on the house and cut off the Seals' retreat with Sir Paul. But while he was there, intact, there was hope, for he represented the only legitimate instrument of government on the island and, as Sandford and Vigilante put it, "Should he authorize the intervention there could be no doubt of its legality."[84] Fortunately, the late Tom Adams made it possible for him to do so. Sir Paul got a request for assistance out to Barbados.

The idea that Grenada was merely a pretext for action by a frustrated President, burned by the Beirut bombing of Marines, is too contemptible to discuss, although it recurs in numerous surveys of Operation URGENT FURY. You have to go to *Granma* for that kind of calumny and some there were who did. The facts are straightforward. Under its Chair of Dominica's Eugenia Charles the OECS made a unanimous request for assistance. Later, law-school sophists would aver that the decision was not unanimous since Grenada itself was not present. It was not there since our Governor-General, who had in any case initiated the appeal and can so hardly have been against it, was being held at gunpoint in his house. Similarly, Sol Linowitz's idea that the "dispute", whatever that was, should properly have been put to the OAS was somewhat one-sided since one party to it were in their graves. This, though, was the Rio Treaty idea, originally designed for South America. Meanwhile, mediation by the Commonwealth, as proposed at the Port-of-Spain CARI-COM meeting following that of the OECS, involved the notion of a fact-finding team being sent over to (wait for it) Hudson Austin!

No, the "lesser" Antilles needed immediate muscle and they knew where to apply for it. In the point-of-order brouhaha that followed on the intervention nobody saw fit to mention that there had already been such an intervention in the area. Early in 1980, after Milton Cato and his Labour Party won elections in St. Vincent, a hothead called Bumper took Union Island, a constituency of St. Vincent, and had to be seen off by police planes from Barbados, to whom Cato made appeal for help.

Much rules-of-evidence tut-tutting then ensued in the editorial columns of the *New York Times*, finally eliciting this reply from the *Wall Street Journal:*

one very big problem facing such emerging or fragile democracies as that in Grenada is that the dark and unfamiliar people who live in these places are not quite worth, say, the 16 Americans who died on their behalf. We have quoted before and will quote again the New *York Times* comment on yellow rain: "Reports that the Russians used toxic agents in Afghanistan and Indochina have not been fully confirmed. Besides, they describe small-scale use against unprotected people in remote areas.[85]

That *besides* says it all.

It is unedifying for us Grenadians to run all the legalistic objections to the intervention to ground. Anyone who wants to do so will find a lot of law-school ammunition available in William C Gilmore's *The Grenada Intervention: Analysis and Documentation.* Those of us who had to live out the bloody psychodrama at first hand are likely to dissent from his findings. Jewel was no private tyranny, so much Duvalierism. The Russians were directing it. Nor was what we saw an invasion. At a disgracefully hostile American press conference (which I watched), and in a UN debate later that same day (which I did not) Eugenia Charles declined the term. And O'Shaughnessy describes this modest woman as "a ruthless international operator" and "a media star."

The term *invasion* carries with it the concept of illegitimate and forcible encroachment into territory. Eugenia Charles denied that Grenada was being invaded on several grounds, including the fact that the region was now one, integrally united thanks to modern media. Equally, Sir Paul Scoon declined the term on the BBC, which Payne, Sutton and Thorndike report as follows: "Significantly, in that same interview, he said: 'What I asked for was not an invasion but help from outside.'"[86] Correct. He got it.

For precisely what were the British doing about their Commonwealth brethren on the isle of spice? On Monday 24th Sir Geoffrey Howe was still fielding anti-American questions in the House, while the British High Commissioner on Grenada was assuring all and sundry there was no cause for alarm, though a Cunard cruise liner, pinpointed for possible evacuation, had just been fired at by PRA shore batteries. About the only difference between Commissioner Kelly's office in St. George's and the *Titanic* was that he didn't have a band. O'Shaughnessy claims that Mrs. Thatcher was "deliberately misled" at this point. Were I a

British citizen in such case, I would hope she were.

On October 19th an AmEmbassy plane out of Barbados was turned back from Pearls and then-Ambassador Milan Bish counseled non-permissive evacuation (i.e. where the host government may impede departure). Ships carrying troops to Beirut were diverted the next day. On the 21st Charles "Chuck" Gillespie reported the OECS request for aid from Barbados, Schultz receiving it at 2.45 a.m. on Saturday 22nd, the President being briefed at 5.15 a.m. Rather naturally, the latter needed to look around corners before making a decision and then, after a kooky incident on the Augusta golf links later that day, Reagan was again awakened, this time at 2.37 on the morning of Sunday October 23rd, to learn about the Beirut bombing of sleeping Marines, one whose death toll of over two hundred staggered me. For I happened to have been at Sandhurst when the only bomb it took in the war sheared off part of the New Buildings, including the room I shared with John Weir (later killed with the Scots Guards in Italy and brother of the poet Nigel, shot down in the Battle of Britain). That bomb was a 750-pounder, considered large at the time, being probably unloaded by a returning Dornier. The hit accounted for no more than eight cadets (the wounded included the actor Richard Todd). The Lebanon tragedy was amazing, but it did not deter President Reagan from his Caribbean obligations.

Guyana, then under Forbes Burnham, was party to the CARICOM meeting in Trinidad, which followed that of the OECS States. Although CARICOM is supposedly concerned only with trade and commerce, "Odo" Burnham heard of the possibility for a US rescue of Grenada and promptly leaked it to Cuba. Why? I asked a prominent Grenadian at the time. "Because Burnham is Burnham," came the reply. That, and his general indebtedness to Cuba (much of it also on airstrips). If he had not leaked the news, there might have been no bloodshed at all on the island, a landing mode of operation having been originally planned for Pointe Salines. Yet Burnham did more, he offered asylum to the Coard/Austin gang, one or two of whom are still in Guyana. The leak, a complete betrayal of confidentiality, alerted Castro and put yet more pressure on the White House.

At 6.00 p.m. on the 24th Reagan signed the operation order to intervene on Grenada in response to the OECS request. The Caribbean leaders were so informed. The US Chiefs of Staff, in particular, Admiral Joseph Metcalf III on USS *Guam*, coordinated the signal, and, to put it in a nutshell, 82nd Airborne soon had the enemy down sixteen ways to Sunday.

1. It is included in: Bruce Marcus and Michael Taber, eds., *Maurice Bishop Speaks: The Grenada Revolution 1979-83*, Sydney, Pathfinder Press, 1983. Yet there must be dozens of redactions of Bishop's speeches, from various Marxist presses, including his own Fédon publishers. Pathfinder Press gives its provenance from a number of cities. I have not collated all these for variants.

2. The only diary of these events by a native Grenadian is: Gerry R.S. Hopkin, *Grenada Topples the Balance in West Indian History*, "Printed by Mr Merlin" 1984. Bishop is treated as a "beloved humanist." Alas, there are a mass of misprints and Grand Mal is referred to as "just south of the capital" when it is, of course, to the north.

3. William C. Gilmore, *The Grenada Intervention*, London, Mansell, 1984. This book concludes with fourteen Appendices (36 pages) setting out many basic documents.

4. Grenada, Ministry of Finance and Planning, "Grenada – IMF Negotiations: Summary Report and Recommendations," August 30, 1983.

5. *New York City Tribune*, April 22, 1985 p. 10A. See also the alarming analysis of an early Jewel shortfall in their budget in *Grenadian Voice*. As I am one of the very few to own a copy of this document, I cannot tax my fellow scribes for ignoring it.

6. "Line of March," pp. 6-7 (Orthography sic).

7. From Castro's funeral tribute to the Cubans killed in Grenada, as reprinted in Britain's *Guardian*, November 19, 1983.

8. Armando Valladares, *Against All Hope*, New York, Knopf, 1986.

9. Bishop, *Forward Ever!*, p. 97.

10. Payne, Sutton and Thorndike, *cit.*, p. 22.

11. "Like an expectant dog barking for his supper," Bishop said of the genial Adams, destined to die tragically young, "he rushes in to please his new master Reagan." As if Bishop were not trying to please his own master. In fact, Tom was the nickname of J.M.G.M.Adams, son of Sir Grantley Adams, Barbados' first Prime Minister. Tom died age 53 in 1985. I treasure the last letter he wrote me, just after intervention. Errol Barrow died in June 1987.

12. *Granma Weekly Review*, November 2, 1980, p. 12.

13. H. Michael Erisman, "Cuba and the Third World: The Nonaligned Nations Movement," *The New Cuban Presence in the Caribbean*, ed. Barry B. Levine, Boulder, Colo., Westview Press, 1983, p. 165.

14. Payne, Sutton and Thorndike, *cit.*, p. 50.

15. Anthony P. Maingot, "Cuba and the Commonwealth Caribbean: Playing the Cuban Card," *The New Cuban Presence in the Caribbean*, p. 27.

16. "Grenada: A Preliminary Report," Washington, D.C.: Department of State, December 16, 1983, p. 20; this document, with its detailed rundown of weaponry both provided and to be provided to Grenada under agreements with Russia, North Korea, Czechoslovakia, and Cuba caused a sensation on the island when released. It was reprinted seriatim in *The Grenadian Voice*.

17. "The Vanguard Leninist Praxis," *Grenadian Voice*, September 14, 1985, p. 13.

18. "In my view the great British achievement was the development of 'capitalist democracy', to show the world that democracy in political life and the social 'free market' in economic life are a workable combination." Dennis J. O'Keeffe, "Swann-Song of Prejudice," *Encounter*, December, 1985, p. 75.

19. "Line of March," *cit.*, p. 4.

20. V. Martin Oppenheimer, *The Urban Guerrilla*, Chicago, Quadrangle Books, 1969, p.58.

21. "Grenada: A Preliminary Report," p. 32.

22. Robert A. Pastor, "Cuba and the Soviet Union: Does Cuba Act

161

Alone?", *New Cuban Presence in the Caribbean*, p. 191.
23. Pastor, *cit.*, p. 192.
24. G. Cabrera Infante, *Infante's Inferno*, Translated from the Spanish by Suzanne Jill Levine, with the author, London and Boston: Faber and Faber, 1984. The Cabrera brothers were among the minor literati associated with Carlos Franquis *Revolucíon*.
25. Antonia Jorge, "How Exportable is the Cuban Model? Culture Contact in a Modern Context," *The New Cuban Presence in the Caribbean*, *cit.*, p. 222.
26. Franqui, p. 170.
27. Payne, Sutton and Thorndike, *cit.*, p. 68.
28. J. W. Treeby, "Some Notes on the Economic Mineralisation of Grenada," in Groome, *cit.*, pp. 11-12.
29. *Free Press International Report*, January 14, 1987, p.8.
30. Bishop, *Forward Ever!*, p. 94.
31. *Granma*, November 2, 1980, p. 2.
32. Mayo Loiseau Gray, *New York Tribune*, February 16, 1984, p. 4B.
33. Andrea Lee, *Russian Journal*, London: Faber and Faber, 1982, p. 52.
34. Colin Dennis, *The Road Not Taken,* Kingston, Jamaica, Kingston Publishers, 1985, p. 52.
35. *Daily Gleaner*, June 3 and November 18, 1981.
36. *Barbados Advocate*, December 11, 1985, p. 5.
37. William McGurn, "An Eye for an Eye," *The American Spectator*, December, 1985, p. 13.
38. *Time*, December 23, 1985, p . 23.
39. Thomas Fleming, "Shelter from the Storm," *Chronicles of Culture*, January, 1986, p. 6.
40. There are four main Cuban intelligence agencies, all of which nearly all English-speaking journalists muddle up: the DGI (as above); the DOE (Dirección de Operaciones Especiales); the DA (Departmento América), which supplied Torres Rizo for Grenada; the DGRE (Departmento General de Relaciones Exteriores).
41. "Line of March," *cit.*, p. 9.
42. V.S. Naipaul, *The Middle Passage*, Harmondsworth, Penguin Books, 1969, p. 45.
43. Ibid., p. 27.

162

44. A typical recent example of the Down-With-Us misanthropy of the National Endowment for the Arts was the $25,000 Fellowship awarded to Peter Saul who specialized in vicious caricature of President Reagan. The *New York Times* (November 10, 1985, Section 2, p. 29) described the Saul award as "on the plus side for the endowment." The U.S. *Measure* regularly publishes examples of educational demagogy.

45. Maureen Stone, *The Education of the Black Child in Britain*, London, Fontana, 1981, p. 83.

46. From the creed of the Ras Tafaria man in: *The Tafari Movement in Kingston*, by M.G. Smith, Roy Augier, and Rex Nettlefold, University of the West Indies, 1960.

47. Dennis *cit.*, p. 17.

48. *Education for All: The Report of the Committee of Inquiry into the Education of Children from Ethnic Minority Groups* Chairman: Lord Swann, FRSE. Her Majesty's Stationery Office, 1985.

49. Shiva Naipaul, *Beyond the Dragon's Mouth*, London: Sphere Books, 1985, p. 383.

50. *Daily Telegraph*, September 1st, 1985.

51. V.S. Naipaul, *Middle Passage, cit.*, p. 245.

52. Stone, *cit.*, p. 70.

53. *Ibid*.

54. Maurice Cranston, "American's Neo-Whigs," *The American Spectator*, February, 1987, p.27.

55. R. Emmett Tyrrell, Jr., *The Liberal Crack-up*, New York, Simon and Schuster, 1984, pp. 44-45.

56. Adam Wolfson, "Heart of Darkness: What Governments Do to Blacks in the Rest of Africa," *Policy Review*, 1985, pp. 42-46.

57. Jesse Jackson, "Jesse Jackson's Manifesto: A Call to Black America," *Chicago Tribune*, April 18, 1976, Sec. 2, p.1

58. Anthony Sampson, *The Money Lenders*, London, Hodder and Stoughton, 1981, p. 154.

59. Wolfson, p. 43.

60. Yonas Deressa, "Rebel Aid," *National Review*, April 24, 1987, pp. 36-38. The author is President of the Ethiopian Refugee Education and Relief Foundation. See also the article by Yonas's brother Dereje in *Salisbury Review*, vol. 4, no. 2, January 1986.

61. Holger Jensen, "Mozambique: Winning the War Against All

Odds," *Insight: The Washington Times*, January 12, 1987, pp. 33-35. After typing a page of these exotic African names, often purloined by American revolutionaries, I wonder what effect it would have had on the Mexican revolution if we had all referred to the fiery Zapata as plain Mr. Shoe.

62. V.S. Naipaul, *Middle Passage, cit.*, p. 76.
63. Brian Ng Fatt, "Taking a deeper look at Calypso," *Trinidad Guardian*, December 11, 1985, p. 35.
64. Quoted by Searle in *Race and Class* XXV: 1 (1983), p. 58.
65. Major Eugene D. Seiter, Jr., "All-Source Production Section," *Military Intelligence*, January-March, 1985, p. 11. I apologize to Gene if, by this time, he has been promoted to general officer, as he richly deserves to be. At p. 23 of this issue, incidentally, may be seen a picture of our home during the hostilities.
66. *Grenada Newsletter*, August 10, 1980; this extra-insular bulletin was a fount of stories about torture in Richmond Hill prison.
67. Sandford and Vigilante, *cit.*, p. 152.
68. The job is tolerably well done in the "Bishop Trial Report" special supplement to the Barbados *Nation* of December 2, 1986, though the reader should be warned that some of the chronology cited is incorrect.
69. Ogarkov is reported to have told Einstein Louison: "Over two decades ago, there was only Cuba in Latin America. Today there are Nicaragua, Grenada, and a serious battle going on for El Salvador" (*Human Events*, November 16, 1985, p. 12).
70. Shiva Naipaul, *Journey to Nowhere*, Harmondsworth, Penguin Books, 1980, p. 87.
71. From Maurice Bishop's Notes on the CC meeting. It does not seem to be true that Maurice was tortured during this house arrest, as alleged in the Barbados *Nation* special supplement on the trial cited.
72. Perhaps not so paranoiac, at that. Pincher Martin theorizes that Hugh Gaitskell was poisoned by the KGB in 1963.
73. Morris S. Thompson, "The day Grenada's leader went to the wall," *Newsday*, as reprinted in the London *Guardian*, May 24, 1985, p. 12. Abdullah's statement from which this is drawn can be found in full in the Barbados *Nation* Special Supplement, of December 2, 1986.

164

74. This sign was left for some time as a memento of our collective island nightmare, but despite what visiting journalists say, it has long since been effaced, together with another nearby that read, POLITICS DISCIPLINE COMBAT READINESS EQUALS VICTORY.
75. Transcript, RFG, October 19, 1983.
76. Payne, Sutton and Thorndike, *cit.*, p. 138.
77. *The Times*, November 5, 1983.
78. Payne, Sutton and Thorndike, *cit.*, pp. 138-139. According to this legend the bodies were dropped in "the sea off Point Salines, where the current is particularly strong." It is particularly mild. I swim in it thrice a day. The same authors describe Fort Frederick as "across the bay" from St. George's. Which bay?
79. *Granma*, October 30, 1983.
80. Sandford and Vigilante, *cit.*, p. 176. So much, too, for the objection that such Cuban workers were not pseudo-soldiers.
81. *Human Events*, February 7, 1987, pp. 10-11.
82. Payne, Sutton and Thorndike, *cit.*, p. 155.
83. *Ibid.*
84. Sandford and Vigilante, *cit.*, p. 9.
85. *The Wall Street Journal*, November 1, 1983, p. 30.
86. Payne, Sutton and Thorndike, *cit.*, p. 157.

PART THREE: AFTER

3. AFTER

Let's Do It

October 25th, 1983, a day now celebrated as a national Thanksgiving holiday in Grenada, broke wet and muggy; this is the height of our rainy season and when the sun comes out after a shower you're in a steambath. Temperatures rose over ninety that day.

Myth: A Delta team sent to free political prisoners in Richmond Hill prison had to turn back under fire before it could reach the prison, which turned out to be abandoned. A Navy SEAL team sent to take over a radio station moved in at first light and was repulsed by enemy fire. The result: the SEALS had to blow up the radio station, rendering it useless as a pacifying tool during the invasion. Another SEAL team, specializing in speed, stealth and quick getaways, was sent to rescue Governor-General Sir Paul Scoon but was pinned down for 24 hours before Marines came to its aid.[1]

Reality: Delta Blue Light, specializing in anti-terrorist hostage rescue situations, a detachment created in the seventies which had bad luck in its Desert One rendezvous in Iran, was never anywhere near our prison. This was never "abandoned." It was relieved in an orderly way on the 26th and political prisoners only freed. No SEAL team was sent to "take over" RFG. The radio station, which throughout the night had been broadcasting inflammatory instructions to Grenadians to pour down to the beaches, was put out by rockets fired from an armed HH-53. Richard Gray watched its destruction from the terrace of his Cinnamon Hill residence: "I watched them call off the coordinates and WHOOF! WHOOF! It was bloody marvelous. It needed to be bombed."[2] It did. And 82nd at once set up their Spice Island station for us on the same frequency.

Those SEALS winched down into the grounds of Government House from Blackhawk copters (in the first combat use of that work horse), were trapped with the Governor-General for less than twenty-four hours. Finally, it is to be noted that this myth of *Time* is given us light years after the event and is probably being used as fact by some researcher. Thus is history made. All the news that fits we print.

The rescue of the Governor-General was delayed because the Special Forces were charged with sparing civilian lives and Lucas Street is heavily populated. On the less populated windward coast Pearls Airport was rapidly secured by Marines of the 1-84 Amphibious Ready Group, off the *Guam*. Then shortly before dawn the major objective, inclusive of the Cuban camp, was achieved. Five Hercules C-130s, attended by as many Spectre gunships (able to pour down 20 mm Gatling-gun fire), approached the Pointe Salines peninsula in formation. Each C-130 contained some fifty US Army Rangers of the 2nd Bn, 75 INF. They had left their staging base two hours before.

It might be interjected here that the helicopter is an all-important article of this kind of warfare. The AH-64 Apache is said, despite *Time* magazine, to be far superior to the Soviet Mi-24 Hind copter gunship (used in Afghanistan). The British were considerably handicapped in the Falklands by accidental loss of a number of helicopters. For the vectored thrust of a jumpjet like the Harrier, so successful in the Falklands, depends on enormous fuel reserves. The Harrier has a tremendously high "disc load," meaning that it burns fuel fast when taking off, hovering, or landing. A conventional helicopter's "disc" carved out of the sky by its rotors has a load of about nine pounds per square foot given a 50-foot rotor span (the V-22 Osprey's tilt-rotor is about 40), whereas the Harrier's is 1,000 per square foot.

In any case, so much for the idea that eight hundred Rangers dropped on Pointe Salines at 6.00 am.[3] Nor did even as many as five hundred tackle the job.[4] Less than two hundred initially jumped. Less than ten of those were combat vets, Vietnam vintage. Of these Lt. Col. Ralph Hagler, leading the command bird, was a decorated Vietnam vet, with five hundred jumps to his credit. He was the first man out, after turning to shout back, "Rangers, be hard."[5]

It is perhaps unnecessary to add here that jumping out of an aeroplane is contrary to the human instinct to continue life and in itself requires great courage. Cyrus Vance, when Secretary of the Army in the nineteen sixties, acknowledged that "People in the airborne had style, zeal, and motivation."[6] US 82nd Airborne knew it, coming from Fort Bragg with its drop zones named after World War Two assaults. Theirs is not the eat-rattlesnakes, Rambo brand of courage, but the real variety known as grit.

In any event, Hagler's mission group had been planning to land in their craft. Thanks to Forbes Burnham's perfidy they met fierce gunfire, the Cubans under Tortolo having had time to site and sandbag their anti-aircraft guns, as well as cement stakes into the runway, and otherwise block it with vehicles like steamrollers, bulldozers, tractors (some still extant, as I write).

Not nearly enough credit has been given to this drop which was the lowest in combat since World War Two, allowing most men only seven seconds on the silk – Colleen and I treasure the signatures of some of them. The reason for this low altitude approach to the windy drop zone was as follows: aerial photographic surveillance had shown four 23 mm anti-aircraft pieces on the hills at the end of the strip. Using topographical maps, Hagler calculated that these guns could not depress sufficiently to hit the transports if they came in under six hundred feet. As he laconically put it, "500 feet allowed us to fly in under the threat."[7]

It was a risk, especially as auxiliary chutes would be useless, and the men had trained at more than twice that height. Directly the "jump" signal had been given there was a frantic scramble to rig up for an airborne assault – "The next thing we knew," reported 1st. Lt. Raymond Thomas, "they were opening the doors." Each Ranger pack weighed well over a hundred pounds, being crammed with everything from Claymore mines to mortars, spare ammo, water. Many carried a M-60 machinegun, a rifle, a .45 pistol, and frags (grenades). As Sgt Terry Pholand put it, "You didn't jump out that door, you fell out."

They did so Ranger-style, that is with weapons exposed, and using T-10 parachutes. When first alerted some of the men had imagined this to be just another EDRE (Emergency Deployment Readiness Exercise), but realized it was serious when issued live ammunition and atropine styrettes. A rough chronology at Pointe Salines was the following: on D-Day October 25th the Rangers fell from the skies, securing the strip of obstacles by 7.15 am; the next day we had the 160th Avn Bn dropping on us; the third day major elements of 82nd Abn Div from Fort Bragg came in and relieved the Rangers.

The latter dropped into a driving wind of twenty knots and heavy fire from the high ground above the strip at Frequente Gap. Some, scrambling over others to get out, dropped at 150 knots air speed. All cleared their planes in twenty-one seconds. One man landed in the sea, harmlessly enough. One broke his leg. The rest kept the heads down of a number of well trained Cubans who rained small-arms fire down on them from the hills. Navy A-6s streaked in to help from the carrier *Independence*. The Rangers sent a group back to mash down the stakes the Cubans had set in the runway and hot-wire the heavy vehicles left to block it. I thought this last a neat performance. It isn't every day you get the assignment to hot-wire-start a Russian steam-roller and drive it away. But when I later put this to a fairly senior officer involved, a slow smile creased his face as he told me, "Those guys used to be a bunch of car thieves in California. They could start anything." Rangers ain't gentlemen. They proved that within hours of landing. A group of Cubans made a sudden determined charge in three Soviet armored carriers, coming from the True Blue side of the runway, down the hill towards Hardy Bay at the Rangers. This was just what the latter were waiting for. They pumped those carriers as full of holes as a Swiss cheese with their 90 mm recoilless rifles.

A coda to this particular carnage, the largest single head-on enemy engagement of the campaign, came when two well-scrubbed US officers arrived at our gate. One was a veterinarian who came to see if our dogs were all right. Before leaving he said, "Don't eat any pork." Though not Rastas we hadn't intended doing so. It transpired that the bodies of Cubans killed in this shoot-out had accumulated under some trees to the north of Hardy Bay, where their pig farm was. The pigs had got loose. I remembered from my own days in service how time-consuming and unpleasant corpse disposal could be ...

That night the Rangers dug in through torrential rain. "I've never seen a rusty Ranger yet," quipped Hagler. Next morning they had to evacuate the medical students from their Grande Anse campus, a tricky task since the Cubans had re-formed in the way, and civilian life had to be safeguarded. An end-sweep by Navy CH-46 choppers did the job, though only after the Rangers had made a human corridor for the students to run through, while they themselves took machinegun fire from the Soviet Embassy above, one which all American elements respected despite repeated Russian violations of conduct codes.[8] Hagler got the students back, loaded sixty in each copter, to the Pointe Salines strip.

This had become mayhem, as more and more planes landed, and 82nd deployed. To its G2 there now reported the 519th MI BN, charged with tactical exploitation and interrogation, whose plaque presented to my wife and me "for support" I glance at proudly as I write. Now that the Governor-General had been rescued, and temporarily sheltered in our house, this US Intelligence unit went up the hill to the main Cuban camp and their own Divisional HQ.

There they found about seven hundred unidentified Cuban and Grenadian prisoners-of-war slopping around the huts under less than a dozen guards. There was no perimeter wire and a good thousand Grenadian civilians, mostly refugees from the village of Kalliste under sniping, were milling about trying to find water and lodging. In the course of the next month that MI unit, getting some three hours sleep a night, had organized the entire area into a civilized entity, carried out more than 2,400 interrogations, and exploited five tons of captured documents.[9]

Hagler stuck around for one more important mission, to secure the Egmont Harbour-Calivigny PRA base on the 27th. This was well equipped for defense and it was here that three Blackhawks crashed, their rotors dismembering and killing three Rangers on the ground. This collision was ridiculed by the *Washington Post* – who else? – but was due to one of the pilots being badly wounded in arms and legs. The wrecked copters were slingloaded out. PFC Tim Romick, 1st Bn, 75th Rangers, won a Purple Heart, presented to him in Womack Community Hospital at Fort Bragg by General John A. Wickham Jr. As mentioned, Calivigny was demolished after warning runs by Corsairs, whose airbrakes make a wail reminiscent of those siren-equipped Stukas I heard in North Africa.

The medical students were evacuated to the Pointe Salines strip and on October 26th, seventeen flights brought out *at their own request* 599 Americans and 121 foreigners. Marines then took Fort Frederick, which was heavily defended. Friends close to it describe the PRA ack-ack guns toppling down the long hillside every which way. But the take-out was pin-point accurate and, in the case of Fort Rupert, it was just as well it was. Unknown to the assailants, a storage cellar there was packed with dynamite; had the site been bombed rather than rocketed, enough TNT to take the whole of St. George's skywards would have detonated.

In this attack a Cobra was brought down in flames on the GBSS cricket ground. The pilot was able to crawl away but, though he surrendered to approaching PRA, his body was riddled with shot and tossed in the nearby lagoon. This kind of treatment was frequently meted out by both PRA and Cubans: "Talk among the troops was that Cubans on Calivigny mutilated and castrated captured Americans before killing them."[10] Paying tribute to the Air Force interrogators working with him, Captain O'Shaughnessy adds: "Without this breadth of experience, the identity of the individual who mutilated a Marine pilot's body would not have been known."[11] They got the man but he was not punished for his barbarity.

Then, from Barbados, we heard that the Queen's Park Power Station had been secured. The old Santa Maria Hotel, where I had first stayed on Grenada, and which had become Bishop's Headquarters, was taken out. There remained the Richmond Hill ridge. This runs above the capital, housing the prison, what was Stan Friday's clinic, an old folks' home, the Crazy House (as the mental hospital is known), and the Kennedy Home for Handicapped Children, all of whom had been crouching terrified in their cellar. Despite its name, and the rude bust of JFK outside it, the Kennedy Home has no connection with the famous family, though doubtless every tourist passing by imagines it to be endowed by the philanthropic Kennedys. This entire area, from which picture-postcard views of the capital can be seen, was subject to a lot of fire night and day, including even some light artillery rounds.

Subsequent to this assault on the institutions there was much outcry in the press that Americans had bombed a hospital. The truth is that the Crazy House was a 250 year-old structure with three-foot thick walls, which made a tempting shelter for the PRA, under a Red Cross sign. They not only used it as a fire base but handed out weaponry to the inmates. Of these there were sixteen, including some homicidal maniacs (one had recently cut off the heads of two woman at Westerhall). So, after due warning

passes, Marine A-7s battered the old fortification down. There
certainly were casualties among the patients, thanks to the PRA.
There were not among the civilians in the area.

I visited Crazy House shortly after its destruction. It was still a
grim place, its barred cells dank and dark, its sanitation medieval.
Food for the patients was still being cooked in old cauldrons
inherited from the soldiery of two centuries past (though none the
worse for that). The new mental hospital built at Mount Royal by
US AID has been provided with a plethora of therapy equipment; it is a modern facility, cheerful and encouraging. All the
same, I shall not soon forget attending the last Christmas at Crazy
House, when a dance was given for the inmates by nurses and
doctors. Relatives attended, bringing up presents and food for
the afflicted. Seeing the insane wheeling and turning in their last
dance in that old fort was a weirdly moving experience.

It was during this final fire-fight that the chopper containing a
brilliant political officer from AmEmbassy Barbados, Larry
Rossin, was repeatedly hit, its navigational equipment wrecked,
and pilot wounded. The Blackhawk managed to limp away, just.
But Rossin, a good friend of ours, was reported killed to his wife
Debbie. It is good to know he is alive and well, and now serving
America elsewhere.

The Questions of the Questioners

After the main St. George's police station was burnt down on the
once shady Esplanade, the major intelligence loss, more and
more of the PRA started shedding their uniforms and guns in the
bush. You are still likely to see youths wearing camouflage pants
in St. George's, but that does not indicate sympathy with the
PRA. Stray Cubans were rounded up. The tidying and investigation fell to the 82nd Abn Div of Fort Bragg, manning checkpoints, searching and clearing, winkling out snipers, weapons,

and personnel. On any given day in that period I could go through as many as a dozen searches of car and person between Pointe Saline and St. George's, many enforced by red-bereted girls.

This *ratissage* at both major checkpoints, Alpha and Bravo, was invariably polite and efficient, if a trifle rank-heavy. Local Grenadians were intelligently employed at such points. The degree of language ability in this American army new to me was surprising. If the interrogation platoons came ready for Spanish they did so not only with Puerto Rican personnel. Russian and German-speaking sources had to be assessed in this heterogeneous compound and I even met one interrogation technician who was fluent in Urdu!

At these checkpoints there were ruses for catching stray Cubans. A soldier might sit to one side of the track, listening to music on a transistor coming from one of the many Venezuelan stations nearby. Directly language came on, the soldier's eyes would flick over the vehicle. Eye recognition is easily identifiable.

I once gave an unsuspecting ride to one of these intelligence monitors. He got in, thanked me, and noticed that I had my dial set on the main Spanish-speaking station out of the island of Margarita, a Venezuelan free port. For five minutes he led me down a puzzling garden path – how wonderful the Cubans were, and so on – until I twigged. We had a good laugh over some Carib draught in the Crab.

This countersubversion phase soon moved into final (?) stability. The Marines had left, the Governor-General was restored to his house, and an Advisory Interim Council (of nine members) formed, until elections might be held. The Russians were seen off. The checks were essential as regards the Russians. Captain Stephen Donehoo put it: "An example of the breadth of responsibilities given to Company B was the screening of Soviet Embassy personnel upon their departure. Baggage inspection resulted in the confiscation of a large cache of Soviet weapons and ammunition that Cubans were attempting to smuggle off the island."[12] SIGINT (Signals Intelligence), with Vinson Secure Nets, divided the island into six sectors, and soon the entire group of radicals responsible for the massacre in Fort Rupert were rounded up, interrogated, duly charged, and put in prison. (More of them later.) On October 28th, 1983, Sir Paul Scoon broadcast to the nation. On the 30th, while gratitude services were being held in churches all over the island, Hudson Austin was captured, skulking in drag, in a house belonging to a German at Westerhall. Andrew Bierzynski, a Minister under Gairy and Jewel alike, gave the tip-off to catch him.

By now elements of the multi-island Caribbean Peace-Keeping Force were streaming in, with XVIII Airborne Corps moving into Grenada on the 31st. Though the south of the island was still without power and water, Scoon called for a full re-opening of all shops and business. The populace responded. The walls became decorated with GOD BLESS AMERICA signs, USA FORE-VER adorning what had been called Kaunda Square in Tempe. Then, at risk, Tony Buxo directed 2-505th. Infantry to Bernard Coard's hideout. An ophthalmologist who had, like myself, been trained at Sandhurst, Tony identified several Cuban and Grenadian revolutionary leaders to US Forces; the story of his courage was recounted in *Paraglide*.[13]

Coard wore no disguise (his very bulk would have given him away) but his wife pleaded pregnancy, based, it was found, on a pillowful of greenbacks stashed in the front of her dress. Austin and Coard were taken to the ships, before being put in prison. The last Marine left Grenada on November 3rd. On the 5th island-wide interrogation was consolidated at Pointe Salines.

The 1-505th Infantry stayed to ensure the peaceful transition to the temporary government which took full control on November 15th. The search-and-clear operations of this unit were routine, though attended with risk. It is said that the last bullet fired in anger on Grenada was on October 31st. There were cases of snipings after this, as well as combat-related hazards that any soldier knows. Recon troopers of the 82nd pursued sporadic hostility well into December. One incident involved a group of armed Cubans in the north.[14] An Airborne Captain had made a sweep and put down in some bush, where he was told by a pipe-smoking crone that she knew of two Cubans hiding nearby. However – "Leave them to us, Daddy." I also heard stories at this time of Cuban skulls seen on stakes in the country, but tend to disbelieve them. All the same, my wife and I vividly recall all the Red Alerts in this period.

People used to ask me whether there were any Cubans left hidden on the island today. No. Thanks to heavy intelligence gathering, using sophisticated automation and captured documents, it only took 525th MI Group seventy-two hours to pick up the key sixty or so "Most Wanted" extremists. Those PRA who faded back into the population were collated into an "At Large" list, with every single rank and residence known. The file of in-country Cubans was as complete.

The interrogations were carried out impeccably. The Cubans even enjoyed them (I have a photo of one doing so). Many would have liked to go back to Fort Bragg immediately, but after Mariel defections of the lower orders were discouraged. The bonehead liberal press complained that PRA hard types were being housed in packing-case crates in the sun, for lengthy screening. It is true you entered such a hut on hands and knees, at the crawl (a PsyOps touch?), but inside they were cooler than a pup tent. I went into one. Each occupant had a foam rubber bed, unlike their opposite number in Richmond Hill prison. In any event, these crates were only used in the brief phase when detention authority was granted to US forces; the amnesty program, calling on all such hard cases in the defeated machinery to report to the Caribbean Peacekeeping Force in St. George's, met with a surprisingly positive response. Pulling guard duty, patroling, confiscating arms, giving medical attention, supervising the p-o-ws, the men of the 82nd gave a fine impression. These support troops, it should be emphasized, left no prisoners; they only left in Richmond Hill prison a number on charges of murder and/or conspiracy to murder. "No one's up there because he's a communist," as one 82nd officer put it to me.

I remember a young Lieut coming up our drive in a Dodge truck and slapping some cartons of C rations on our kitchen table. After he had gone I thought – *C rats*! Holy Smoke, exactly forty years ago, I had been a young ensign in the British army cadging C rations from "the Yanks" whenever possible. They were so much more varied, as well as more nutritious, than our stuff. All through North Africa it had been bully beef and M. & V., the latter a succinct summation of the English table, since it stood for Meat and Vegetables (any meat, any vegetables). I ate suet pudding in 110 in the shade near Sousse.

At Pointe Salines I shared our rations with locals around, particularly one who had crawled through the bush, braving fire in the curfew, to see if we were safe and provided for. Personally I went for the sliced peaches first, then as now. I noted that the chocolate cookies had been much improved, the new fudge kind being positively four-star. If the grub was the same, however, the men were different. I had to toss out the window the stereotype of the gum-chewing GI Joe of Bill Mauldin's *Stars and Stripes* cartoons. (As also the conscript seen in Vietnam movies like *Platoon*.) After so many years among the scruffy Cubans this was like living with another breed, scrubbed, tough, intelligent, fit, and – yes – abstemious. General Farris' instructions to all Commanders, US Forces, Grenada, concluded:

One of the most important elements of our mission in Grenada is to support development of a freely-elected, democratic government and minimize the impact of our presence on the island ... We have done so many good things here, and you and your troops have earned an enviable reputation for goodness, fair play, and respect for others. As we wind down, do not let some isolated unfavorable incidents tarnish that record.[15]

He need not have worried. There were none. By my book these were exceptional soldiers. We, in the Brigade of Guards, were also such, we thought. But square-bashing, and ceremonial duties, were designed to eradicate individuality (a month at our Depot at Caterham was all you needed for that), whereas in the electronic warfare of today initiative is highly prized. Indeed, such was shown by the Scots Guards in the Falklands.

That assumption of superiority of any men who know their role perfectly made it possible for those of the 82nd I met in Grenada to regard the spittle of the liberal press back home with a sort of amused contempt; their Intelligence officers used to quietly show me specimens of the muck thrown at them by the *Washington Post* or *New York Times* (which we shall examine below). They did so with the wry resignation of the completely confident. Keith Douglas, the poet with whom I was at school and at Oxford and whom I met in the Western Desert before he was killed, put it well of such men when he wrote of his own pride of regiment: "We knew we were better than anyone else, and cared for no one."[16] Such cool disregard, however, is the prerogative of volunteers, such as served in both Grenada and the Falklands, and we do not have enough of them.

Unlike the Cubans, US Forces were respectful of private property. Thanks to extensive damage to our switching system and cable plant, largely fouled up by Bulgarians in an effort to create an elaborate eaves-dropping system, telephone service was out. US SIGINT soon contrived a secure point-to-point circuit. On this absentee houseowners in the States were contacted for permission to rent. They were recompensed by USG who established a generous Claims Office in St. George's. This was a very different story from the grab-and-gimme days of Bishop and the Cubans.

Of those post-intervention days Colleen and I treasure memories of General Jack Farris, commander of XVIII Airborne Corps and Fort Bragg, a Vietnam vet all wire and whipcord, sitting on our terrace at sunset and reminiscing with Colleen, General

Browning's daughter, over the great names of World War Two. As a child, Colleen had perforce grown up in Camberley Staff College quarters, her chums the offspring of names to be legends. Pam Wavell was one such friend, Slim's children others. Farris warmed to the mention of Slim and I sensed he was the same kind of foxhole General. He always seemed surrounded by calm, clean, confident officers, full of private jokes, like members of some *ancien régime*.

Rather naturally we admired Jack Farris who so coolly endured the calumny of the Stateside press. Once, for instance, *Newsweek* had occasion to point out that he had stood beside Sir Paul Scoon at one briefing with a holstered pistol. But since when might our general officers not go around armed? This petty nit-picking on the part of the press will be examined in the next section and was typical of the kind of criticism, wholly uninformed, that both Farris and his black ADC Captain Saunders had to put up with, not from Grenadians but from American press personnel.

At 4.45 pm on Monday June 10th, 1984, Grenadian and American flags were run down from in front of the gutted Holiday Inn on Grande Anse beach, US military headquarters since October 1983 and today a Ramada hotel. Later on there was a fireworks celebration (and not that only!) and next morning Col. Earl Horan presented the flags to the Grenadian Police Commissioner, Russell Toppin; whereupon the remaining sixty-seven US military left on the island boarded their C-130 for the seven hour flight to Fort Bragg. The Grenadian intervention was officially over.

Before he left, Jack Farris came round to say goodby to us. Colleen baked him a cake, with stars of rank iced on it, and we wished him and his well. He gave me two parting gifts that defined his presence and personality: Barbara Tuchman's enormous study of Stilwell, and Nigel Nicolson's biography of "Alex" Alexander, Stilwell's alter ego (at least in their first meeting in Burma). I had last seen General Alex in Italy when some of us were pulled out of the line to be on parade in a field near

Benevento, in South Italy, as he presented the VC to Bill Sidney of the Grenadier Guards (today Lord De L'Isle). That was, in fact, the only time I ever saw the unlucky Lord Gort, who joined Alex to mingle with us mere mortals in a tented mess afterwards. Personally, I have Jack Farris tintyped in memory as a combination of the two men whose biographies he gave me: the no-bullshit Stilwell coupled with the modest gentleman Alexander. In brief, the Grenada intervention left me with several military eye-openers, of which two follow.

First, I was impressed by the very great accuracy of take-out bombing and rocketing available in warfare today. How many lovely structures in Europe would still be standing if the rival armies of World War Two had had such expertise at their disposal? No doubt was left in my mind, after consulting LIC (Low Intensity Combat) Manicheans of the 82nd, that they could take out a golfball on your front lawn without disturbing the Louis Vuitton handbag on your poolside table. I learnt, for instance, that on the Yuma Proving Ground a totally new generation of air-to-ground rockets is superseding the antique "Vietnam era" single-warhead, mechanical-fuze rockets. The "S" model Cobra has a wholly computerized fire-control system, into which firing equations are inserted. Unlike the gunners of Keith's and my war, the present version sees a read-off set of numbers plus a pair of sighting points, generated by the aircraft's laser range-finder. As the points intermatch with the target, the capability to disperse munitions over an impact point many miles away is substantially increased – a House of Lord's way of saying that all hell is let loose.

Secondly, the distaff side of this new army impressed me. For one feature of our liberating force was the presence of alert, intelligent, fit, good-looking girls under berets. To be frank, I had long grown tired of those propaganda pictures of female Russian soldiers peering over their guns on the walls of Stalingrad. At that moment in history the Soviets, with greatly depleted manpower, used women in combat *very sparingly*. They no longer do so at all. In fact, in a force of over four millions the USSR has only ten thousand women enrolled, mostly in medical and clerical positions. The KGB is virtually all male.

Similarly, Israel, whose pretty girl warriors are frequently photographed (e.g. Yael Dayan, Moshe's daughter), has less than 3% employed in its military, all in traditional roles, and has never used women in combat since its 1984 war. East Germany has no women in its military in any role at all. On the other hand, US Air Force enlistees are today 11% female, while combat training at Fort Benning now includes a course on sexual harassment.[17]

Numbers of women served in Vietnam, none in direct combat, though one Army nurse, 1st. Lt. Sharon A. Lane, was killed by hostile fire in a rocket attack on her hospital there in June 1969; a statue of her stands at Aultman Hospital, Canton, Ohio, from whose School of Nursing she graduated. In any case, many of these women underwent greater hardships than a lot of the men; the well documented story of the Australian nurses in Sumatra in World War Two is one of the most appalling instances of Japanese brutality, eventually featured on BBC-TV as "Tenko."[18] Statistics are not always kept of these heroisms, with the result that when the US Supreme Court ruled on women and the draft it did so in the dark; even today the Department of Defense seems foggy about the actual number of female veterans of Vietnam. Canada is presently said to be experimenting with women in combat roles.

As for the Cubans, those in Grenada were male. There were a couple of nurses in a Puesto Medical on Pointe Salines to whom I talked occasionally, but they did not carry arms. They used to swan around in the sidecars of ancient motorcycle combinations and were cloyingly "feminine". One could have doubled for any hoop-earringed cantina girl in a Pedro Armandariz film of Old Mexico.

Nicaragua, meanwhile, whatever the feminine quotient in the Sandinista forces may be, came up with the dominatrix of the day in Nora Astorga, a feminist parody out of Sacher-Masoch. For butch-cropped Nora, the Sandinista Ambassador to the UN no less, was used by the 1979 revolutionaries to entice General Reynaldo Perez Vega of the Somoza National Guard to her bed. This she leapt out of at the moment of the General's consummation and watched while the soldiery she let in gouged out his eyes, hacked off his genitals, taped them in his mouth, and clubbed him to death.

The girls assigned to 82nd were sharp and active. I wouldn't have wanted to test the "female upper body strength" of any one of them. Doubtless some of this owed to the new strenuous roles opened up to ladies of late: there were, for instance, 72,000 policewomen in America in 1986 as against only 22,000 in 1970, and 96,000 women truck drivers in 1986 as compared with a mere 42,000 in 1970.[19] Here increase in city populations has to be taken into account, obviously enough.

No women performed combat in Grenada, though I watched a couple search a house for Cubans in true *Dragnet* fashion. They shared one half of a long tent with the men and there was no fraternizing. Pretty Liz Milliken, a Spec 4 who helped guard the US Embassy at Ross Point, attracted a lot of attention, while another such, a dead ringer for Goldie Hawn in *Private Benjamin*, spent her days off with us, leaving her M-16 in my study. When she came to say goodby to us before leaving, night had fallen, and I accompanied her through the dark of our grounds to the gate, where I asked the wrong question – Would she be all right? "I got sixty rounds if anyone wants to mess with me," was her response.

I suppose I was interested in this particular liberation having had two sisters in the British services in World War Two. Neither carried arms and British female military still does not do so. I was told that originally, indeed, 82nd had not planned to take in any women soldiers since Grenada was ex-British. I understand also that the notion peeves a lot of British girls who hold records in free-fall female sky diving.

The US Air Force and Navy still forbid the ladies combat assignments by Title X of the Code. The sex-integrated military came about when conscription ended in 1973 and ERA began crying prejudice at exclusion of women from combat duties. (There were moments when I wouldn't have minded such exclusions myself.) As one of their proponents, Antonia Chayes, put it: since women were likely to be casualties in any future war, they should be given the chance to get some promotion for fighting – "If we want to protect women from high risk casualty, we will have to bury them underground."

Thus, with eighteen male Americans dead (one dying subsequently), the revo was over. In common with Hitler Bishop liked to name his years, giving them vague abstractions bannered up here and there. For Hitler 1940 was The Year of Trial. The proper slogan for 1983 had seemed to give Bishop especial trouble, however. I heard him laboring away on the radio for half an hour on the subject, trying to decide as to whether it should be called The Year of Academic and Political Education or The Year of Political and Academic Education. Eventually, he told us, the Central Committee had decided in their wisdom for the latter, since there could be no academic education without political education. Bro Bish got his in 1983.

That November a CBS poll was taken. 91% of the Grenadian population were grateful for the intervention, 76% being certain of a total Cuban take-over. A January 14th, 1984, a straw poll conducted by Professor William Adams of George Washington University found 59% of the population in favor of increasing the American presence, both civilian and military. Eric Gairy took a signed petition to the US Ambassador requesting retention of US troops on the island. The leader of the NNP (New National Party), and our present Premier, Herbert Blaize, concurred: "To the Americans who are here to help us we say, stay until we can help ourselves."

There were demonstrations for the same. Children walked shyly up to US soldiers and gave them coconuts, others nutmegs.

One medical student jogged in star-spangled shorts and a T-shirt reading SUPPORT YOUR LOCAL POLICE STATE (i.e. the Coard regime). REAGAN FOR GOVERNOR-GENERAL bumper stickers appeared. "I've never been so proud to be an American citizen," said another med student, Stuart From, who had watched the jets come in and waggle their wings in encouragement. On the first C-141 to arrive back at Charleston AFB, S.C., with fifty-nine students, a letter of "sincere and heart-felt gratitude" was composed and carried to the Air Force pilots who ferried that mission.

The actress Mayo Gray, who also stood to lose her home in Grenada, wrote a love letter to those whose actions saved the island:

> Last August the front page of *The Village Voice* heralded *Love with a Proper Revolution*, which turned out to be an unabashed mash note to the Sandinista commandantes of Nicaragua by Argentine novelist Luisa Valenzuela ... I too feel an urge to indulge in a rhapsodic love letter, stirred by the mystique and actions of the American armed forces in Grenada. So this is for you, Jose, Don, Mike, Tom, Rick, Earl, Jack, Ann ... and to the hundreds who beguiled this American with your prowess and esprit, can-do exuberance, wry humor, and a tender-toughness ... they conducted the operation without carnage, with minimal loss of life across the boards, and with honor.[20]

Through A Glass Darkly: The Press in Grenada

Watching the Grenada intervention at all too close hand, in truth from across the road, I was reminded of our Prime Minister Maurice Bishop's friend, the late Samora Machel of Mozambique. A visitor to our island, Machel defined the role of the press in our time as being to "liquidate liberalism, individualism."

I believe I received my epiphany on media war coverage in the democracies when chatting on my terrace at Pointe Salines with some 82nd officers about the movie *Under Fire*, which they had seen. The movie depicts three war correspondents in Somoza's Nicaragua. American mercenaries are shown gunning down handsome Sandinistas (one wearing a Baltimore Orioles baseball cap), and by the end of the film the three have dropped all pretense to neutrality, they are committed anti-Americans. Were not my guests, professional soldiers all, disgusted with this depiction?

Not really. Their temperate placidity brought me to realize the special relationship of the volunteer forces; the conscript armies of World War Two joined up, as I did in England, because everyone was doing so, because the country was being threatened by foreign powers. The volunteer election, on the other hand, is predicated on the suspicion that the ordinary citizen, in today's technological world, hasn't a clue as to the dynamics of the threat posed to his country, and his own existence. He is not armed to judge such, nor is his Congressman, or Member of Parliament.

Contemporary "objective" journalism reposes on a secrecy which a famous attorney for the *New York Times*, Floyd Abrams called "the essence, in good part, Your Honor, of good journalism." On the matter of refusal of source identification Justice Burger once replied, "The newspapers and newspaper reporters claim for themselves the right which this argument would deny to the government." As Richard Reeb puts it, "the media do not believe that the public has an unqualified right to know everything but, rather, only what the media themselves choose to reveal to that public."[21] Referring to a book suspicious of new media power by Renata Adler Benjamin Stein writes, "The freedom of the press, as Miss Adler notes, may now be so great that it has squeezed out freedom of speech for everyone else.[22]

Operation URGENT FURY took place after the Falklands war, but partook of that operation's suspicion of publicity. In both cases it was decided that you cannot play today's electronic warfare on television, nor did I meet a single 82nd soldier whose aim in life was to be a video idol. It is, rather, the contemporary journalist's ambition to be played by Robert Redford.

The Falklands campaign lasted for seventy-five days and for the first fifty-four England received no direct pictures therefrom. HM Fleet HQ initially disallowed any press members aboard. Only two BBC correspondents were allowed to accompany the task force out, and no satellite facilities were put at their disposal. All tapes had to be shipped home by mail bag, often reaching London three weeks after the event.[23]

The reporters who accompanied the Falklands assault, like those who went in with the Normandy landings, did not question the justice of the operation involved. They went in an informative rather than interpretive role. This was not the case of those American and British reporters fighting to get on planes to Grenada in October 1983. They had come to hit the Reagan administration. Congressman Ted Weiss (Upper West Side, New York City) called for impeachment of the President. The *New York Times* likened the Grenada mission to the Soviet invasion of Afghanistan, calling the USA a "paranoid bully."[24]

Indeed, even directly after Bishop's assassination prior to intervention both the *Washington Post* and *New York Times* pointed accusatory fingers at Reagan – it was, of course, all our fault. Down with us again! Press presence in the Falklands was well summarized by war historian Alistair Horne:

Despite the extreme frustration of the pressmen with the Task Force, the British operation was undoubtedly much aided by the rigid clampdown on news. In marked contrast to Vietnam, there was no live television from the battlefront ... I have often reflected that, had there been live TV coverage in World War II, there would have been no D-Day+1; while in World War I, fighting would have been called off some time before the Battle of the Marne.[25]

A *Philadelphia Inquirer* cartoon went further back, depicting Washington stealthily crossing the Delaware when suddenly his helmsman peers round – "General, we gotta turn back; we forgot to tell the press about our surprise landing."

The first reporters to Grenadian shores after intervention were mostly American. I watched some of them made to lie down on the hot airstrip tarmac to be searched. Later, incensed by such lack of respect, some US press bodies got together to sue Defense Secretary Caspar Weinberger. The only reason they desisted was that general counsel to the *New York Times* made it clear they wouldn't win. Katherine P. Darrow said, "I'm not sure there is a First Amendment right to be on the beachhead. Reporters are there because the Government lets them be there."

The London *Observer*'s Hugh O'Shaughnessy chartered at great expense a boat from St. Vincent with *Time*'s Bernie Diederich, a bearded giant of a man far superior in knowledge of the area to his predecessor William McWhirter. For the *New York Post* Charles Lachman also chartered a boat – of fiberglass, to slip through the radar screen – and his photographer Mike Norcia took some of the best pictures of the fighting. Local lore was not high in such journalists, however. In his book O'Shaughnessy completely confuses Gervaise and Herbert Blaize (our present Prime Minister), while Lachman tells us he landed on Grenada twenty-five miles north of St. George's – namely in the sea.[26]

After hostilities ceased journalists poured onto Pointe Salines and by the end of the year Colleen and I totted up that we had hosted (excluding delegations like the Congressional Black Caucus) forty-four journalists from sundry countries, including one girl member of the Japanese Communist Party whose chief virtue was she didn't have a beard. Apart from Chris Thomas of the London *The Times* and the *Daily Telegraph*'s Richard West nearly all these people were anti-Reagan.

Reminded by such press that World War Two in Northern France was covered by multitudes of Ernie-Pyle journalists, I could only respond that, fortunately, I did not participate in the Normandy landings, but that my end of the war, in Italy, saw few journalists at all. In any event, the Normandy invasion was overwhelmingly popular with the home countries, as was the Falklands operation (with exceptions, the BBC being criticized for a pro-Argentinian or enemy stance).[27]

In the light of the 1987 "Irangate" hearings, or investigations, it is chastening to be reminded that England's MoD or Ministry of Defence (roughly the equivalent of the American DoD, or Defense Department) inherited Churchill's secrecy strictures of World War Two and deliberately tried to avoid the kind of media shaming which undermined the American foray into Vietnam. "For the bulk of the Falklands war, the camera might as well not have been invented. The crisis lasted for seventy-four days, and for the first fifty-four there were no British pictures of any action."[28] More to the point: "To the American-born defence correspondent of the *Economist*, Jim Meacham – who actually served as an officer in Vietnam – civil servants and soldiers often observed: 'This is why you Americans lost the Vietnam war, because you had a free press'."[29] Lieutenant-Colonel North said virtually the same.

In fact, there were a number of American, if not British, correspondents invited to the Anzio beachhead by the publicity-conscious Mark Clark. US reporters of this area included the excellent Eric Sevareid and Sidney Mathews. When Clark reached the link-up between Cassino and Anzio forces he had the moment re-enacted for photographers with himself in the scene. On arrival in Rome Clark immediately had himself photographed at St. Peter's. After this the Pope consented to meet US pressmen and photographers to cries of "Hold it, Pope" and "Attaboy." Sevareid was sickened. To be sure, Pyle, eventually sniped on Ie-Jime in the Pacific, had a deep sense of communion with front-line fighters, as did others such, notably the *New York Times'* Richard J. H. Johnstone, who won a Purple Heart.[30] Too, I reminded our Grenadian press guests that when a reporter and photographer from the *Miami Herald* went in with forward troops in the 1965 Dominican Republic action, both were wounded and later blamed the military for not protecting them.

As for television it was ironic that liberal David Marash, then of CBS, produced in 1981 a four-part documentary on revolutionary Grenada that should have been taken far more seriously than it was, since it evidenced intimidation of Grenadians in America, the torture of prisoners in Richmond Hill prison, and even executions of prisoners by Cubans.[31] Who knows today of these atrocities? No one seems to have revealed the appalling conditions under which uncharged political prisoners, or "detainees," had to live in Richmond Hill prison. During the curfew whole families were picked up and put inside. On intervention a four-year-old boy was found wandering, lost, around the compound. Lloyd Noel, Jewel's original Attorney-General and its first menshevik, has briefly described the life of political prisoners sent "up the Hill." One hour in each twenty-four to empty slops, two visits from family a month, no access to priests. In "Jonestown," the detainees' name for their underground lightless cells of 9 x 6 feet each, they did not know night from day, living off stale bread and water daily.[32]

For Machel was right. In the liberal world the task of the press is to liquidate individualism. In *1984* Big Brother erases events from memory. Russia creates its own history.[33] Lidice was obliterated from the map by the Nazis revenge for the assassination of Heydrich. Today Dal'stroi, the largest extermination camp in history, is a similar physical blank; it is not even mentioned in the 1985 *Encyclopedia Britannica* although Auschwitz and Dachau are, their victims amounting to less than half those exterminated by the Russians in the single camp at Kolyma.

Take Dan Rather (CBS): having interviewed Castro (in his pyjamas) and shown his son Fidelito (fondling a puppy) Rather was at pains to inform viewers that his footage of the Grenada mission was "censored" by USG, as if that automatically proved it biassed. He suggested that, had open-minded reporters been allowed to land with forward troops, another story would have come out. Another did.[34] CBS took its own poll, coming up with a vast plurality of the population pro-intervention, and coinciding exactly with Trinidad's St. Augustine Research Associates poll of December, 1983. These figures were never aired on CBS Evening News. They were Lidice-ed.

Concerning the Medical School evacuation O'Shaughnessy tells us that Chancellor Charles Modica "repeated that his students were in no danger." But Modica amended his first position completely:

> Now that I have a fuller assessment of the situation that existed in Grenada over the past week ... that the military authorities were in fact making it virtually impossible for me to accomplish getting aircraft on the island to get you off safely ... There is no question, in conclusion, that your safety could not be guaranteed and the action of the President did have a sound basis regarding that issue.[35]

Then this change of stance becomes itself suspect, of further skulduggery in the White House, according to Heather Bennett of COHA (Council on Hemispheric Affairs) who writes in the *Miami Herald* that the med-school administrators "later harmonized their statements with those of Administration spokesmen after a White House carrot-and-stick meeting held as the U.S. landing was taking place." This is playing Heads you win, tails we lose.

On the day the *New York Times* announced Grenada's liberation it called the elected democracies of St. Lucia, St. Vincent, Dominica, Barbados and Trinidad all "right-of-center" regimes. None of these governments at the time could have been called rightist, though two omitted might have been (Seaga's Jamaica and Vere Bird's Antigua). "What, in any case," the *New York Times* editorialized, "could Cubans have done from

Grenada that they cannot do better from Cuba?"

This extraordinary strategic ignorance was echoed by Sol Linowitz in the *Washington Post*, despite the fact that *National Defense* for May-June, 1981, had carried elaborate charts of the Grenada threat, giving diameters of combat ranges for MiG-27s, showing their potential for oil-lane coverage and penetration into Venezuela, one of Castro's bugbears at the time. And to characterize such diverse individuals as Eugenia Charles, Tom Adams, John Compton, and "Son" Mitchell under the umbrella hate-term "rightist" is surely gutter journalism. (Why has no newspaper in England or America, for that matter, called Dominica's Rose Douglas, the recipient of Libyan funding, by his proper political name?) Indeed, the excitable sneers of the *New York Times* at "President Feelgood" are only a step away from Maurice Bishop's press calling the same "an eater of babies."

Press bigotry as regards the Grenadian intervention was, of course, fueled by interested politicians. Not long after it I hosted the Black Caucus in Grenada at the Red Crab pub, where the revo was said to have been concocted. It was led by Oakland Congressman Ronald Dellums and Georgia State Senator Julian Bond, both on the list of those who helped raise funds for the defense of Stephen Bingham, the Yale-educated attorney once accused of passing a firearm in San Quentin prison to Black Panther hero George Jackson, convicted murderer of a Soledad guard. Dellums' name was also to be found supporting the New York-based Grenada Foundation, together with those of John Conyers and Pete Seeger; this foundation allegedly helps front the new MBPM (Maurice Bishop Patriotic Movement) and its island tabloid *Indies Times*. Both Dessima Williams, Jewel's Ambassador to the OAS, and its Cuban "Press Secretary" Don Rojas are seen on US TV advocating a return of the revo. It should perhaps be remembered that the man who first put Castro on CBS TV was Robert Taber who founded the Fair Play for Cuba Committee, which folded after one of its members, Lee Harvey Oswald, assassinated John Kennedy.

When it became apparent that the intervention was a political success, both at home and on the island, the burden of US press criticism turned into an attempt to indict the services for blundering incompetence and cowardice (shared by such operations as the *Mayaguez* rescue and the Iran raid). In particular was US intelligence at fault. "Among the most glaring shortcomings," writes Richard Gabriel of the Grenada rescue, "was the intelligence failure."[36] Scott Minerbrook repeats the charge in the *Washington Post* – "faulty intelligence and hurried, sloppy planning.[37]

There is no space here in which to confront the catalog of incompetence alleged by such critics. Why did our intelligence not know more about Grenada? Briefly, it did. On March 25th., 1983, President Reagan sounded an early warning on television, during which he showed aerial photos of Pointe Salines, including the new airport, Cuban huts, the block building for senior Cuban personnel – and our home.

Yet while these pictures showed arms storage sheds they could not show the arms stocked inside them, any more than could the CBS photos of the "hot" Soviet freighter *Alexander Ulyanov* with its arms for Nicaragua in containers or below decks. One principal Russian threat in Grenada was impervious to satellite photography, or to any physical approach at all, namely the cliff-protected Egmont Harbour submarine facility being created. Sonar submarine detection is notoriously difficult in our warm waters whose thermal layers blank out transponder buoys dropped from the air.

Gabriel suggests it a failure that so little military information came out of Grenada when "the island was open to anyone who wanted to visit it right up to the invasion." But imagine the uproar there would have been had US agents been found in place on intervention. I watched Cubans site their anti-aircraft guns about the Pointe Salines peninsula, and fire them too, but it was hardly an "intelligence failure" not to report this to the Pentagon. In fact, all US residents on the island had been recorded by

AmEmbassy Barbados and sent flyers refuting Bishop's lies point by point, and warning all aboard of Jewel's manifest direction.

Another distortion by Gabriel was echoed around the press, namely that US forces were issued with "tourist" maps. It was never mentioned that there was no time (less than a night) in which to provide anything else, nor that the government "tourist" map is excellent, complete with terrain contours and so on. When my battalion in North Africa was detailed to land on the tiny island of Pantellaria, in the first amphibious Mediterranean landing of the war, we had no maps at all. We were shown a large drawing on a blackboard and told to get on with it. In the event, the Germans abandoned the small airstrip and after a few shots from our ships the Italian garrison surrendered.

Scott Minerbrook's attack starts off: "No one questions that the invasion accomplished its stated objectives." Having disposed of that item of trivia, he cites Jeffrey Record of the Institute for Foreign Policy Analysis that "the South Pasadena fire department could have taken Grenada." Gabriel says much the same: "In the end Grenada was a military success largely because it could be nothing else." The *New York Times* Editorial of November 10, 1983, takes this attitude further: "So the invasion is finally justified because Americans needed a win, needed to invade someone."

This is unfair and untrue. It does not take into account the safeguards imposed on American troops for the civilian population nor the presence of Russian Spetsnaz commandos. Langhorne A. Motley, Assistant Secretary for Inter-American Affairs, told the House Armed Services Committee: "our primary focus remained on the protection and removal of U.S. citizens from the zone of danger." The bulk of Minerbrook's article is reserved for the alleged looting of valuables by American forces while Gabriel specializes in stories of helicopter pilots machine-gunning livestock, old women, and babies in their cribs. They are not alone in delightedly depicting American forces as incompetent and/or   corrupt. Well after the event,

Times's January 13, 1986, story of US Special Forces is one long recital of blunderings, malfunctionings, chopper collisions, and it ends with grossly inaccurate descriptions of the Grenada action. Moscow's Active Measures disinformation service could do no better. Minerbrook tells us that a Vietnam-vintage Hughes OH-6 Cayuse helicopter was shot down. It was never there.

As remarked, trying to correct these errors, seriatim, did little good. The left press seemed determined to believe its own prefabricated version of events. When I rebutted a pro-Bishop piece in the London *Guardian* by Victoria Brittain, a lady whose name I took to be a parodistic pseudonym (and who was innocent of any visit to Grenada), I received droves of letters from readers, all venomous, most obscene, and one longing for the day New York City would be atom-bombed. I learnt the same again at an International PEN meeting in New York in 1986 when a little gray-haired lady called Grace Paley rose to say of Secretary Shultz, "he is as responsible as anyone for the tortures and the deaths in South Africa and elsewhere."[38]

Even more revealing, perhaps, than the British press of the time was the attitude of British delegations that visited us post-intervention, and which lost no leather to the US Congressional Black Caucus. The borough of Islington may not have been well known in the islands, nor neighboring beauty spots like Camden, Finsbury, Hackney, all of whose Councils call themselves "progressive,"[39] but in the year of our revo Islington, like Hackney a self-styled People's Republic,decided to "twin" itself with St. George's. Comrades of the Vanguard Leninist Praxis exchanged congratulatory visits. For today Islington, which I recall in my youth as a tube station on the way to a soccer stadium in Highbury, boasts a bust of Lenin in its Old Town Hall, a street named after Nelson Mandela, a church for Yoruba Nigerians, and compulsory Bengali in some of its schools.[40] A group of parents who tried to fund a Catholic Secondary were disallowed it. Malcolm X lived there.

The borough is proud of a caff' that forbids men – Hackney has tax-funded homes for lesbians, Haringey orders courses to "promote positive images of lesbians and gays" (nursery schools not exempt) – and it frowns on the sale of golliwog dolls. It was thus to their horror that members of the 1983 Islington delegation to Grenada, headed by the MP for Islington North, Jeremy Corby, saw golliwog dolls on sale in their twin city in the sun. Their eventual report was widely circulated, on taxpayers' money, and is still received as truth in that Trotskyite clerisy to which a lot of intellectual England responds.[41]

It sets off, at a time when nearly all US troops had left the island: "The delegation's main finding is that Grenada continues to suffer under a military and political occupation by the United States and its allies, and that the majority of working people in Grenada are opposed to the continued occupation ... The Governor General has assumed dictatorial powers ... Detainees have been tortured and maltreated ... a show trial is being planned." In short, the Islington Report is an anti-American tirade designed to depict US forces as so many slovenly, incompetent, and dissolute rapists, picking up "girls of 13" and introducing prostitution to the island – "There are rumoured to be two cases of Herpes on the island already." How many are there in Islington? Its Report yields nothing to Gabriel's visions and revisions of our days and ways. Even so, its contempt for any sort of accuracy is astonishing. With regard to tourism the Report tells us, "Cunard and other cruise operators had canceled all stopovers in Grenada while we were there"; but the cancelation occurred under the Bishop regime, the cruise ships reappearing after intervention (that of the Cunard *Countess* coming in playing *Yankee Doodle Dandy* full blast while most of St. George's lined the Carenage).

As for finance, Islington opines, "The fiscal management of Bishop's government was scrupulous" (the line reported to *The Observer* by O'Shaughnessy); in fact, Coard's figures were a ruler measuring itself, since two sets of books were kept of the island's ruined exchequer. Then, "Many were cynical about Westminster-style politics which involved them every five years for five minutes" is a tired echo of an echo (by Bishop out of Lenin out of Rousseau), while on-site Grenadians would have thought little of the Islington allegation that "Large amounts of Plessey materials were missing as they had been used to fake the Soviet arms cache pictures so widely reported in the western media." This is incredible. Are we being asked seriously to credit the idea that the famous electronics firm of Plessey Airports imported Russian arms in bulk, for photograph?

The Report concludes with comments on "The Position of Women," predictably fulminating against "sexual harassment by US troops" (a pity the delegates did not see the Cubans in action on our beaches). Referring to Phyllis Coard's National Women's Organization, North London wags a final scolding finger: "The NWO women were also very angry about claims circulating that Cubans raped Grenadian women. They reported that Cubans were about the only men on the island who did housework." Now the Islington Report was not put together by wild-eyed Shi'ites but by British MPs. And their calumnies were repeated by a member of the House of Lords, Tony Gifford, claiming that Headache Layne was "tortured for 16 hours" in prison and that Bajan police "resorted to beating and torture" to obtain the signatures of defendants to the murder trial.[42]

The situation in respect of the Councils of large English cities (London, Leeds, Sheffield, Manchester) is baffling, with local authorities using tax-levy funds openly to oppose the elected national government in matters of defense and foreign policy, which fall outside their scope. Professor David Regan's pamphlet *It Costs A Bomb* instances such cities financing free magazines and films to propagandize against the Thatcher government (Sheffield showing *Dr Strangelove* and *The China Syndrome* for its Hiroshima-Nagasaki Commemoration). I am even told that Oxford City Hall now flies a CND (Campaign for Nuclear Disarmament) flag from its roof!

This concern for black people by whites in high places is

unmatched in Russia. When the Russians brought out a Bishop stamp, the face on it was a travesty of We Leader, having been whitened and softened to look like some calendar-art Christ. A journalist chatting with a Russian delegate at the first anniversary celebration of the Grenadian revo reported the latter as saying of our sinking island economy, "But what do you expect? The whole place is run by blacks."[43]

There can now be little doubt where most of the press stood in this lamentable distortion of the intervention. But the public's right to know was also affronted by the legal profession in America. The American Bar Association (Section of International Law and Practice) produced its committee report on the intervention on February 10th, 1984, at a moment when defense in the trial of the Coard faction had filibustered for postponement on postponement. The impediments put up to proceeding in the Maurice Bishop murder trial became absurd, as we shall see, making for a parody of democracy that clearly encouraged the vengeful to settle scores in vigilante fashion. In our case, the procedural niceties of American legalistics certainly set no example for the reverse. Only a country where everyone seems to be suing everyone else could produce the point-of-order fanatics from our law schools who threw up the Rio Treaty, the Vienna Convention, and the UN and OAS Charters as roadblocks to the rescue of a people helpless in the face of a murderous gang. The ABA report is a depressingly heartless one.

It claims that the OECS request was invalid since not unanimous, Grenada being absent. This is good law school stuff since a few pages further on the report admits that Sir Paul Scoon (reduced to "Mr." in their pages) was impeded from attending any conferences by the presence around his dwelling of Soviet amphibious armored cars. Of course, Sir Paul, in whom executive authority was clearly vested by Article 57 of the 1973 Constitution, not only initiated the appeal but subsequently ratified it. The ABE report further charges that the peacekeeping force was not multi-Caribbean since Montserrat and Nevis did not send troops. In fact, Montserrat, a Crown Colony still, sent a few men, while at the time Nevis was not joined with St. Kitts, under Kennedy Simmonds, in independence and had, in any case, no security troops.

It is when one comes to the provenance of the ABA report that one plumbs the dregs of bias, in the 117 footnotes that at times threaten to drive the text off the page in their scholarly zeal. "U.S. hostility to the regime of Prime Minister Bishop had been immediate and virtually unrelenting," explains note 36. In fact, both Ambassadors Ortiz and Shelton did all they could do to conciliate Bishop from the start, even with dollar assistance. The picture given of Washington by ABA is Bishop's. Nor do the lawyers mention the "unrelenting" hostility of Bishop to the USA.

Surely it is curious that the ABA footnotes rely almost entirely on ultra-left sources, particularly the London *Guardian* (who had no one on Grenada, until the BBC's Nick Worrall came to string for them much later). If British sources were to be used for this highly American document, why not the *Daily Telegraph*, whose experienced New York bureau chief Ian Ball put two men on Grenada post-intervention, or *The Times*, or *The Economist* (whose detailed series Tom Adams of Barbados hailed as the best penned on the Grenada crisis)?

As for native coverage, why so much reverence in the ABA document for the *Washington Post* over other sources, such as *Time* or *The Wall Street Journal*? But the mind boggles when the ABA's footnote 24, at page 20, relies for backup on one F. Castro in "Gramma (the English language organ of the Cuban Communist Party)"! Our learned lawyers refer to *Granma*, so named after Castro's boat out of Mexico, and it is neither in the English language, at least not originally, nor particularly reliable as a source of facts.

The result of such provenance is that, at pages 25-26, the ABA report considers General Hudson Austin's Revolutionary Military Council, having just murdered Bishop and his minions, the de facto government of Grenada *because it had been able to impose a 96-hour curfew*! For the ABA, then, the criterion for sovereignty was armament. Its report washes off the blood of Grenada's agony by dismissing the murders as "an internal struggle" (page 60).

Understandably enough, several journalists worked their dispatches up into books. O'Shaughnessy's was the first and frankly almost unreadable in parts due to typos and misprints, transposed paragraphs, etc.[44] O'Shaughnessy's first view of St. George's reminds him of "the set of some beautiful, extravagant Italian opera." Although O'Shaughnessy could not have known of Jewel's double-bookkeeping scam, his adulation of Bernard Coard, "the cautious Coard" who balanced our books and produced a surplus, is astonishing. For, in case we had forgotten, Coard was really a capitalist: "Coard for his part initiated policies which apparently strengthened the capitalist complexion of the Grenadian economy." Or again, "While the Reagan Government itself had to borrow billions of dollars to finance its spending Grenada was, under Coard's guidance, living modestly within its means." We came out of intervention with an external debt of US$150 million.

Torture in Richmond Hill prison was "shown to be unfounded." By whom? On the contrary, it was coroborrated. There was "better behaviour from the army and police." At which point my copy hit the opposing wall. Come off it, Lord Copper. There wasn't an army, as such, under Gairy, so how could the PRA be better? As for the police,Bishop largely disbanded the force, the PRA assuming their authority. As for the increasing arrests without charges, "the reviewing of cases was then done more informally by Bishop himself as Minister of the Interior." That *informally* is worth pondering.

The book is typical of several that have been published since intervention. In fact, it is not a book. It is a stick, one with which to beat Ronald Reagan, who is "paranoiac," "a dangerous cretin," and so on, Eugenia Charles of Dominica who is both "a ruthless international operator" and "a media star," and Tom Adams. The white hats are worn by those like Bishop's imported Marxist Chris Searle and the discredited journalist, thrown out of Barbados, Ricky Singh. Of Bishop himself O'Shaughnessy tells us, "He had not become, and never was to become, an admirer of the Soviet system of government." No? I must have been listening to someone else for four and a half years. Under Bishop Grenada voted Soviet in 92% of the votes of the 1982 UN General Assembly. O'Shaughnessy's text is crowned by a sixteen-page Appendix from Fidel Castro, and no wonder.

As for Mrs Thatcher, he clearly loathes her yet wants to use her position regarding the alleged illegality of the intervention, and her general fury at being kept in the dark by Washington. The KGB General Sazhenev, who was to deal with our destiny in 1984, is *never mentioned* in O'Shaughnessy's book. Indeed, why not take one step further into this quicksand of disinformation and essay that fount of truth *Pravda*, for December 20th, 1983? By some miracle *Pravda* discovered that Bishop had been murdered, by the CIA of course, via a source in New Delhi:

> The weekly magazine *New Wave* has published facts incontrovert-
> ibly demonstrating that the murder of Grenadian Prime Minister
> Maurice Bishop was carried out by the U.S. Central Intelligence
> Agency on orders from the White House ... Based on the
> testimony of Grenadian eyewitnesses who fled the island after its
> occupation, the magazine writes that the CIA succeeded in
> recruiting the chief of the Prime Minister's personal bodyguard
> and one of his subordinates, who carried out Washington's order
> and shot Bishop.

If the intervention was "illegal" and "unnecessary" (pace O'Shaughnessy) what would such critics have prescribed for any sort of meaningful freedom on the island? The truth is that the press visiting Grenada post-intervention generally shared in a new and virulent anti-Americanism sweeping the intellectual West, which I shall try to identify in the next section. The Khomeini phenomenon is perhaps its most crackpot example. In Grenada, however, Jewel belabored a past that never existed and underestimated young America's dislike of the New Age Liberals. "This is the first time since Inchon that we've done something like this without screwing it up," admits the generally hostile Jeffrey Record.[45]

In conclusion, there comes a point in such affairs when abuse of the truth by the media can be said to prevent the government from fulfilling a decision. In the so-called Iranscam hearings of summer 1987 the investigative committee seriously handicapped the country's dynamic by requiring top official after official, busy on other matters, to spend days testifying (often to the same questions asked five times). In Grenada, as in the Falklands, the media were incensed that they, the self-elected elite, the self-appointed guardians of democracy, were not given first choice of what to reveal to the public. And to be kept out by the yokels of the services was the last straw.

Again, there was an echo of this same sense in England during the Falklands war. The BBC, referred to in World War Two by Churchill as "an enemy within the gates," was hauled into the Tory Media Committee in the persons of Chairman George Howard and Alasdair Milne, attaint, for some, of something pretty close to treason. In the "ox-roast" that followed both men apparently behaved with a supercilious arrogance, a class hauteur, that infuriated the services, the irate Milne refusing to take part in the proceedings after the first few minutes while Howard "stood like an eighteenth-century Whig grandee – which in many ways is what he is – confronted by a group of angry tradesmen and looking as though he'd like to set the dogs on them."[46] Milne was Winchester and New College, Howard Eton and Balliol; the editorial seats of the *New York Times*, *Washington Post*, *Boston Globe* are replete with the beneficiaries of privileged educations, even though such recipients firmly insist that they are self-made men. So in Grenada the press had indeed, in Machel's phrase, liquidated liberalism, the mushy arrogance of which can be detected in the comment of ABC's Barbara Walters that "the news media in general are liberal. If you want to be a reporter you are going to see poverty and misery, and you have to be involved in the human condition."[47] Which human condition? This sloppy syllogism excludes conservatives, presumably, from feeling compassionate about poverty or the human condition. But Walter Cronkite, erstwhile CBS anchor man, backs her up: "I think most newspaper men by definition have to be liberal."

The press didn't know that Bishop had started a fratricidal circus on Grenada, of which he was its self-elected highbrow clown, adjudicating jesuitical heresies in the island God made from the rainbow, and ending up one of nature's true Barnums quacking "The masses ... the masses" in a pair of underpants. A Monty Python character, to be sure. But the clown has his consequences in the audience. Bishop was one of those whom Donald Westlake has called "buffoons with fangs," the architect of not-so-funny horrors to come: "Burlesque and tragedy," Westlake went on, "go hand in claw, never more so than in the case of the comic-opera rulers of some recently independent African nations, who wave cartoon fists that draw real blood."[48] One thinks of Idi Amin alone and screaming at the severed heads of assassinated enemies preserved in his freezer, a true Kurtz figure. One thinks of Bokassa beating schoolchildren to death for objecting to their uniforms. The press never saw Bro Bish for what he was. They came to Grenada with preconceived notions ... the human condition and all that.

But Cronkite, when asked why most journalists have to be biased liberals, retorted that no, they simply tended "to side with humanity rather than authority." This makes for a convenient division of the world; but it is a factitious one. What if authority sides with humanity, as it did in World War Two England? The America media habit of always pretending to give two sides to every issue (except apartheid) would hardly have done justice to

Auschwitz, and it would have meant equal air time for Joseph Goebbels.

For a recent study of the American media shows such to consist of a largely rich, secular, and cosmopolitan group, far more liberal, or plainly left-wing, than the US society as a whole.[49] The proportion of leading American journalists (or limousine liberals, as they have been called) supporting Democratic candidates did not drop below 80% from 1964 to 1976, while a recent survey of attitudes of students at Columbia University's School of Journalism (which costs an arm and a leg to graduate from) showed only 4% voting for Reagan in 1980; 75% of them believed that the US was exploiting the Third World. Castro was rated more positively than Reagan and the Sandinistas higher than Margaret Thatcher. That's about how in touch with electorates they are. Indeed, Linda Ellerbee of NBC has frankly declared: "We report news, not truth..."[50]

David Horowitz, the disillusioned co-founder of the America-hating *Ramparts* magazine, so successful in the sixties, was asked what he had learnt from his experience. He replied, "My experience has convinced me that historical ignorance and moral blindness are endemic to the American left, necessary conditions of its existence."[51] Those last words are worth pondering, too. In one response to antagonistic press heckling after being evacuated safely to America, a young medical student, Jeffrey Lake of Montrose, Pa., put it in a nutshell – "All I can say is, you had to be there."

The press was not.

The New Anti-Americanism

I am hardly the first to observe the phenomenon of anti-Americanism in otherwise intelligent people, but it was brought home to me in a new dimension after the intervention. Here in

Grenada were a lot of West Indians scrawling pro-American graffiti on their walls, the while a scribble of scribes was telling us how heartily the United States was hated on the Isle of Spice. As a boy in England I grew up on anti-Americanism – of a kind. That kind was not political, it was social snobbery, the sort of thing seen at its fruitiest in Evelyn Waugh and in a sophisticated form today in the *Sunday Telegraph*'s editor, Peregrine Worsthorne (a name that says it all). Frankly, this snobbery was handed down by parents who had never seen America, nor more than two or three Americans.

In those days there was no TV, nor Concorde jets. I traveled schoolwards from Malaya in the old P & O liners which yielded the acronym *posh* (Port Out Starboard Home). When I went to North Africa in the British Army in World War Two, the Egyptians (whose territory we were defending under treaty, though you wouldn't have known it) and the Libyans alike considered England the dominant industrial power, the Moloch or Babylon of our times. After the recent Libyan Embassy incident in London, when a British policewoman was shot, however, Colonel Qadhaffi referred to the British as "stray dogs" of the CIA, and Britannia as a "hag." Times had changed.

The British revulsion of my youth was based on the famous language difficulty identified by Shaw. In fact, Nancy Mitford, author of a popular book on U (upper-class) usage, despised America as much as did Waugh, though infringing the code that the most non-U thing to do was talk about U speech. Both were conservatives and as such tend to resist change, particularly in language.

In the late fifties the House of Lords lengthily debated whether an *a* or an *an* should precede *hotel*, finally finding for the latter, Lord Conesford suggesting that "every one of your Lordships would say 'a Harrow boy' but would also speak of 'an Harrovian'" (provided they would descend to the topic at all, I would add). Fowler was against *an* historian, but Fowler, like the royal family, was non-U. The point is that the language in which we receive ideas is all-important and variation sounds, at first, like error. We hate neologisms. And the heavy accenting of syllables in sequence, called the American drawl, we were brought up to look down on, or think funny (like Braid Scots or the Doric); US was non-U though at the same time we admired movies enlivened by it, starring the likes of George Raft, Humphrey Bogart ... and Ronald Reagan.

Such was the America of us schoolboys, of all ages. One must use the past tense of it today since the BBC, instead of feeding U-English, and related values, pedagogically downwards, now does the reverse. During the sixties, so Jeffrey Richards tells us, "it became for the first time in history fashionable to be working class, so much so that some of the upper and middle-class young adopted *ersatz* regional working-class accents, to disguise their now unfashionable antecedents."[52] I know what he means. BBC English is today a mid-Atlantic mush. My own pronunciation sounds ludicrously outdated whenever I revisit England now, particularly when I catch myself dropping g's off present participles in the West Indian manner.

Largely as a result of this upbringing, transition to "the States" for such an Englishman was in some ways more difficult than for a Pole or Greek or Italian. Less psychological capital had to be invested in the new land, which was, apparently, an erroneous extension of one's own. Someone coming out of another language tended to take a deeper plunge. Wilbur Shepperson's *Emigration and Disenchantment*, a University of Oklahoma doctoral dissertation, shows that the British assimilated less easily in America than those who could not speak the common tongue. We were, in short, the worst immigrants.

But our dislike was not of a political system, nor of a man. Today's European anti-Americanism is of another kind, rather than degree. I defy anyone to find the rank mindless loathing evinced by today's radical Europeans in any of Churchill's memoirs, though Churchill was educated at Harrow, a school only exceeded in social esteem by Eton, where Harold Macmillan was dragged up, and from which he drew most of his Cabinet. Note that Macmillan got on admirably with Eisenhower. Nor let us forget that NATO was originally proposed by Ernest Bevin, Foreign Secretary to Attlee's Labour government. The present West German Green Party, with parliamentary representation, seems to be in open attack against the principle of any democratic choice at all (including for cable television).

The language filter which, for a while, saved England from such extremes meant that in France leading intellectuals, cut off from US culture in the war only to be drenched by it on liberation, often looked plain silly, André Gide praising Kathleen Winsor (of *Forever Amber* fame) in his postwar journals and Marcel Duhamel translating *Tobacco Road* beside him. Yet at this same time Simone de Beauvoir visited the belly of the beast and returned with *America Day by Day*, an account full of such wildly irrational anti-American preconceptions as to be unassailable, together with photos of Bowery bums. Diana Trilling had a go at some of the book's cruder errors in *Partisan Review*, but didn't faze their author. I was teaching at the University of Rochester at the time, as de Beauvoir passed through for some self-promotion, and seldom have I met such a dogmatic lady. Back in France she was able, as late as 1961 when US soldiery was thin on the ground there, to turn to Albert Camus in a restaurant in Chinon, where she had spotted two GIs, and proclaim that she was reminded of the Nazi occupation. Surely one is tempted to give up all hope when Europe's so-called intellectuals equate Nazi occupation with American liberation from that yoke.

De Beauvoir gave the communist cliché of *Amerika*, while the view of Cyril Connolly or Evelyn Waugh at the same time was one of offended esthetes (music at meals, cosmetized corpses). The communist vision of this generation, articulated while some of them like Boris Vian ("Le Menteur"!) were fabricating American thrillers on the side, undoubtedly cloned the no-holds-barred hatred to come. Previously, out of an earlier generation, Bernanos and Jules Romains had also had a dyspeptic dislike of

America, the latter horrified by the Chicago slaughter yards (far more sanitary than most *abattoirs* in France); neither arraigned democracy in the process. But a document like the Islington Report of Grenada is nothing more than unadulterated mendacious hatred of the USA – mainly for being successful.

Thomas Fleming, editor of *Chronicles of Culture*, observes hatred of one's own country as differentiating old-style American radicals for the new. Thomas Debs, and even Big Bill Haywood (who went to live in Russia but found "this isn't Idaho or Colorado"), were basically loyal to the United States; the reverse is the case of modern liberals. As Fleming puts it:

> Perhaps the first thing to observe is that what the American left really hates are the friends of the United States, especially those that profess some commitment to freedom. The form of government does not seem to matter much ... the closer a regime is to America (politically or culturally) the more likely it is to be attacked for its failings .... It is not that their Marxist principles drive them into the arms of the enemies of the United States, but that it is the liberals' hatred of their own country which leads them to embrace any ideology so long is it is the opposite of what we stand for.[53]

The new European anti-Americanism seems somewhat to have bypassed the French, or the more guarded among them, and to have located itself, with Russian blessing, on something called the West, technology, the Rastas' and Bishop's Babylon, of which America is the avatar, regardless of the success of Japan, Singapore, Taiwan, etc. What the barmen in Groppi's in wartime Cairo threw drinks in my face for representing has merely crossed the Atlantic, that is all. Instead of asking how technology can be used for the betterment of man, the new anti-Americans say, Eliminate it. Return to Nature (snail darters and clams and so forth). "I am for the demolition of industrial civilization," says Rudolf Bahro, East German exile and executive member of the

Green Party. *Split Wood Not Atoms* exhort the new peace groups. This book was a tree.

Such has been the thrust of England's Greenham Common protesters, whose Soviet pocket money has been found alongside Scargill's, and colleague groups in Holland. The same self-cleansing semantic occurred in the American peace communes of the sixties, as indeed it did in the Digger movement at the end of England's 1642-49 revolution.

Parenthetically, what reasoning should be available in the new anti-Americanism seems to have been particularly compromised by the Church. It is fascinating to note the number of clerics in present peace meetings. England is full of them. In West Germany we find apologists for the new anti-Americanism in Helmut Gollwitzer, a clergyman, and Dorothea Solle, a theology professor. Denmark abounds in that Punch-and-Judy figure, the anti-American peace pastor. In 1972 Sweden's subsequently assassinated Olaf Palme likened the US bombing of Hanoi to the Nazi bombing of Guernica. Even so, it was disheartening to find the same bias in the US Catholic Conference of 1985, and the Bishop's subsequent pastoral on peace. Apparently the guardians of the largest single-faith community in the United States are Pied-Pipering their flocks across the same line into partisan politics.

The quibble here was this: that by letting the idea of nuclear deterrence into our minds we were immoral and, as a matter of fact, already guilty of using nuclear weapons, just as if I undress a girl in the street with my eyes I have done it with my hands. The Magisterium must chuckle at such Aquinan niceties, as must Soviet Russia. In rebuttal to Dinesh D'Souza's *Policy Review* article "The Bishops as Pawns" Edward Doherty of that Conference tells us: "I did not say that a Soviet occupation of the United States would be good from a moral point of view; only that if such an occupation did occur, Americans would still have the same means of defence available to the Poles and Afghans."[54]

Which is what? The liberty to die by a Russian gun. This is

what was recommended for us in Grenada by critics cited above. From the Russian point of view, and now evidently that of the USCC, possession of nuclear weapons is the same as their use. In addressing this issue, D'Souza (a former Dartmouth student actually bitten by a black Dean) points out: "Deterrence is not a prelude or a moral equivalent of use; it is an alternative to use. We have nuclear weapons to avoid using them."[55] America has avoided using them for nearly half a century. Unfortunately, the paradoxes of clerical thought, now spread to America, seem simply another disguise for hatred of that country. D'Souza writes: "Mr. Doherty told me, in unequivocal terms, that the current U.S. deterrent is immoral and that Soviet occupation of this country would be preferable to the status quo."[56]

England and America now subsidize dissidence out of public funds. Into this reactionary, back-to-nature brew communism pours its poison. Why not? Those who lap it up are such easy bait. For philanthropy never works. It is the surest way to make yourself hated. The IMF and World Bank advance their billions and end up snarled at – look how mean America is to want its money repaid. Those vicious bankers. In Grenada our populace heard the filth poured on America for four years and it had remarkably little effect on them, judging from the pro-American euphoria on liberation. The welcome Grenadians pressed on their rescuers was part of a feeling that ran through all levels of the country when American forces stabilized it – something akin to VE Day in London, I imagine. This hospitality took place when food was short after the curfew and islanders had been told by Jewel how unnecessary consumer luxuries of the West were, and how guilty Americans, in the face of African famines, should feel consuming them.

Extension of this neo-medievalism is given in a recent book by Gunter Gaus, one of Helmut Schmidt's diplomats in East Germany, wherein we are told that that State, by avoiding electoral democracy, has conserved the true or *echt* Germany, a frightening thought. The iron fist within the velvet glove of this dialectic is clear: Join with us and we will reunite Germany – with the East. The new anti-Americanism is thus, first and foremost, a rearguard action against civilization itself, of which democratic government is an outrider. In West Germany Solle has poured scorn on the voting process in the same words used by Bishop when parroting Lenin. This is based on the patronizing assumption that the given populace (and they differ) is unable to make long and careful scrutiny before entering the voting booth.

In fine, much European anti-Americanism has little to do with America, and does not want to learn about it. America is simply another protest button standing for everything detestable. In Grenada we listened to Bishop accusing the United States of sponsoring concentration camps and biological warfare, of being "the evil which liquidated Hiroshima." Some hearing those last words may have recalled the Bataan and similar death marches, where little Japanese mercy was shown, the machine-gunning of nurses on Sumatra, the Burma Road horrors, and the unspeakably cruel Japanese prison camps such as Singapore's Changi, where my father just survived three and half years at the close of his life. We do not hear the liberals agitating about the fact that today Japan allows no immigration at all, indeed boasts of its racial purity.[57]

On liberation Grenada must have been just about the most pro-American place in the world. It lacked the professional America-haters of *The Village Voice* or the *New York Review of Each Other's Books*, which once featured on its cover an instructional diagram (all wrong) of how to make a Molotov cocktail.

In *Areopagatica* Milton wanted it all let out; if truth and error were allowed to do battle in the same arena, truth would always win. This democratic conceit seemed for long to be the attitude of the pipe-smoking US Ambassador in Bonn, the late Arthur Burns. However, the Russians are making sure that error now goes in with a gun, both in Nicaragua as in Grenada. For this foray into anti-Americanism is integrally linked with Cuban adventurism in the hemisphere. Prior to 1960 the Soviet Union left Latin America more or less alone. Nor was Russia encouraged to change this policy by the overthrow of Allende in 1973, completed, as it was, by conservative coups in Uruguay, Argentina, and Bolivia. But at this point Castro started unifying insurgency groups, from Guatemala down to Chile. In Colombia, of special interest to Nicaragua thanks to the strategic passageways past the San Andras and Providencia Islands, President Betancur proved a temporary block to terrorist expansion; but when he ordered the Bogota Palace of Justice, being held by the April 19 Movement (M-19), to be stormed, the latter killed eleven supreme court justices.

All these groups – the Salvadoran FMLN (led by a lot of Che Guevara look-alikes), Peru's resuscitated *Sendero Luminoso*, the Guatemalan EGP, the M-19s, the Venezuelan *Bandera Roja* – were collected by Castro in his April, 1983, meeting in Esmeralda, Cuba, and lessoned on the new pan-Latinism. Such is not all that different from the Africanism of Nkrumah, claiming that the Anglo-Saxons dominating the area are qualitatively inferior to the Latins to whom it belongs. Thus a Latin "nation" (cp. a black nation) should be set up to combat the United States. To this end all that the Soviet Union need supply is armament, and in 1981 it delivered 66,000 tons of the same to Cuba. Castro found himself able to support 31 major factions in 11 Latin countries. He seems finally to have convinced the Politburo of his directorship of the region, Sergio Mikoyan conceding in *Latinskaya Amerika* that "only the armed road has led to victory in Latin America."[58]

By a whisker it didn't in Grenada, but as we shall see below it did in Guyana. It didn't, signally, in Malaya at the end of World War Two, as we shall also inspect; but at this point it is pertinent to pick up on Coard and his cronies, charged with murder after the intervention.

The Maurice Bishop Murder Trial

On intervention those suspected of murdering Maurice Bishop and his Ministers were variously rounded up, as mentioned. They were charged after they had made frank statements to Barbados police (Grenada having virtually none by this time). Though the carnage had been considerable the State, under its interim government, could only try on evidence and had to limit itself to the alleged murder of eleven persons.

The accused first numbered twenty, but one was discharged by the Magistrate of the Preliminary Inquiry in August, 1984, while another, Fabian Gabriel, who gave one of the most gruesome accounts of Bishop's bloody end, turned Queen's evidence. In the event seventeen men and one woman (Phyllis Coard) were charged with murder and/or conspiracy to murder in the deaths of Maurice Bishop, his Ministers, pregnant mistress and others in October, 1983). *Regina versus Andy Mitchell et al.* became the longest and largest murder trial in West Indian history.

In fact, the long and hair-splitting legal delays, to be touched on below, produced eventually a collective yawn in the region, few local stations covering the hearings at all regularly, and even some of Grenada's own papers preferring cricket to the complexities of the courts. In contrast with the bloody events the meticulous niceties of the law once again made democracy look ineffectual or anemic.

This quite incorrectly redounded to the disparagement of the government. For once the matter had gone to the courts the government, both interim and then elected, had no say in the matter. The trial was outside their jurisdiction, and the delays cannot be blamed on them. Furthermore, serious constitutional matters were raised within these years of apparent inaction; precedent-setting motions, and appeals, were put before the court, into which the government could not enter. It was confined to the role of spectator.

When Maurice Bishop spoke at a meeting in New York at the end of May, 1983, he was likened by supporters to Luke Skywalker challenging Darth Vader – "The standing, screaming, stomping ovation must have lasted a full three minutes."[59] Payne, Sutton and Thorndike agree, claiming that "Bishop's visit was a triumph."[60] They do not add that it was a select crowd of the converted who attended that address, nor that an equally large number of real Grenadians were demonstrating against Bishop in the streets outside the auditorium. And for screaming and stomping you should have seen the crowd outside the St. George's courthouse when the accused were brought down from prison to be charged. I watched them taken into this first session of the PI and there was no doubt but that the crowd were ready to tear them limb from limb. Rocks were hurled at the Coards in particular, one injuring a policewoman. It seems to have been much the same during their original transfer to the *Guam*: Charles Lachman of the *New York Post* recounts how "at 11 a.m. we saw the Grenadian political strongman Bernard Coard and his wife Phyllis being escorted into a Navy helicopter following their arrest Saturday. The Grenadians who watched with us screamed for their heads."[61]

For their own protection the PI was thereafter moved to a room in the prison called the Lion's Den, to reach which, even with a pass, I had to percolate six checkpoints, at the last of which I had to surrender my watch. That element of farce which so often seems to haunt black revolution became the order of the day as, first Phyllis Coard was brought in on a stretcher, allegedly weak from a hunger strike (though it was found she had watered her bowls of soup to make them appear untouched), then Goat Redhead developed a remarkable limp in court, supposedly due to police brutality, and General Hudson Austin sported a plaster cast on an otherwise healthy arm. Coard himself, who had survived an attempt by other prisoners to dry-drown him with a hydrant, apparently spent the years of repeated adjournments immersed in that aura of melodrama with which he liked to surround himself, studying the sacred texts and occasionally composing Brahminical commentaries on just where the blasted revo had run off the rails. He claimed to suffer from "emotional stress", and no wonder.

For it was not until April, 1986, that a jury was finally empaneled and the case taken to its conclusion. Forensic ingenuity by counsel for the accused, using procedures the latter had scorned, succeeded in contriving a three-year filibuster, threatening to exceed the "reasonable" time between being charged and tried in the country's Constitution. Some of these delays were allegedly orchestrated by Ramsey Clark, whose concern for the accused was such that he more than once came down to visit the scene of the crime, and consult with Bernard Coard.

For a long time, however, the accused would not accept court-appointed counsel (paid for by the indigent Grenadian taxpayer), then refused to obtain their own. Endless procrastinations, which infuriated the Grenadian populace, are too complex to capsulize succinctly here but generally rested on the challenge that the High Court of Grenada by which the accused were being arraigned was illegal.

This ploy was tried, with rather better basis, at Nuremberg.[62] In Grenada the point was this: by tearing up the 1973 Constitution on his first day of office Bishop hoped to obviate any appeal to extraneous, extra-insular judiciaries, as might have qualified his own form of "justice". He did not wish appeal to be made to the Supreme Court of the Associated States of the West Indies. Now the Coardites argued that if the Constitution were restored, as *ipso facto* it was, then they should be heard by that wider West Indies court rather than by the purely insular one they themselves had set up, for their own arcane purposes.

But there had been changes. The West Indies Appeals Court withdrew from jurisdiction over Grenada after the annuling of the Constitution, and subsequent fiat rule by Cabinet (viz the Central Committee or Maurice Bishop). After some difficulty in getting legal lackeys to man his own court, Bishop found that the island's appeals system had become that of the EC, or Eastern Caribbean, one unfriendly to him and one which, after his murder, was understandably reluctant to accept Grenada with "That Case on the Hill" outstanding.

The truth was that Bishop had once again flubbed it, if perhaps on Cuban instructions. He tore up the Constitution but *kept on* the Governor-General, though there are those, in law schools, who argue that he could not have done one without the other. The importance of the Governor to Jewel for recognition purposes has already been pointed out. But this same retention of the highest office in the land meant that, having been a permanency throughout, his office and its rights uninterrupted, Sir Paul Scoon could, by virtue of the executive and legislative powers vested in him, *both* reinstate the Constitution *and* retain the Grenada High Court. If Bishop had held elections as promised directly after his coup he would probably have won (against an absent Eric Gairy) and then been able to write his own Constitution in a rigged parliament. However, Havana may well have counseled against any risk at the ballot box at all.

So the last of Jewel were hoist by their own petard, not to say noose. Finally firing all their lawyers they resorted to recalcitrance, turning the courtroom into a Mad Hatter's Tea Party. Most mornings it took prison guards half an hour to round up and transport them to the court where they chanted and jigged and shrieked, quite in the manner of some revivalist meeting, if to a different drummer – "CIA spies", "This a Yankee court", "Torturers". Justice Denis Byron, a Kittitian and former Puisne Judge of the Eastern Caribbean Supreme Court, had repeatedly to clear the defendants from the dock, bringing them back individually for witness identification and once considering using gags. Coard required that President Reagan be called. The jury foreman had a heart attack in court.

At last, after Coard (refusing to take the oath)[63], had been allowed to address the court for six days on end, on every one of which he excoriated America, the trial terminated. One need hardly add that for the local cane-cutter or nutmeg grower the entire exercise had come to appear some sort of bauble of the law schools. There were even mutterings about organizing a jail break and letting those same cane-cutters and nutmeg growers organize their own justice. For after the brutal bloodshed the tergiversations of the law hardly seemed to conduce to democracy at all, rather to its reverse, vigilante justice by an outraged citizenry frustrated for years by legalistic technicalities and demanding at least some perception of right and wrong. After all, somebody killed Maurice Bishop.

Indeed. After an eleven-day summing-up of extreme caution by Judge Byron the island was electrified on the afternoon of December 4th, 1986, when the jury retired to consider the best part of two hundred counts (eleven for each accused). Including five women they took only three hours: to acquit one man (Raeburn Nelson) who had convincingly pleaded innocence and attended every session of the court without disruption, and to find the rest guilty on all counts. That same afternoon the Judge donned the black cap and sentenced fourteen to death by hanging, as is mandatory in Grenada for murder. These included Bernard Coard, Phyllis Coard, and General Hudson Austin. Two PRA soldiers guilty of manslaughter were given prison terms of forty-five and thirty years respectively. A life sentence is construed as fifteen years in Grenada and the Judge clearly eschewed it. And, though England outlawed capital punishment in the mid-sixties all the islands retained it on independence, sometimes dealing it out for rape (as twice in Trinidad in a recent year). For once it seemed to the patient Grenadian populace that justice delayed was not justice denied. Even The Coards' Jamaican lawyer, Ian Ramsey, was given a two-year prison sentence for contempt of our Grenadian court.

Guyana: The Caribbean Basket-Case

The Soviet Caribbean strategy depends on an image of invulnerability. Since Russia began seriously interesting itself in the area, circa 1960, it has gained an adventurous vassal, in Cuba, and made power probes into Grenada, Nicaragua, El Salvador, Honduras, Guyana, Suriname, all against a depressing background of American lack of resolve.[64]

"There is no communism to speak of in Fidel Castro's 26th of July Movement", averred Herbert Mathews in the *New York Times* in 1957. Today, thanks to John Kennedy's half-heartedness during the Bay of Pigs invasion, to Carter's "no need to panic" reply to revelations of a Russian combat brigade in Cuba (thus effectively sanctioning their presence), we are look at the following ninety miles off America's cost: 16,000 Soviet personnel; a Cuban army ten times that number (excluding reserves and militia), of whom some fifty thousand are serving in sixteen countries far from their borders; a Soviet nuclear warhead facility (at Punta Movida); electronic intelligence facilities (at Lourdes) able to eavesdrop any Stateside phone conversation at will; attack submarine pens; squadrons of hostile aircraft (from Hind D gunships to the nuclear-capable MiG-23BN) contemptuously overflying not only US territorial waters but even US aircraft carriers; a plant for manufacturing biological toxins; SAM missiles and torpedo craft; an infrastructure of terrorist infection of the region, co-ordinated with narcotics trafficking and the KGB. The only COMECON member outside the Eurasian landmass, Cuba is today considered by Russia worthy of more than half its worldwide assistance. The country – or should we say arsenal? – is a secure Soviet base just off our shores. And now Nicaragua, with the largest armed force in Central America, lies athwart the isthmus itself.

General ignorance has certainly been a factor in smoothing over Russia's path into this back yard. How many Americans or

English know that originally the Cuban Communist Party worked *with* Batista (to topple President Carlos Prio) until Fidel turned to Leninism for power, rather than doctrine. When the Cubans came to Grenada in 1979 their intelligence officers spelt out in white stones opposite my house SIEMPRE 26. One of the first things Colonel Hagler's Rangers did on airborne arrival in 1983 was to remove those silly stones. Their replacement, in the form of a billboard, read: THIS IS AS FAR AS THE BASTARDS ARE GOING.

That philosophy appears to be the only one the Russians understand in the region, as doubtless elsewhere. And after Cuba and Nicaragua can we doubt that Mexico, which sheltered Castro's exile base and assisted the Ortegas and Grenada's Maurice Bishop, will be far behind? In response what are we to expect of a Congress that seems more intent on declaring war on Chile and South Africa than on protecting our borders?

For a long time Russia was tentative about putting a paw forward into the Caribbean. To the USSR Cuba and Nicaragua are no more than strategic assets. This was shown in the period when Russia chastened an increasingly egocentric Castro by withdrawal of subsidies; as a result there was a considerable amount of outright sabotage, as well as vocal dissidence, in Cuba. While the Gorbachev generation grew up free of any military inferiority to the United States, its leaders well know that their treasury is not bottomless; indeed Moscow has shown considerable impatience of late with its Cuban burden. But while it is taking risks unimaginable thirty years ago (Afghanistan) it is obliged to show, during interim periods, the appearance of a juggernaut momentum in its general imperialist advance. You may stay them, but you won't halt them. There have been very few external rescues from communism; a comparison between the cases of Grenada and Malaya will be pursued below. There have been no cases of an internal overthrow of an indigenous Soviet proxy – yet. El Salvador, Suriname, and Angola represent a brief halting of the bear's approach. The case of Guyana, formerly B.G. or British Guiana, so operative in the betrayal of the Grenada intervention, strikes a note of absurdity, likely to be duplicated in Africa, with both major parties longing to be Soviet surrogates and impeded from uniting by the primadonna egotism of their leaders.

Guyana is an object lesson in Caribbean Soviet vassalage, but I doubt that the average liberal even knows where the country is. It has had a pro-Soviet political system for over thirty years and got out of it nothing but economic bankruptcy – and some arms. The PPP (People's Popular Party) was founded at the end of the Second World War by the American-educated dentist Cheddi Jagan and Linden Forbes Burnham. The PPP won control of the colonial legislature in 1953 and two years later split, its position at present writing. Burnham's smaller faction formed the dominant PNC (People's National Congress) and, in the belief that the more openly pro-Soviet Jagan had been stopped, England granted Guyana independence in 1966. Jagan became, and still remains, an opposition leader opposing nothing (except cronyism and general corruption).

After Burnham had been in power a decade or so, and had started seriously draining his once viable economy, he turned to Russia; but that country had not then the self-confidence in the Caribbean they have today. Besides, the Kremlin mistrusted this new black opportunist who flirted with anyone who would give him money, including revivalists like James Jones. After 1975 Burnham began courting Cuba, with regular visits to Havana and the importation of technical "assistance". He was a good actor; I once saw him laughingly pooh-pooh the idea of any Cuban presence at all in the country, when there were probably close on a thousand; indeed, five were expelled for "illegal activities" in 1978. Burnham died in August 1985. Odo, as he was known to his friends, if he had any left at the end of his life, died under throat surgery performed by Cuban doctors; he was embalmed by Russian technicians at the same time as Joyce Hoyte, his successor Desmond's wife, was also under the Cuban knife in a

Havana hospital. But his body was brought back from Russia and buried in 1987.

Amid the usual allegations of fraud, physical violence, the banning of foreign observers, and the apparent beating of Cheddi Jagan, Guyana "elected" Desmond Hoyte, a fifty-six-year-old lawyer, to succeed the odious Odo, the PNC winning forty-two of the fifty-three seats in the National Assembly, while Jagan's PPP was whittled down to eight. This at a moment when Jeane Kirkpatrick characterized Guyana as one of the most densely packed forward Soviet bases in the world.

Today Guyana, a physically beautiful country, resembles an impoverished African sub-state, rather than a neighbor of sophisticated Venezuela and Brazil. It is a beggar country, desperately in debt to the IMF, the poorest in the Caribbean with a per capita income below even Haiti's. Hemorrhaging currency, this "suitcase economy", as it has been called, has nothing to show, beyond armaments, for its long sycophancy to the Russian-Cuban axis. Even the importation of toilet paper is considered a drain on foreign-currency reserves, while a packet of Kleenex costs ten times its US price on the black market. At the last meeting of CARICOM he attended Burnham reneged on his large debt to Trinidad, offering to pay off part with sugar and rice, both over-produced commodities in the region. Odo had already pre-sold his rice to Cuba, anyway. And he also sold out Grenada.

What has been the reaction of Guyana's population to this dismal record? It is a little over half a million, of whom East Indians are in a small majority (look at their cricket teams). But, unlike Trinidad's Eric Williams, Burnham never seemed proud of those marvelous varieties of racial mix we see in several of the islands, and which endow them with some of the loveliest women in the world; he always ostentatiously favored the African element, though facially looking Carib himself.

Guyana is divided down the middle by the Essequibo river. From its backlands come good bauxite and fine lumber. Our house in Grenada is built with purple-heart wood floated downriver to the capital, Georgetown, in rafts. From the rivers divers pull out gold and diamonds. I know at least one emigrating Guyanese who brought out all his wealth in such river diamonds, which are not susceptible to electronic screening at airports. Today no Guyanese is allowed a cent of foreign currency in his or her possession and the pockets of emigrating nationals are searched at Timehri International.

Despite crackdowns on Ras Tafari, despite killings and beatings in its prisons (which appear to be run by the prisoners), Guyana has the highest crime rate in the world. Airline pilots sometimes decline to leave their aircraft overnight. There has been the telltale managerial exodus. One representative of such was Odo's personal pilot, a colorful Pole who got out to England in 1939 and spent the war dropping agents into France; Colonel Julien Pieniazek flew out of Guyana to Grenada under fire. I know two others who have done the same.

In March, 1983, Guyana assured Cuba and Russia of its continuing "socialist policies" and invited four hundred Cuban military in to train its army of over six thousand. Arms arrived at a rapid clip from North Korea (whose concern for the Caribbean had not previously been evident), while next door Suriname's stew bubbled over. There Desi Bouterse, a close friend of Maurice Bishop, overthrew a moderate democratic government leagued by the Dutch in a February 1980, coup. Less than a year later we find Bouterse signing treaties with the Soviet Union and welcoming in Russian personnel. The now customary Cuban "ambassador" arrived in the shape of a senior DA officer called Oswaldo Cardenas Junquera. As the Cuban presence increased the country became increasingly uneasy.

Loud in his praise for Bouterse, Maurice Bishop visited him in December, 1982. This visit prompted widespread demonstrations. Cuban flags were torn off Paramaribo hotels, housing Cuban personnel, and Bishop was compelled to leave in haste, though not before, it was strongly rumored, he had counselled a clampdown on the unrest at Castro's instruction. Bouterse arrested and "shot while attempting to escape" some thirty opposition leaders, including lawyers, journalists, union leaders, and his own Minister of Sport (such always seem to be unlucky in the region). Their bodies were publicly exhibited, broken bones and all.

A second popular uprising met with more executions, this time of both men and women; I met some of the refugees from this purge in Grenada. There was no doubt which way Bouterse was headed. Indeed, Tass expressed itself grateful for the massacre to "young progressively-minded military who overthrew the corrupt colonial regime and led the country onto the road of democratic transformations in the interest of the broad mass of the people". Anyone still awake after such clichés could note that Bouterse never overthrew a single colonial, since the Dutch had led the country into independence years before; that little help was forthcoming from a listless Holland; that the Soviet Ambassador to Suriname, a senior KGB officer, remained in place throughout; and that in July, 1983, Air Cubana flew its first TU-154 airliner from Havana to Paramaribo.[65]

Virtually none of this appeared in any of the US press that I was watching, though occasionaly the *Miami Herald* takes an interest in the area. Most journalists I have met have little idea where Guyana and Suriname are situated. Suriname is the smallest independent country in South America and it is heartening to learn that butcher Bouterse now seems to have met the same bloodthirsty split in his ranks as did his mentor, Maurice Bishop. For some time a Bush Negro called Ronnie Brunswijk, said to have been Bouterse's bodyguard, has been heading a practically weaponless Jungle Command of his kin, to oppose his Marxist master. It couldn't happen to a nicer guy.

Needless to say, bases in Guyana and Suriname considerably increase Atlantic combat ranges for the Soviets. From them Soviet Backfire bombers can destroy refineries and cut oil lifelines in the ABC islands (Aruba, Bonaire, Curacao) which between them refine an average of 588,000 barrels of black gold daily. At the apex of this triangle sits Nicaragua, with its Soviet T-54 tanks, SA-7 surface-to-air missiles, heavy ferries, and 122mm multiple rocket launchers, a fire power only matched in the region by Cuba's. Costa Rica and El Salvador have virtually none such at all. Nicaragua is counted on to continue the onward thrust of Russian imperialism. Apart from extensive revetment of the Sandino airfield outside Managua, plus runway extensions at Puerto Cabezas, Nicaragua's military field at Punta Huete already boasts, at 3,200 meters, the longest strip in Central America, capable of taking any craft in the Soviet arsenal, and speeding it northwards. No wonder Sovietologists tell us that Moscow thinks the Sandinista success to be as important as Castro's in Cuba.

For not only are there over ten thousand Cubans operating in Nicaragua today, with the experienced General Ochoa directing them as he did in Ethiopia and Angola, but the country has become the central spider of area subversion, giving hospitality to offices of the PLO, the Argentine Montoneros (whose leader Mario Finnenich was arrested in Brazil in February, 1984, after a briefing mission to Managua), the Peruvian Sendero Luminoso, the Chilean MIR, the Uruguayan Tupamaros, even the distant Basque ETA, regardless of the Antiguan and Haitian hotheads. Suriname and Guyana sit at the struts of this triangle, both of them having set themselves up against democracies bequeathed by enfeebled or embarrassed colonial powers. Castro and the Ortega brothers, on the other hand, confronted *and continued* dictatorships. Moscow prefers it that way.

So Burnham's Guyana became Haitianized. Its economy now stands on barter agreements, river gold, clandestine gun/drug running. It lacks any consistent schooling at all. Students work in the fields and are graded by their political loyalties (as was becoming the case under Jewel in Grenada). At the end of Burnham's life Guyana had become the customary "floating orchestra" of communism, initiating agreements with North

Korea, China, Bulgaria, Cuba. It created twelve major air bases of the 8,000-feet category, with all-weather hardtops and control towers, microwave navigational aids, fuel storage, hangers and barracks. Apart from all this it offers no less than forty-five intermediate air strips of 6,000 feet or more (presented to visiting press as roads).[66] The runway requirement of a MiG-23 is less than three thousand feet, only the Bear reconnaissance bomber requiring more than 7,000 (depending on load). The backland savannahs, Edgar Mittelholzer country, have indeed thus been transformed into Ms Kirkpatrick's nightmare. Before he died, Burnham was asked about these airstrips since it could not be said, as was said of our Pointe Salines in Grenada, that this concatenation of bases, with barracks and camouflage, was for tourism. Guyana has none. Burnham's churlish replies to such reporters as got through to him (e.g. Virginia Prewett of the *Washington Times*) amounted to a snub. He had cast his card.

Having become Premier after destabilizing strikes brought down his only real rival in 1964, Burnham became President-for-life in 1970; this became a bar joke throughout the islands but for those compelled to live in Guyana it was less amusing. Hoyte, his Vice-President, assumed the Presidency on August 6th, 1985, after Odo's death and, as leader of the winning party thereafter (though by no means its strongest man), Hoyte confirmed his Presidency which, locally, allowed him to appoint a Prime Minister who automatically became his Vice-President. The Guyanese President also names the entire Cabinet. It is not designed to be a losing situation.

The new Premier, Hamilton Green, was a black Moslem racist, a tail that wagged the dog as Guyana at once started to enter into yet more agreements with Moscow and continue its general infringement of human rights. Even the left-leaning World Council of Churches (WCC) had repeatedly cabled Burnham about their dismay concerning the disruption and prevention of church meetings throughout the country.[67] Guyana's new regime started off by kicking out a Catholic Bishop.

So Burnham was "elected" in 1968, 1973, and 1980 (when he wrote his own Constitution); during this time he nationalized the country's wealth, in particular the Canadian-owned bauxite mines and the British sugar estates of Booker McConnell. The venality of his voting procedures became notorious, with ballot boxes found floating on the river and ghosts voting from all over.

Further, Burnham kept his press muzzled by libel actions decided by his own judiciary (Hamilton Green being awarded US$5,000 in such a suit in March, 1985). Shortly before Burnham died, the *Catholic Standard*, edited by the liberal Father Andrew Morrison, felt the brunt of this ploy, while another Burnham coercement was government rationing of newsprint. Burnham expelled the editor of *Caribbean Contact*, a weekly financed from America and Canada which is, in fact, consistently pro-Cuban, if possibly no more so than the *New York Times* or the London *Guardian*. By banning Amnesty Hoyte simply followed in his master's footsteps. Why worry? Burnham left his party a considerable army and, for his civilian bully boys, used the Cleveland fugitive from justice David Hill (Rabbi Washington), whose House of Israel thugs beat up opponents far more mercilessly than Gairy's Mongoose Gang, allegedly stabbing the much-liked Father Darke to death in 1979. Burnham never seems to have bothered unduly about the proper pose, the proper rhetoric, like Bishop, though riding here and there on his white horse he was known to mouth the usual shibboleths about "socialism".

Towards the end Bishop must have felt Moscow riding hard on him. After the arrival of Sazhenev in Grenada Tass installed wire services. Bishop yearned for an upgrade in Moscow's mind. Officially, Grenada was *novaya* ... *narodnodemkraticheskaya gosudarstvennost* – in the phase of "new ... popular-democratic statehood", – Kremlin code for a State not fully Leninist, yet proceeding that way (like the East European countries around 1950). "Developed socialism", full Leninism, comprised the inner circle, the USSR, Mongolia,[68] Vietnam, and Cuba.[69]

Shortly before he died Burnham told the Caracas *El Nacional*, "I have always maintained that I am socialist in the sense that I accept Marx's tactical argument," although, in his first campaign against Jagan he took an anti-communist stance; and I very much doubt that he could define "Marx's tactical argument" any more than could those DGI officers I hobnobbed with on Pointe Salines, or any more than might have the young Jamaicans taken to Cuba with Colin Dennis for terrorist training. "Most of the men I speak about," Dennis subsequently recounted, "were incapable of differentiating between socialism and capitalism."[70]

Referring to himself repeatedly as a "military man," Burnham had no military career at all that I can uncover, nor ever saw a bullet fired in anger, despite the medals down to his ankles. He was about as much a war hero as Marcos. He was interested in power, with rum a close second, and, unlike Bishop, he hung on to power, which is what Russia requires in the first instance of its client States. After all, for Burnham it was not so very difficult. He controlled his Leninist PNC, with, most of the time, his only serious opposition being Jagan's Stalinist PPP and Eusi Kwayana's WPA (Working People's Alliance), also Marxist-Leninist, etc. It was a situation in which Moscow could scarcely lose and in Odo's lifetime did not do so. After the 1985 elections Hoyte began to look even more *apparatchik* than his celebrated predecessor, though this may have been due to pressure from Green, who had seen that Moscow mistrusted Burnham and wanted to encourage it to dip feet further into the water. Nevertheless, one wonders whether Guyana is democratically redeemable at all, either by military coup, as in Grenada and Suriname, or by intervention from Venezuela with its ongoing territorial suits against its English-speaking neighbor.

I have said that Guyana provides us with an object lesson in Soviet vassalage. First of all, Burnham really got nothing but arms out of Russia. Secondly, those critics, like O'Shaughnessy, who opposed the Grenada intervention on the grounds that somehow its people would have thrown off the RMG yoke and restored democracy, must answer why a very substantial opposition in Guyana was never able to do the same. For the Soviet-Cuban card has two faces; on one side it offers total power; on the other, economic destitution. It remains to be seen whether Guyana will continue to imitate the sinking Cuban model, to the detriment of its already pitiable people.

Malaya and Grenada: A Comparison in Communisms

Jean-François Deniau quotes a Soviet official as follows:

> We took Angola and you did not protest. We even saw that you could have beaten us in Angola ... and that you did nothing to win. And when, to save ourselves, we sent in thirty thousand Cuban soldiers, Ambassador Young, a member of the American cabinet [in fact Ambassador to the UN], said it was a positive step and an element of stability. All right, we noted the fact and included it in our analyses. Then we took Mozambique. Forget it, you don't even know where it is. Then we took Ethiopia, a key move. There again we noted that you could have replied via Somalia or Eritrea or both. No reply. We noted that and put it into our analyses. Then we took Aden and set up a powerful Soviet base there. Aden! On the Arabian Peninsula! In the heart of your supply center! No response. So we noted: we can take Aden.[71]

It is the history of our times and certainly of the present writer's life, the first part spent in Malaya where a bloody communist take-over was attempted after World War Two, the last part spent in Grenada, ditto. In both cases Russian communism was overthrown by force, contradicting the Brezhnev doctrine that power seized by communism is irreversible. No matter that Malaya, the FMS or Federated Malay States[72] of my youth, may have fallen today under a Moslem fanatic, another rutilant Khomeini, it was handed over to the Tungku as an elective democracy, as was Grenada to its own people in 1983. Both victories cost blood, in Malaya quite a lot of it.

By now it is surely incontestable that the principal diplomatic winner of World War Two was Josef Stalin. As hypnotized as Roosevelt in the presence of the Generalissimo at Yalta (see FDR's letters to his son Elliott), the Allies watched while the world was parceled out for Russian domination at a moment when Russia was physically drained. By now the Soviet Union is on a permanent war footing, the amount of its GNP going to its military paralleling that of Japan or Germany just before World War Two.

Jean-François Revel reminds us that at Helsinki in 1975 "The West presented the U.S.S.R. with two lavish gifts: we recognized the legitimacy of the Soviet empire over Central Europe, which it had illegally grabbed at the end of World War II, and we offered massive and almost interest-free economic and technological aid. In return, the Soviet Union promised a more moderate foreign policy and respect for human rights within its empire."[73] Surely the Politburo must have fallen over each other laughing at that provision. The Helsinki "accord" legalized the conquest of some 700 millions of beings: empire enough.

As in the Caribbean (though it was then considered more of an American lake), Stalin hoped for rapid post-war communist expansion in the Far East. Who, surveying today's map of Asia, can say he hoped in vain? To be sure, there were brave resistances in Southeast Asia then. Burma made its bid, there was the Hukbalahap revolt in the Philippines, and of course there was Vietnam, already launched into its agony by the Moscow-trained Annamese, Ho Chi Minh. South Korea was narrowly pulled out of the cauldron by UN intervention, the first time US troops fought under a flag not their own. But Korea was merely returned to its uneasy status quo; no communists were expelled from North Korea, it was a defensive act of sanitation. Today UN rescues from communism are pipe dreams. Only Malaya was recovered intact in the most difficult and costly intra-

Commonwealth war the British have ever known, and that includes the Falklands.[74]

Approximately the size of Florida, the Federated Malay States (inclusive of Singapore) where I grew up was England's richest Crown Colony, as well as its loveliest. Rice, rubber, tin came out of jungles which, until recently, housed elephant, tiger, rhino. Its postwar population was just over five million. During the thirties a militant communist network spread into the FMS from the Soviet Far Eastern Bureau in Shanghai, Cominterm of the area. Together with a seedy character called Loi Tok, or "The Plen" (Plenipotentiary), Ho set up a Malayan Communist Party (MCP) in Singapore in 1930. He then returned to Hong-Kong (as Nguen Ai Quoc), and was arrested, though not before he had formed a Vietnamese Communist Party, with world-known results. Until the Japanese overran the FMS in December, 1941, this MCP was chiefly engaged in labor strife, sabotage of rubber estates, and other such mischief-making with psychological effects locally.

Once in control of the peninsula the Japanese went for their traditional enemies the Chinese (numbering some third of the population). Brutal mass murders of innocent Chinese Malays took place, one of the bloodiest being the Batu Caves massacre north of the capital, Kuala Lumpur, from which Loi Tok, by this time MCP Secretary-General, is said to have escaped (though more of this later). The Japanese wiped out the MCP leadership but not the Chinese Malays, a courageous and tough element; my prisoner-of-war father was kept alive by such, food being left in roadside pipes and the like by sympathetic Chinese (some of them former clients), while out on working parties.

From this Chinese minority sprang various guerrilla groups who harassed the occupiers, often bearing wild names like the Dare-to-Die Corps. Some of their chiefs were even decorated by Mountbatten after the war. In the north, near Penang, they received drops of arms from the RAF which many later "lost." After the intervention in Grenada there were at least seven thousand dedicated, if disbanded, PRA soldiers who claimed to have "lost" their Akkas.

In occupied Malaya the popular animus was against the Japanese. So, besides getting dug into the population, the guerrillas helped many British escapees, the Civil Service having been put into Changi Camp, where my father and two uncles starved the war out, apart from spells in the Utram Road Kempetai prison on the mainland.

It was this quite legitimate hatred of the Japanese, then, that Moscow "turned" against the British when restored in 1945, just as in Grenada Bishop tried to "turn" hatred of his predecessor, Sir Eric Gairy, into hatred of America. In Malaya, however, deprived of all communications, guerrilla bands in the jungles of Pahang and Kelantan had little hard evidence the British would ever return.

They certainly looked done for on August 14, 1945, when the Japanese agreed to an unconditional surrender. The Civil Service tottered out of Changi into hospitals, most of them having lost about half their weight. As in Grenada, the police were non-existent, and conscripted troops, chiefly Australian, thin on the ground, as well as anxious to get home for demobilization. This was perfect terrain for communist exploitation and it took the British seven years to dig them out and restore the country to democracy. The Russian orchestration of their near take-over is writ large in all the evidence, from its February 1948 Calcutta Conference of Asian Communists on.

One Selangor CID chief recounted how he and his men got a group of communist terrorists to lead them to their arms cache simply by showing a piece of paper stamped with a hammer-and-sickle seal that he had picked up in an earlier raid on another camp. Ambushed in the Cameron Highlands at this time, my father, in failing health, had given up hope when his chauffeur calmly produced the same from under his cap, and they were allowed to proceed. In Grenada under Jewel later there was the same infantile reverence for things Russian by Bishop and his minions, Soviet Lada trucks running wild with their Russian insignia almost boastfully intact.

As the Malayan terrorists stepped up their attacks against the rubber estates and tin mines, the country's bread basket, murders increased in both numbers and brutality, Chinese laborers who would not join the People's Anti-British Army being tortured and dismembered alive. The fate of rubber planters was brought home in a Ken Annakin movie starring Claudette Colbert, while a *Straits Times* photo of two tots playing in a sandbagged nursery ran around the world (my father then being Chairman of that newspaper's Board). Bitter Perak planters led a delegation to KL demanding "ruthless action" if they were to continue. Finally, in June, 1948, a long overdue emergency was declared.

The tardiness cost thousands of lives. On a lesser scale it could be compared with the irresolution of the Carter administration and the palliative appointment of the liberal feminist Sally Shelton to succeed Frank Ortiz as our Barbados Ambassador. The British delay in Malaya (which was not then independent) owed to the fact that Russia had become our ally in 1941, after having been Hitler's beforehand. It was thus one of the four Great Powers. Attlee's Labour Government refused to allow the Malayan Communist Party to be declared illegal, which would have hastened its end. Indeed, MPs like D.N. Pritt and Konnie Zilliacus actually sent it congratulatory messages! Only belatedly did this House recognize direct Soviet manipulation of the terrorists and send out more troops. They were not enough. Two more murders in high places had to dramatize the scene before Whitehall (under Churchill) decided to hold the colony until self-government could be granted it.

In 1951 High Commissioner Sir Henry Gurney, age fifty, was ambushed and assassinated, gallantly leaving his car to draw fire to save his wife. The following year a handsome young Anglo-Malayan boyhood friend of mine, a man who returned to fight the war and achieved fame by using a wooden horse to escape from a German prison camp, Michael Codner, was cold-bloodedly killed in Tanjong Malim, of which he had just become the much-liked District Officer. But shortly before Mike's death the new Conservative government sent out General Sir Gerald Templer. The rest is history and for once it does not belong to the Russians.

Templer was blown up by a mine at Anzio. In fact, he was in a PU (15-cwt Pick-Up van) when the vehicle in front of his touched off a Teller causing a piano it was carrying (of all things!) to fall on the General.[75] He is today remembered, and rightly so, for his ruthlessness in extirpating terrorism from Malaya – his ascetic appearance, "thin as a rake," adding to the legend. Templer at once introduced curfews, detention camps, collective area punishments, resettlements, identification cards – and the new SAS. Frankly, Templer went about things in a way we never could today, at least in a Third World country, though it is the only way the commie understands. If, after due warning and time, you did not carry an ID card when tapping a tree, it was just too bad.

Yet at the same time Templer recognized the need for enlisting a multiracial populace, in particular its thriving Chinese community, into identity with the struggle for democracy. Jack Farris was the same in Grenada, where a misled youth had to be re-educated into recognizing the communists as the common enemy of mankind. Once that step had been taken by his Intelligence, Templer was able to end the emergency. Directly it was stood up to, the MCP drew in its horns, captured documents suddenly counseling courtesy to civilians; finally, the bodyguard of a Central Committee member, Supreme Military Commander Ah Kik (no kidding), the equivalent of Grenada's General Hudson Austin, actually brought in the decapitated head of his boss – surely one way of guarding a body.

Having watched at first hand both Malayan and Grenadian communist probes, I must be excused a certain sense of *déjà vu*. The mimicry of the Russian model was almost pedantically similar in both cases: as Lenin put it, in *The Events of the Day* for August 21, 1906, "A ruthless guerrilla war of extermination against the governmental perpetrators of violence, which undoubtedly means killing them by means of 'guerrilla actions,' appears to be timely and expedient."

First, the puppet Quislings: Chen Ping in Malaya, Bishop in Grenada. Next the cut-throat rivalries: Chen Ping versus Loi Tak and Bishop against Coard, for a strong theory has it that Loi Tak, Chen's predecessor and bosom friend, informed on the whole MCP apparatus to the Japanese to save his skin, hence their easy extermination of most of it. Certainly the PRG's Central Committee condemned Bishop to outer darkness and death as "petty Bourg," while the MCP called Loi Tak "the greatest culprit in the history of our Party" and had him executed when he fled to Thailand.

The party structure and semantic of both Soviet surrogates were identical, with both loudly decrying any Russian sponsorship. The MCP directives and diaries captured by British SAS could double for the documents hauled in by 519th MI in Grenada in 1983. The indoctrination of children is numbingly similar, with its training manuals, cries for self-criticism, harsh treatment for deviation, robot-like repetitition of rhetoric, division of communities into litmus-test progressives and enemies, with attendant hit lists, martyrs, brothers. Finally, we see the same steady infiltration of Russia's principal export – arms – via sampan and junk to Malaya, via Cuban freighters to Grenada. Between 1972 and 1982, when America's total number of nuclear weapons decreased, the USSR outspent the USA in conventional weaponry by $700 billion, a sum which, if utilized by the latter country, would have given it every defense program planned for it and subsequently denied by Congress; this includes the B-1B bomber wing now under attrition at Dyess Air Force Base in Texas.[76]

Too, the rhetoric has the identical bullfrog chauvinism, the same codes and disguises, the MCP's Anti-British Army being rechristened at the end the Malayan Races Liberation Army, which can have meant as little to riverine Malays as Bishop's vaticinating slogans did to nutmeg-growers in Grenada. Of course, in today's Caribbean, Soviet adventurism has to embrace a more disparate spectrum of surrogates; it had to make bedfellows of Bishop's Jewel, of Tim Hector's ACLM (Afro-Caribbean Liberation Movement) in Antigua, of Jacques Dorcillian's PUCH (United Party of Haitian Communists) in Haiti. Dorcillian, incidentally, is married to a Russian.

Other parallels are routine by now. In 1945 the returning British found police records, fingerprints, gun licences, widely destroyed throughout Malaya. The Grenadian RMG saw to the same in conflagrations in the St. George's police station and the Butler House headquarters, the erstwhile Santa Maria Hotel. Similar erasures of tapes and files happened when Seaga went after the Brigadistas in Jamaica.[77]

These parallels should at least prepare us for the communist advance, as will be suggested below. Thus it is significant that Havana has recently resuscitated Carlos Marighella's *Mini-Manual del Guerrillero Urbano* and is diffusing it where it can throughout the region. First published two decades ago in the Cuban review *Tricontinental*, the *Mini-Manual* is a terrorist how-to-do-it kit that identically echoes MCP and PRG instructions, allowing for advances in technology and presupposing someone who can really put up a functioning Molotov cocktail. Knowledge of the *Mini-Manual* might have saved many lives in the seventies and eighties.[78]

For Marighella saw the role of the media as partner of terrorism not only by reporting (and thus creating panic) but also, as a Czech resistance fighter of the past perceives, by "fictionalizing about the terrorists" and so creating an entity that did not exist.[79] Terrorists are media stars if ever there were such. And looking back on Jewel, The London School of Economics' Philip Windsor gives us a truly Marighellian statement: "The Constitution itself has been suspended under Maurice Bishop, but not the process of law".[80] Marighella died in his fifties in a gunfight with Brazilian police in São Paulo. Along with Fanon he saw sheer violence as a unifying factor; that is, once you have killed you are "cleansed" (i.e. of bourgeois morality). Compare the esteem given to Jamaican "Rankings" in Cuba. This combination of orphic ecstasy and military aggression was what succeeded in giving the Nazis their sense of messianic *Gemeinschaft* also.[81]

There is something truly Kafkaesque in reading these blueprints – redprints? – for revolution and the end of thought that should have warned us of the nature of terrorism to come. Verily the sage said it: those who cannot learn from history are destined to repeat it.

The Last Backyard: Who's Next?

A year to the day after I had watched Tomcats whirl like leaves down the Ponte Salines peninsula I saw the first commercial jets put down on the runway which novelist George Lamming called "a magnanimous contribution of the Cuban people to the bold creative revolution by the late Maurice Bishop."[82] At the ceremonies to complete what President Reagan had started, with a blessing by Monsignor Cyril Lamontagne and a hearty rendition of *Now Thank We All Our God*, we Grenadians recalled the American lives given on our behalf, a loss memorialized on the campus of the St. George's School of Medicine, to which Reagan paid tribute on February 20, 1986. We were then able to wander around the terminal building and see the vast ratio of kitchen space to dining area planned by the Cubans, the reverse of normal commercial eateries, viz. enough kitchen space to feed an army with dining area for a platoon. Further evidence of Cuban long-range intentions were apparent in the huge fuel tanks that would serve their military distance aircraft rather than commercial jet-liners.[83]

Now, what had happened in the interim after intervention? For it was generally assumed that Grenada at once enjoyed a cornucopia of US aid. A typical State Department release of the time proclaimed that all was well in our best of all possible worlds: "As soon as the fighting ceased, the U.S. Agency for International Development (AID) began to ferry emergency supplies by air, including generators, water tanks, medicine, food and infant supplies valued at $475,000."

No doubt this was true, but as those first commercial carriers touched down on the Pointe Salines strip I can vouch that the area had no piped water, no telephone, about four hours of power a day, an intermittent radio station, and absurd roads. All this has much improved by now, but it was initially tough to get the island going again. It will always be so. We do not have the resources. Nutmeg prices were down and our chief competitors, the Banda Islanders in Indonesia, were exploiting our difficulties. The CBI, as indicated, has made little dent in the Windwards. Post-intervention tugging at our bootstraps was made the more onerous by virtue of the fact that the public services, the infrastructure of the island, were still all in Jewel hands. The head of the CWC (Central Water Commission) was a Bishop appointee to the overthrown Ministry of Defence; all his held-over functionaries had an interest in making American aid look inferior to Cuban aid, and it was not possible for the democratic interim government, even had it so desired, to go around axing everyone. A small island like ours simply does not have in hand a constant cadre of experts waiting to staff its utilities. There were at least three verified cases of sabotage (of loaned Hawker-Siddeley generators) at our Power Station in 1984. For a while no work could be done in a wide range of activities.

All the same, though the Washington print-out of our life may have been overly optimistic, the island was free. You have to have been under communist domination to know what that means. We had a free press. Elections had been scheduled, the usurping Cubans seen off, their creatures detained on murder charges.

In his book *Game Plan: A Geostrategic Framework for the*

238

Conduct of the U.S.-Soviet Contest, former National Security Adviser Zbigniew Brzezinski writes of America's confrontation with Russia today as "a struggle between two imperial systems ... a two-nation contest for nothing less than global predominance." I find this extraordinarily sloppy thinking. America is constantly on the defensive against an offensive Soviet Union. It cannot be said that America is imperial, in the sense of seeking and holding territory. US troops withdrew immediately after liberating Grenada – perhaps too soon in the view of some islanders – but Soviet troops are still in Afghanistan. I have not noticed the United States seeking "global predominance," merely the safety of its citizens and borders. Nor is the "contest" simplistically "two-nation."

The Central American region is much more complex than this. As two Costa Rican journalist-professors have pointed out, the American Congress is inhibited from action by seeing foreign strategy in terms of Vietnam.[84] As a result, it repeatedly misses opportunities. When Jewel was overthrown in Grenada, Suriname at once became wobbly. Bouterse could easily have been undermined, with help from Holland. A month later Edén Pastora and Alfonso Robelo solicited a meeting with the Sandinistas, demanding freedom of the press and elections. They were repudiated as "*traidores*." Their initiative could have been far more widely publicized and exploited. Pastora clearly got bored when it was not. Now the region swarms with Russia's "revolutionary search services," as it euphemizes the promotion of client regimes that will further its own strategic interests. Ever since the Kissinger commission to make policy recommendations on Central America in 1983, worst-case scenarios of the area have been a dime a dozen, bar-stool pastimes, all haunted by Vietnam.

Guatemala: this civil democracy is not Vietnam. Two months spent in it in 1987 initiated me to typical communist methods of penetration. Like the citizens of El Salvador and Costa Rica, the Guatemalans are a pacific and freedom-loving people. There is no Somoza or Battista about there (though there was, as usual, a once forceful army). However, there are young robbers in the hills who make a living by preying on poor Indians. Suddenly these *ladrones* are using Kalashnikovs for their ends. A US AID officer I'd met in Grenada took me to a village only a few kilometers from lovely Lake Atitlán (where the peasants themselves send out protective patrols) and showed me where he had recently delivered a pay packet to an Indian foreman for distribution. Only a few minutes out of the village he had heard the crackle of AK fire. The brave guerrillas had swiped the lot. Where did the robbers obtain this expensive hardware? One needs but one guess; and thus indebted to the local Communist Party they can never leave its arms. Such countries will therefore become increasingly pincered between Nicaragua and Panama. General Daniel Ortega Saavedra pays an increasing number of goodwill visits to Panama's strong-man military commander, General Manuel Antonio Noriega, both almost tripping over their medals. The latter has been running an emergency rule for half a decade. The two exchange hate-America stories and lies about the Torrijo-Carter treaties.

Cuba: Castro loses his touch. Rumors reaching me from Cuban workers in their cups had it that, despite Fidelito, despite Celia Sanchez, the fat-bottomed dictator is as queer as two left shoes. I had long suspected as much, before reading Carlos Franqui. The brutal persecution of homosexual males in Cuba was initiated by Castro, through Ramiro Valdés, a repulsive neurotic who claimed to have a homosexual-detection machine; Valdés became a fanatic anti-gay, finally asking for capital punishment for such deviants. He was calmed down, but not until large numbers of supposed homosexuals had been sentenced to hard labor in re-education camps, where they were made to wear a letter P, for pederast, across the backsides of their striped prison suits. Such zeal protests too much. As Franqui reflects: "historically the greatest persecutors of homosexuals had themselves been homosexuals."[85] One has only to think of Ernst Röhm in Nazi Germany.

So suppose Castro weakens, or his troops do, or his terrorist training does. There was certainly a lot of sabotage by Cubans during the period of withdrawn Russian oil subsidies. A purer robot, a Cuban Jaruzelski, is required. Castro is wasted, marginalized – they missed with the Pope but they won't here, in their own killing ground. The assassination will be attributed to the CIA almost before it happens. America will be once more in the dock.

Nicaragua: The domino is well and truly down, though the party still has racial problems (with Miskitia) externally and festering rivalries internally: "the Ortega brothers, President Daniel and Defense Minister Humberto, have reportedly created jealousy and animosity among other Sandinistas for their aping of Cuba's Castro brothers, Fidel and Raúl."[86] Factionalism destroyed communism in Grenada and Malaya, we have seen, and apparently it threatens Soviet South Yemen. It has certainly dogged El Salvador.

In 1982 probably the most respected guerrilla leader in Central American was Salvador Cayetano Carpio (then sixty-two) who, together with Edén Pastora Gómez, then the Sandinista Minister of Defense over in Nicaragua, felt that Castro completely underestimated the guerrilla task in El Salvador, especially the loyalty of its army. They were proved correct. It was the Bishop-Coard schism writ large. Carpio was (at first) fiercely Stalinist – the sensational capture of Nidia Díaz's diaries showed Salvadorian guerrillas being sent for training to the Soviet Union – and repudiated the influence of the Cuban DA, then under Castro's friend Manuel Pineiro, nicknamed Barba Roja, Red-beard. In this he was initially joined by Dr. Fabio Castillo, who had run for President in 1966. Both suspected the Salvadoran Communist Party of various forms of weakness, Carpio surmising that Melida Anaya Montes, a 54-year-old former schoolteacher and ranking official in the Castillo-Carpio camp, was opposing him. Accordingly, she was found murdered in Managua on April 6, 1983, after a visit to Cuba. Her body had received eighty-three stab wounds. Pineiro flew over to help from Havana while Carpio went to Libya. Within a few days evidence erupted that one of Carpio's henchmen had done the killing. Almost incontrovertibly behind it, Carpio was offered an extended rest in Cuba. He preferred to shoot himself in the heart.

Honduras: The Cinchoneros living off kidnapings, their leader, Reyes Mata, captured but released on amnesty and repairing promptly to Cuba via Nicaragua. Then back in Honduras in July 1983, with a band of a hundred guerrileros, who betrayed him. Reyes Mata was tracked down and killed. The list lengthens, indeed could be prolonged to include almost every country in South America also. But, above all, is there one country where our resolve is likely to be tested more crucially on our southern border? In the Soviet strategy for Central America Mexico is slated to fall.

So much fantasy? Even before assuming office Jeane Kirkpatrick put it plainly:

sooner or later, whatever our present policies, we'll be forced to deal with the problem posed by the Soviet-backed Marxist-Leninist trust in Central America. Either we deal with it now in El Salvador and Nicaragua or we will have to deal with it in two or three years time in Guatemala and Panama, or in five years time in Mexico.

Less. Mexico was the first country in the Western Hemisphere to recognize the bolsheviks, in 1924: hence Trotsky's asylum there and eventual assassination. Mexico is the only Central American country to maintain *unbroken* ties with Castro's Cuba, and the only OAS member to refuse to break ties with Cuba in 1964. It was, of course, from his exile base in Mexico that Castro took *Granma* out, to mount his revolution.

Nor let us forget that Mexico has been hospitable to the Sandinistas from the start, as well as to international terrorists and drug smugglers. This insidious penetration, aimed principally at major American cities, was revealed through US prompting in 1986. A Mexicana airliner, bound for Los Angeles, exploded after take-off, killing all 166 of its passengers. A radical Arab group claimed to have planted the bomb in retaliation for the American attack on Libya. Mexican authorities woke up and suddenly discovered scores of illegal Cubans and Lebanese with counterfeit passports and plans to blow up US installations. Shortly after this an American drug informant in Baton Rouge, Louisiana, who had given details of such drug-trafficking operations, was wiped out by a Colombian hit squad that had entered the US clandestinely from Mexico.

The Sandinistas have close ties with M-19, the Colombian April 19 Movement, responsible for the murders of eleven Judges at the Bogotá Palace of Justice in November, 1985. Shortly before this the Colombian Defense Minister General Miguel Vega announced he had captured planning documents of FARC (the Communist Revolutionary Armed Forces of Colombia) outlining the potential of a 36,000 "People's Army" in the country. Anyone who has motored from Ecuador to Colombia recently will know the seriousness of Customs searches there.

Admittedly, Panama may be an equal culprit in this respect. More than once I have been an in-transit passenger on a South American line which allowed passengers to stop off for an hour or so on Panama's airport shopping mail. It is a busy place. Since not screened on reboarding I could have pocketed almost anything from anyone. But Mexico is the seed of serious trouble. It tacitly encourages the breaking of US borders as safety valve for its failing economy. Its enormous debt is increasing. Its President was booed at the opening of the 1986 World Soccer Cup.

With the Mexican economy sinking the exodus across the Rio Grande will make the Mariel boat escape look like a Sunday school picnic. Lightly policed by the INS this border would be crossed by armies of wetbacks striving to get free. Instead of a couple of million Mexican illegals we shall have twenty. Nor would they likely be discouraged, should Jimmy Carter or Teddy Kennedy turn up in the White House. They would then be allowed to stay as "undocumented" aliens, a term that has always irked me since I waited my own term out as a legal alien, since it suggests that the illegal, far from brazenly breaking the law, has merely mislaid or failed to complete a few documents. In other words, if I deserted my wife and married a few other women and got away with it, I would be an "undocumented" bigamist.

But the Mexican scenario becomes more disturbing as you extrapolate it. MIT's Lester Thurow has done so, arguing that a country with $100+ billion in foreign debts has considerable leverage over its creditor: "What better way for the Mexicans to tweak the Yank's nose than to default on all of the debts."[87] In that case America would have to close its nearly 2,000-mile southern land border. With what? The National Guard? Not nearly enough. With the 82nd? The 101st? Far too valuable. Needed for LIC (Low Intensity Conflict) all over. It would have to be done with troops pulled back from Europe. And the Russian bear would smile and smile.

Frankly, by 1986 the problem of Mexican immigration into the United States had become too large to mention. Sundry professors were flatfooting forward to tell us the crashingly obvious, that close policing of our border would be "divisive to Mexican-American relations."[88] You'll bet it would. Mexico's population is projected to reach one hundred million by the turn of the century, with a per capita income less than a tenth that of workers north of the border and an enormous unemployment rate, as the country's youth comes of age. In the Winter 1986 issue of *Strategic Review* Sol Sanders analyzes the possibility of the same conflagration overtaking Mexico as we have watched grip Nicaragua: "Would Washington wake up one morning, after the first shots had been fired in a new upheaval in Mexico, to find literally millions of refugees swarming across the poorly defended U.S. border?"

It is hardly defended at all. At the start of 1987 the US Border patrol astride that immigration Klondike around Brownsville Texas, with its industry of pro-Hispanic lawyers, social security and employment letter forgers, was rationed to one for every ten miles of riverbank, with no more than eight officers on watch at a time. A couple of thousand more INS agents were supposed to have been added in 1986 but have not materialized a year later; while guidelines out of Washington are increasingly lenient towards the illegals, who seem to enjoy schools, government services, and federally funded health clinics to which they are not entitled. The liberal answer appears to be to give up and let them all in: after all America is a nation of immigrants, and so on.

But the facts are there. In 1982 the U.S. turned back 750,000 illegals from the common border. By 1984 this figure had risen to 1.2 million. Nor does this account for those who got through, legally or illegally. And consider the problem of drug trafficking. Mexico has 6,500 miles of porous coastline. Illegal drugs are an $80 billion-a-year industry in the United States. This cannot wholly be put down to the fault of native Americans demanding dope, cocaine has been made deliberately *more* addictive by the chemical farms of Latin America. Castro boasts of turning America white with cocaine. Your city junkie may be begging for his fix, but he did not ask for it to be made *more* addictive.

What, then, about the UN? Under Third-World control *ce machin* (as de Gaulle called it) either actively supports the Soviet Union or blows off steam at America. Israeli settlements on the West Bank are imperialist, Vietnamese colonization of Cambodia is not. With those countries that share our concerns, at least on paper, we share a paper alliance. James Buckley has well put it:

When an American meets a European counterpart at an international conference, he is apt to find the experience marvelously seductive. European professionals tend to be intelligent and urbane; we and they speak the same intellectual language and share the same values. But any time the conversation goes much beneath the surface, the fundamental differences that distinguish the American experience from the European emerge. By and large, America has retained a sense of purpose, self-confidence, and hope. Beneath the European surface, however, one can detect tired societies unable or unwilling to think through to ultimate consequences, societies for which there are few causes to justify the risk of confrontation.[89]

As an ex-European I would agree with the erstwhile Senator's assessment, while pointing out that Europe has been so badly hurt by such confrontations in this century as to be understandably leery of another. All the same, forget about the UN.

During a radio address on April 13, 1979, Maurice Bishop boomed: "We are not in anybody's backyard."[90] I heard this speech live and could not have agreed more. Our area of the Caribbean is not in America's backyard; it is its front gate. An Editorial in *The Times* put it as follows:

Many of the two dozen small and undefended states of the Caribbean are actually closer geographically to Washington than is California. Half of America's total exports and imports, two-thirds of its shipping trade, three-quarters of its oil imports pass through the Caribbean, Panama Canal or Gulf of Mexico.[91]

It is not only the oil lanes that are vital to America and the free West, but the passage of everything involved in America's security, by which I mean minerals like cobalt, manganese, titanium, chrome. As much as 90% of America's cobalt is brought in by this route, whose vulnerability was shown to us in the last war. Throughout 1942 Churchill can be seen growing more and more concerned about the tanker fleets proceeding northwards from the oil ports of Venezuela, Mexico, and Aruba. Chapter 7 of his *The Hinge of Fate* features a map showing the so-called U-Boat paradise, with large concentrations of German submarines in the southern Caribbean and around Trinidad; and these were submarines operating without any secure base in the area. One member of such a wolf pack put into St. George's harbor at the time and left unscathed. In February 1942 tonnage lost in the area amounted to 384,000, seventy-one ships. On March 12th of this year we find Churchill imploring Harry Hopkins for safer convoying of this shipping:

> I am most deeply concerned at the immense sinkings of tankers west of the 40th. meridian and in the Caribbean Sea ... in little over two months, in these waters alone, about 60 tankers have been sunk or damaged, totalling some 675 dead-weight tons. In addition to this several tankers are overdue.[92]

Since Churchill wrote those words these sea roads have become immeasurably more vulnerable thanks to speedier communications, making the Caribbean's relation to America that of the Channel to England in World War Two.

In short, it is a border and the American President takes an oath of office to defend his country's borders. To a joint session on April 27, 1983, Reagan put this plainly: "I say to you that tonight there can be no question: the national security of all the Americas is at stake in Central America. If we cannot defend ourselves there, we cannot expect to prevail elsewhere. Our credibility would collapse, our alliances would crumble, and the safety of our homeland would be in jeopardy."

The Grenada rescue was of major importance, both for strategic and psychological reasons. Coming not long after the Falklands campaign, when the empire struck back with a vengeance, it evinced a new valuation of the region by Washington. Nicaragua and Mexico are mainland America, a fact that the Contadora group declined to recognize. And as N.D. Sanchez put it in a 1983 article in *Foreign Policy:* "There is no doubt that if

El Salvador falls, Honduras – then flanked on two sides by hostile neighbors and already the target of insurgency – will follow."

Sociologically, the change in US immigration laws, plus a cooler welcome to ex-colonials in England (for which Windward Islanders needed no visa before independence), means that Caribbean natives have lately emigrated in greater quantity to North America than to England. Furthermore, hospitality for such natives is inclining to be warmer in the States than in England.

Of course, there remains the Queen, God bless 'er, with her palace toy called the Commonwealth. On the morning when the Rangers dropped over Pointe Salines, Her Majesty summoned Thatcher to Buck House. Doubtless she told her Prime Minister that the OECS appeal for help was "a matter for long debate among British Constitutional lawyers."[93] The Queen was not amused at her turf being invaded by Yanks. However, on site we were in need of action rather than debate and America provided it.

If Mexico is to be the worst-case scenario, what will happen to the islands? The Soviet option for our future is by now obvious. But it may not be the only one. World War Three or surrender is not a necessary alternate. So long as positive democratic examples can be offered up in Central America and the Caribbean they will be chosen over coercion. That, on one hand. On the other hand, 'Low Intensity conflict' (often far from low intensity at the actual flashpoints) is an activity for which volunteer forces, such as those which fought in the Falklands and Grenada, are admirably adapted.

Over 80% of the world's maritime traffic funnels through a few choke points, e.g. the Panama and Suez Canals, the Straits of Malacca, Hormuz, Gibraltar, etc. This shipping is essential to the West. Any cursory examination of a map will show that Russia has been trying to control contiguous land masses in order to close off those choke points, one by one. To this end they are willing to deploy vast land forces, as in the Afghanistan operation.

My own talks with senior US officers in Grenada led me to espouse Alfred Thayer Mahon's theory in *Narrow Seas*: such choke-point operations can probably be sold to Congress more easily than larger commitments. American strategy must be selective and, above all, must *take the initiative*. Grenada was only rescued in the nick of time; but it represented an action rather than a reaction. Most US military I met there were ready to have a go elsewhere. And I wish them luck in the endeavour. In World War Two I lacked such clarity of purpose. In 1939 most of us retired British schoolboys knew we had to go to bat for our country, or else. Many were glad it had come to the crunch. But though I had twice visited Germany in my teens, and had German relatives, I cannot pretend I went in with any real understanding of Nazism. The world was not disfigured, nor did I know the stench of its infection to come. We were callow in those days.

The men and women who rescued Grenada were not. Most recognized communism for the true beast it is. Older now, I think I understand that animal better than I did and, if the islands felt its evil breath and somehow survived, that does not mean the communists will not try and try again in the area. Harboring the largest concentration of KGB personnel this side of the Iron Curtain, Mexico is a time-bomb waiting to go off.[94?] It is not only the staggering debt mentioned that is ticking away; it is the stagnating statist nature of the economy (which so subsidizes the capital's subways that a ride is cheaper than the printing of the ticket for it) – together with the menace of bank expropriations, the road-blocks in front of foreign investments, and the familiar, tell-tale flight of capital – (between 1975 and 1985 Mexicans took $60 billion out of their country into the USA.[95])

Such scant confidence in one's own country spells death – often in a boxcar crossing into Texas. It arises from the failed promises and self-propelled hot-air balloons of rhetoric sent up by various Mexican revolutions in this century, culminating in the present PRI (Party of Institutionalized Revolution). But of course *institutionalized* revolution is an oxymoron of the grossest kind, and predicts a fracture. The PRI appears to be an oligarchy masquerading as Tammany Hall while in fact being a conduit sending northwards subversion, Soviet agents, drugs, and illegals. Nowhere in Central America (and certainly not among the Cubans working on Pointe Salines) have I ever met with the profound and envious loathing of the North American gringo that I have in modern Mexico. It rivals that of Graham Greene. Yet north of the border this hatred is taken to the bosom of left-leaning academics, most of whom hate themselves anyway. The Mexican wetback turns into an Hispanic, a breed beloved of welfare legislators and starry-eyed Assistant Professors alike. Politicians know that, once amnestied, these invaders will all have votes.

A cuban-type Mexico along the US border is not a funny thought, yet it is doubtful that the present US Democratic Congress, fulminating over Colonel North's snow tires, would do much to prevent it. For Castro and Ortegas and Noriega the conception is only moves away; and resolve is all that will stop such moves. After all, America bought the Virgin Islands for their geostrategic importance when its southern flank was far less vulnerable than it is today. But America's 1987 response to such threats was to appoint to Chairman of the House Foreign Affairs Subcommittee on the Western Hemisphere a Congressman who abstained from the 416-0 House vote in 1983 condemning the Russian shooting down of Korean Airlines flight 007, and who filed suit against President Reagan for liberating Grenada.

Thus today the Communist Empire has, for the first time in history, established a military beachhead on the North American mainland, thanks to the lack of will, or plain self-serving pusillanimity of a Congress whose Democratic majority Pat Buchanan (erstwhile Communications Director for the Reagan administration) describes as frankly "opposed to victory." That is more than a word, or merely saying that peace is so pleasant, after all. For instance: in Angola the Cuban-supported communist drive is partially funded by the US Chevron Corp., which lobbies vigorously against UNITA in Congress.

The Democratic Party of Truman and Jack Kennedy and Lyndon Johnson was, whatever its failings, surely opposed to the extension of the Soviet Empire, let alone into what was not its own hemisphere. The present Democratic Party, in particular that wing of it led by Jack's brother the notorious Chappaquiddick Plunger, sees little urgency in stemming the Sandinistas in Nicaragua at all. As Buchanan puts it: "Along with its auxiliaries in the mainline churches and the liberal press, it is conducting this feverish campaign to discredit, defund and defeat the contras, *because it wants the other side to win.*" [96]

Resolve is what is needed. It took the United States seven years to get Stingers into the hands of the Afghan resistance and only then, after some regular loss of aircraft, did the Soviets even mention a ceasefire. Dr. Robert Jastrow, Director of the NASA Goddard Institute for Space Studies, gives America – and, by implication, the free world – five years. By that time mammoth Russian radars, each the size of a soccer stadium, will be in place in phased array, closing out all corridors against missile penetration into the USSR. The Russians were apparently working on these fifteen years ago, i.e. when negotiating the ABM treaty!

Alongside those structures they have been building up a first-strike ICBM arsenal. Such a total defense against retaliation, coupled with a first-strike attack force, surely represents such a challenge that even the US Congress might give heed to it.[97] Instead, Congress reduced Department of Defense budget request by over US$60 billion for fiscal 1986 and fiscal 1987. Who dares, as the saying goes, wins. Sooner or later the Western mind has got to learn that freedom isn't free. Let us hope that the recognition comes sooner than later.

1. *Time*, January 13, 1986, pp. 16-17.
2. *Washington Post*, November 3, 1983, p. D.1.

3. Payne, Sutton and Thorndike, *cit.*, p. 158.
4. Sandford and Vigilante, *cit.*, p. 11.
5. *Army Times*, November 14, 1983, p. 2.
6. Ward Just, *Military Men*, New York: Knopf, 1970, p. 135.
7. *Army Times*, November 14, 1983, p. 10.
8. Mayo L. Gray, *New York City Tribune*, October 25, 1984, p. 4B.
9. Capt. John F. O'Shaughnessy, "Interrogation," *Military Intelligence*, January-March, 1985, p. 14. No relation to Hugh O'Shaughnessy.
10. Mayo L. Gray, *New York City Tribune*, October 25, 1984, p. 4B.
11. John F. O'Shaughnessy, *cit.*, p. 15.
12. Capt. Stephen C. Donehoo, "Counterintelligence," *Military Intelligence*, January-March, 1985, p. 18.
13. *The Paraglide*, November 10, 1983, pp. 1, 6.
14. *Ibid.*, December 1, 1983, p. 8A.
15. *Ibid.*, p. 9A.
16. Keith Douglas, *Alamein to Zem Zem*, Oxford University Press, 1979, p. 147. The last time I saw Keith was when he gave me and Richard Llewellyn (Lloyd), author of *How Green was my Valley*, a ride in Tunisia, see: *Keith Douglas: A Prose Miscellany*, Compiled and Introduced by Desmond Graham, London, Carcanet, 1985, p. 121.
17. Michael Levin, "Women as Soldiers – The Record So Far," *The Public Interest,* Number 76, Summer, 1984, pp. 31-44.
18. Lavinia Warner and John Sandiland, *Women Beyond the Wire*, London, Michael Joseph, 1982.
19. Dinesh D'Souza, "The New Feminist Revolt," *Policy Review*, Winter, 1986, p. 46.
20. Mayo Gray, *New York City Tribune*, October 25, 1984, p. 4B.
21. Richard Reeb, "Grenada: The Media versus America," *The Claremont Review*, December, 1983, p. 6.
22. Benjamin J. Stein, "Free to Libel," *The American Spectator*, February, 1987, p. 18.
23. See: Brian Hanrahan and Robert Fox, *I Counted Them All Out and I Counted Them All Back*, London BBC Publications, 1982; John Laffin, *Fight for the Falklands!*, London, Sphere, 1982; Robert McGowan and Jeremy Hands, *Don't Cry for Me, Sergeant-Major*, London, Futura, 1983; William Fowler, *Battle for the*

Falklands, London, Osprey, 1982.

24. See: Adam Myerson, "Ronald Reagan's Peace Offensive: Containing the Soviets without Going to War." *Policy Review*, Fall, 1986, p. 66.

25. Alistair Horne, "Lessons of the Falklands," *National Review*, July 23, 1982, p. 888.

26. *New York Post*, October 31, 1983, p. 2.

27. See: Robert Harris, *Gotcha! The Media, the Government and the Falklands Crisis*, London, Faber and Faber, 1985.

28. *Ibid.*, p. 57

29. *Ibid.*, p. 62

30. *Ernie's War: The Best of Ernie Pyle's World War II Dispatches*, Edited by David Nichols, with a Foreword by Studs Terkel, New York, Random House, 1986.

31. Evidence for such is reliably given in *The Grenadian*, July, 1981 (an anti-Jewel broadsheet printed in Trinidad).

32. *Grenadian Voice*, February 20, 1986, p. 6.

33. See: Miron Dolot, *Execution by Hunger: The Hidden Holocaust*, New York, W.W. Norton, 1985.

34. Reed Irvine, *New York City Tribune*, January 14, 1986.

35. "The Decision to Assist Grenada," U.S. Department of State Current Policy No. 541, January 24, 1984, p. 4.

36. Richard Gabriel, "Scenes from an Invasion," *The Washington Monthly*, February, 1986, p. 39 (excerpted from the same author's *Military Incompetence: Why the U.S. Military Doesn't Win*, and rebutted as "bordering on libel" by a Ranger who actually dropped on Pointe Salines).

37. Scott Minerbrook's *Washington Post/Los Angeles Times* critique was reprinted in *The Fayetteville Observer* (which serves Fort Bragg), August 18, 1984, pp. 1A, 2A.

38. *Time*, January 27, 1986, p. 36.

39. For an example of English local government in a war against the elected national body, see: David Regan, *It Costs a Bomb*, London, Peace Through Nato, 1985.

40. See: Roy Kerridge, "Magic in Islington," *Encounter*, January, 1986, pp. 30-33.

41. The text cited is: "GRENADA: Report of a British Labour-Movement Delegation, December, 1983," available from 4,

Gray's Inn Buildings, Roseberry Ave., London EC1R.

42. *Guardian Third World Review*, June 7, 1985, p. 11.

43. *Grenadian Voice*, October 20, 1984, p. 4.

44. Hugh O'Shaughnessy, *Grenada: Revolution, Invasion and Aftermath*, London, Sphere, 1984.

45. *Army Times*, November 14, 1983, p. 35.

46. Harris, *Gotcha!*, p. 84.

47. *Human Events*, August 16, 1986, p. 13.

48. *New York Times Book Review*, May 3, 1987, p. 32.

49. S. Robert Lichter, Stanley Rothman, and Linda S. Lichter, *The Media Elite*, Bethesda, MD; Alder & Adler, 1987.

50. Allan C. Brownfield, "How Media Bias Distorts Our View of the World" *Human Events*, May 9, 1987, p. 10.

51. *Human Events*, December 21, 1985, p. 11.

52. Jeffrey Richards, "The Hooligan Culture," *Encounter*, November 1985, p. 20.

53. Thomas Fleming, "La Vie en Rouge," *Chronicles of Culture*, November, 1985, p. 4.

54. Dinesh D'Souza, "The Bishops as Pawns: Behind the Scenes at the U.S. Catholic Conference," *Policy Review*, Winter, 1986, p. 6.

55. *Ibid.*, p. 8.

56. *Ibid.*

57. *Sunday Telegraph*, February 23, 1986, p. 16.

58. David Brooks, "Latin America is Not East of Here," *National Review*, March 14, 1986, p. 33. The Sandinista support of terrorism throughout Latin America is codified in "Revolution Beyond Our Borders," U.S. State Department Special Report No. 132, September, 1985.

59. *Everybody's Magazine* (New York), June/July, 1983, p. 41.

60. Payne, Sutton and Thorndike, *cit.*, p. 116.

61. *New York Post*, October 31, 1983, p. 2.

62. Ann Tusa and John Tusa, *The Nuremberg Trial*, London, Macmillan, 1983.

63. This gave him the right not to be cross-examined, but it also gave the jury the right to ignore everything he said.

64. V. Timothy Ashby, *The Bear in the Back Yard*, Lexington, Mass., Lexington Books, 1987.

65. It is indicative of the low esteem held by Moscow of Grenada that

254

the USSR, through one or another of its "peace" funds, subsidized Grenadian Travel on Aeroflot, but made the Grenadian government pay for any official travel between the island and Havana.

66. "Guyana: A New Threat to the Americas," *Aker Foreign Information Service*, Woodbridge, Virginia, June, 1985, passim.
67. *SOS Guyana*, Washington, D.C., April, 1985, p. 3. Human rights violations by Burnham were repeatedly reported by CANA (Caribbean News Agency).
68. "A comparison of modern day Russian practices parallels the empire and the methods set up by their Mongol overlords – only the uniforms have changed"; "Russia's Mongol Heritage," *Aker Service*, June, 1985.
69. Jiri and Virginia Valenta, "Leninism in Grenada," *Problems of Communism*, July-August, 1984, pp. 8-9. This article feasts off the memos of the Grenadian Ambassador to Moscow, Richard Jacobs.
70. Dennis, *cit.*, p. 38.
71. *L'Express* (Paris), September 3rd, 1982.
72. At least Malaya didn't seriously change its name. My own feeble grasp of exotic geography makes much of Africa vague; some of us got lost after Kenyatta and gave up.
73. Revel, *cit.*, pp. 36-37.
74. V. Harry Miller, *Menace in Malaya*, London: Harrap, 1954.
75. For a recent account of the Anzio fighting, see: Raleigh Trevelyan, *Rome '44*, London, Secker & Warburg, 1981.
76. Tyrrell, *cit.*, p. 191.
77. *Daily Gleaner*, November 20, 1980.
78. Alberto Abello, *La Sovietización del Caribe*, Caracas, Venezuela Publicaciones Seleven, 1982 contains lengthy extracts from the *Mini-Manual*, including its prophetic section on "Terrorismo."
79. Dr. Rudolf Levy, "Terrorism and the Mass Media," *Military Intelligence*, October-December, 1985, p. 35.
80. Philip Windsor, "Some Reflections on Grenada," *Atlantic Quarterly*, 1984, p. 7; not to be confused with the US *Atlantic Monthly*.
81. Oppenheimer, *Urban Guerrilla*, *cit.*, p. 65.
82. *Caribbean Contact*, November, 1983, p. 5. For Barbados-based Lamming the intervention was "an infamous act of aggression.

83. Following the line of Editorials in the British *Defence* for July and August, 1983, Philip Windsor writes, "fuel storage tanks at military airports do not normally stand about in the open" (Windsor, p. 4). This shows lack of knowledge of our terrain. The "tiff" of Pointe Salines was impervious to underground fuel tanks.

84. Jaime Daremblum and Eduardo Ulibarri, *Centro America: Conflicto y Democracia*, San Jose, Costa Rica, 1985, pp. 42-43.

85. Franqui, *cit.*, p. 141.

86. Timothy Ashby, "The Road to Managua," *Policy Review*, Winter, 1987, p. 15.

87. *Time*, February 24, 1986, p. 35.

88. *New York Times*, June 26, 1986, p. D22.

89. James L. Buckley, "All Alone at the UN," *National Review*, December 14, 1984, p. 26.

90. Maurice Bishop, *Selected Speeches, 1979-81*, Havana, Cuba, Casa de las Americas, 1982, p. 9.

91. "The Fourth Frontier," *The Times*, December 10, 1984, p. 11.

92. Winston S. Churchill, *The Hinge of Fate*, Boston, Houghton, Mifflin, 1950, p. 119.

93. Windsor, *cit.*, p. 8.

94. See: Sol Sanders, *Mexico: Chaos on our Doorstep*, New York, Madison Books, 1987

95. John A. Gavin, "Mexico, Land of Opportunity," *Policy Review*, Winter, 1987, p. 32. The writer was US Ambassador to Mexico from 1981 to 1986.

96. *Newsweek*, July 13, 1987, p. 19 (emphasis in original).

97. Robert Jastrow, 'America Has Five Years Left', *National Review*, February 13, 1987, pp. 42-43.

AN APPENDIX OF ACRONYMS

Nothing is more irritating than reading a text in which the eye is brought to a halt by bumping into a block of indecipherable capitals every few lines.

A true acronym is a language playback by which you abbreviate to a word expressive of meaning. It is a *calembour* of a kind, a sort of lipogram you are constructing. ERA (Equal Rights Amendment) was an efficient acronym, regardless of what happened to the endeavor it stood for. So was FAIR (Federated Associations for Impartial Review), or SCUM, short for a Feminist Society for Cutting Up Men.

Sometimes acronyms overlap – a Navy mailing marked MOM was interpreted by one agency as Military Ordinary Mail and by another as Military Official Mail, while there are six or seven CIAs, including the Cotton Importers Association. Sometimes, too, they get in the way, as when the Argentine rugby football Club Universitario Buenos Aires decided to desist from identifying itself by the club's initials – CUBA. At the lower end of such puns might be included special number plates, Elizabeth Taylor using, as Mrs. Mike Todd, ETT 1, while the British sex star Sabrina took S 41 (her bust measure at the time). One brassiere manufacturer, before they all got tossed out the window, used BRA on his plates; it means good in Swedish.

True acronyms, forming words, cannot be translated. De Gaulle was right, for once, in sneering at NATO, SHAPE, and UNO as "bodies known to the world by a collection of letters" (though the last now has a Caribbean application, Unidad Nicaraguense Opositora). In fact, UNESCO, a non-acronym, was at one time preparing an international dictionary of acronyms; it never came out, but then again nothing much did out of UNESCO.

Unfortunately, these days Central American politics are as full of acronyms as are armies. Take this random para from a recent issue of *Military Intelligence*; it is taken from an article on intelligence-gathering in Grenada by a US Major we got to know well and admire warmly:

> Outside the CIOC the principal corps intelligence assets consisted of interrogators, tactical SIGINT collectors and CI personnel. Each asset was tasked against the corps PIR and managed on a day-to-day basis through the CIOC. The HUMINT collectors had integrated with all agencies and coordinated daily operations, thus precluding duplication.

Any questions, men?

As I told the author of this passage, so long as our army can write like this we have nothing to fear from the Russians.

Actually, it is in fact decipherable – HUMINT being human intelligence – certainly more so than pages of General Hackett's *World War Three*, a book made acronymically unreadable for this reader, who otherwise applauded it.

Thus I thought it might be helpful to set out here a few of the essential acronyms that the reader will find in these pages.

ABA   American Bar Assocation
ACLM   Afro-Caribbean Liberation Movement
AFDC   (US) Aid to Families with Dependent Children
AID   Agency for International Development
ANC   African National Congress
BEOG   Basic Educational Opportunity Grant
CANA   Caribbean News Agency
CARICOM   See CARIFTA

CARIFTA	Caribbean Free Trade Association
CBI	Caribbean Basin Initiative
CC	Central Committee
CCC	Caribbean Conference of Churches
CCNY	City College of New York
CDCC	Caribbean Development Cooperation Committee
CIA	Central Intelligence Agency
CND	Campaign for Nuclear Disarmament
COHA	Council on Hemispheric Affairs
COMECON	Council for Mutual Economic Assistance
CPSU	Communist Party of the Soviet Union
CWC	Central Water Commission (Grenada)
DA	Departmento América (Cuba)
DGI	Dirección General de Inteligencia (Cuba)
DLP	Dominica Labour Party
DOE	Dirección de Operaciones Especiales (Cuba)
DPP	Director of Public Prosecutions
EC	Eastern Caribbean
EDRE	Emergency Deployment Readiness Exercise
ETA	Euzkadi ta Azkatasuna (Basque Spain)
FAL	Fuerzas Armadas de Liberacion (El Salvador)
FARC	Fuerzas Armadas Revolucionarias de Colombia
FLN	Frente de Liberación Nicaragüenses
FMLN	Farabundo Martí de Liberación Nacional (El Salvador)
FNMS	Federated Malay States
FSLN	Frente Sandinista de Liberación Nacional
GBSS	Grenada Boys Secondary School
GLC	Greater London Council
GNP	Grenada National Party
GULP	Grenada United Labour Party
IMF	International Monetary Fund
IRS	Internal Revenue Service
JEWEL	Joint Endeavour for Welfare, Education and Liberation (Grenada)

JLP	Jamaica Labour Party
KGB	Komitet Gossudarstvennoi Bezopasnosti (Russia)
LIAT	Leeward Islands Air Transport
LIC	Low Intensity Conflict
LSC	Legal Services Corporation
LSE	London School of Economics
MAP	Movement for the Assemblies of the People (Grenada)
MBPM	Maurice Bishop Patriotic Movement (Grenada)
MCP	Malayan Communist Party
M-19	Movimiento de Abril 19 (Colombia)
NAACP	National Association for the Advancement of Colored People
NATO	North Atlantic Treaty Organization
NJM	New Jewel Movement (Grenada)
OAS	Organization of American States
OECS	Organization of Eastern Caribbean States
OLAS	Organization for Latin-American Solidarity
OPEC	Organization of Petroleum Exporting Countries
PCC	Partido Comunista Cubano
PLO	Palestine Liberation Organization
PNC	People's National Congress (Guyana)
PPP	People's Popular Party (Guyana)
PRA	People's Revolutionary Army (Grenada)
PRAF	People's Revolutionary Armed Forces (Grenada)
PRG	People's Revolutionary Government (Grenada)
PUSH	People United to Save Humanity
RFG	Radio Free Grenada
RMC	Revolutionary Military Council (Grenada)
RMG	Revolutionary Military Government (Grenada)
SALT	Strategic Arms Limitation Talks
SAM	Surface-to-Air Missile
SAS	Special Air Service
SEALS	Sea, Air, Land Forces
SEOG	State Educational Opportunity Grant

SWAPO	South-West Africa People's Organization (Namibia)
UN	United Nations
UNO	Unidad Nicaragüense Opositora
USCC	United States Catholic Conference
USG	United States Government
USIS	United States Information Service
UWI	University of the West Indies (Trinidad, Jamaica)
WCC	World Council of Churches
WHO	World Health Organization
WPA	Working People's Alliance (Guyana)
WPJ	Workers' Party of Jamaica

OTHER BOOKS BY GEOFFREY WAGNER

Novels

Born of the Sun
Venables
The Passionate Land
The Dispossessed
Sophie
Nicchia
Rage on the Bar
Season of Assassins
A Summer Stranger
The Asphalt Campus
The Lake Lovers
The Passionate Strangers
Sands of Valor
The Killing Time
Axel
Boulogne, un Midi ... (in French only)
The Innocent Grove
The Wings of Madness
The Red Crab

Criticism

Parade of Pleasure

On the Wisdom of Words
Wyndham Lewis: A Portrait of the Artist as the Enemy
Five for Freedom: A Study of Feminism in Fiction
The Novel and the Cinema
No Language But a Cry (with Richard D'Ambrosio)
Leonora (with Richard D'Ambrosio)
Language and Reality

Travel

Your Guide to Corsica
Corsica
Elegy for Corsica
Another America

Poetry

The Passionate Land
The Singing Blood
The Period of Mammon